Human Development in Cultural Context

A Third World Perspective

A. Bame Nsamenang

Foreword by Michael E. Lamb

Cross-Cultural Research and Methodology Series
Volume 16

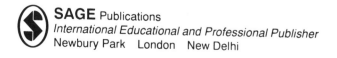

SAGE Publications
International Educational and Professional Publisher
Newbury Park   London   New Delhi

For information address:

SAGE Publications, Inc.
2455 Teller Road
Newbury Park, California 91320

SAGE Publications Ltd.
6 Bonhill Street
London EC2A 4PU
United Kingdom

SAGE Publications India Pvt. Ltd.
M-32 Market
Greater Kailash I
New Delhi 110 048 India

Printed in the United States of America

Library of Congress Cataloging-in-Publication Data

Nsamenang, A. Bame, 1951-
  Human development in cultural context : a Third World perspective
/ A. Bame Nsamenang : foreword by Michael Lamb.
        p.   cm.
  Includes bibliographical references and index.
  ISBN 0-8039-4636-8
  1. Child development—Africa, West. 2. Ethnopsychology—Africa,
West. 3. Developmental psychology—Africa, West. I. Title.
HQ792.A477N78   1992
305.23'1—dc20   92-10600

92 93 94 95 10 9 8 7 6 5 4 3 2 1

Sage Production Editor: Astrid Virding

To Vitavi, Sheri, Diyla and Yeh

Human Development in Cultural Context

CROSS-CULTURAL RESEARCH AND METHODOLOGY SERIES

Series Editors

Walter J. Lonner, *Department of Psychology, Western Washington University (United States)*
John W. Berry, *Department of Psychology, Queen's University, Kingston, Ontario (Canada)*

INTERNATIONAL EDITORIAL ADVISORY BOARD

CONTENTS

FOREWORD

Bame Nsamenang's *Human Development in Cultural Context: A Third World Perspective* presents a valuable and exciting contribution to the social sciences. For the first time, a social scientist from a non-Western country has provided a systematic and complete account of human development that is sensitive to the needs, interests, and ecologies of non-Western cultures and individuals.

The systematic attempt to understand the origins and determinants of human development had its origins in Central Europe around the turn of the century. At this time, of course, Sigmund Freud was developing and expounding his psychoanalytic theory of human development, which provided both a normative account of the phases and stages of human development as well as a conceptual framework within which to view the development of individual differences. Although Freud's earliest adherents were Central Europeans like himself, the scientific study of human development was always more vigorous across the Atlantic than in Europe. With the flood of immigrants forced out of Europe by the Nazi Holocaust in the 1930s and 1940s, North American dominance of the scientific study of human development escalated and persists to this day.

Since the humble emergence of developmental psychology just a century ago, a vast body of findings and theories have accumulated; we know immensely more about child development than we did even two decades ago. This knowledge has not been achieved without distortion or limitation, however. For a start, North American social scientists have demonstrated a remarkable ethnocentrism in developing their accounts of human development. They have, with few recent exceptions, attempted to develop universally valid accounts of human development on the basis of studies focused on a narrow stratum of human existence. Most of our collective knowledge of human development has been wrung from small studies, focused on the young, unrepresentative, and exceptional offspring of the affluent, largely white, overeducated, and unrepresentative parents who constitute the preferred focus of researchers. When Western social scientists have examined non-Western children, it has often been with a view to demonstrating deficiency. In addition, as critics like Urie Bronfenbrenner have argued with eloquent force, Western developmentalists have tended to describe human development as though it unfolded regardless of its social context. They have, in so doing, failed to recognize the extent to which each child's development is constrained and shaped by the cultural, physical, social, and economic opportunities afforded and restrictions applied to it. Even as "ecologically valid" studies of human development have flourished in the last two decades, these attempts have largely involved descriptions of the ways in which the development of white, affluent and unrepresentative children is affected by the quality of the relationships they have with their family members, the nature of the relationships among these other family members, and the fashion in which these families are embedded in community networks. Little attention has been paid to the sociocultural context in which families, communities, and organizations are embedded, however. And surprisingly few social scientists have asked how we can claim to understand human development when our focus falls so narrowly on so select a sample of developing humans.

In his forcefully argued and eloquent book, Bame Nsamenang takes issue with the assumptions and fallacies that undergird research and scholarship of this sort. He demonstrates the crucial role played by the physical and cultural context in delimiting the nature of the opportunities made available to children and the goals of their parents, and in conditioning the directions in which children and parents develop. And Dr. Nsamenang has written a book that does more than simply identify the "universalist fallacy." He has surveyed the published literature with a view to demonstrating the importance and value of a multicultural and multicontextual perspective in constructing a theory of human development. In addition, as a native of Cameroon, he provides an insider's view of development in one part of this country, using this example to elaborate a novel view of development in non-Western, especially African, contexts. The result is a richly argued and well-documented treatise in which scholarly and polemical arguments come together in synthesizing a broad, novel perspective on human development.

Dr. Nsamenang's book will be of great value to developmental scientists of all cultural backgrounds. Those from the Western industrialized countries will find its argument particularly pertinent to their attempts to develop intrinsically valid process-oriented accounts of human development. Those from less developed countries will find it an exemplary account of the ways in which Western knowledge must be interpreted and filtered with caution in the course of developing accounts of social structure and human development in non-Western contexts. Finally, those from West Africa will find here the first attempt to provide a scholarly and culturally sensitive account of development in this important region of the world. All readers will enjoy the engaging and lucid style which Dr. Nsamenang has brought to his topic. This is a book that will be read widely for information, enjoyment, and edification.

—Michael E. Lamb
National Institute of Child Health
and Human Development
Bethesda, MD

PREFACE

During my graduate studies (1980-1984) in Nigeria, I was jeered for expressing an interest in academia. The common feeling was that the graduate school is a place to obtain a better meal ticket and an improved social status. Memories of that moment haunted me throughout work on this book.

Scholars who study human development or social systems in Third World contexts are frustrated by developmental or social science texts that offer no appropriate guidelines and theoretical concepts to give meaning to developmental "facts" and social phenomena in non-Western niches. More importantly, students of human development in the Western world are grossly unaware of the real conditions of childhood and human life in the non-Western world. If social science should essentially remain ethnocentric, scholars with interests and focus in non-Western societies deserve a volume that addresses the social realities and developmental patterns in those ecocultures.

In this volume I have attempted to paint broad strokes of the ecology of human life in the Third World, with illustrative examples from (West) Africa, particularly from Cameroon. I have stressed the need for *developmental research in context,* outlining an ecocultural perspective as a relevant paradigm for human development research in context, especially in the Third World. Although the emphasis is on the Third World, the paradigm can guide the conceptualization of human development in all cultures.

This book is primarily intended to introduce and interest Western social scientists, especially cross-cultural researchers, to the conditions of childhood and developmental pathways in non-Western cultures, with particular reference to (West) Africa. It is also meant to remind and sensitize Third World scholars to indigenous conditions, with potential developmental consequences, in their niches that are often ignored or taken for granted.

I am grateful to a number of people who read earlier drafts of this book and gave valuable comments: Michael E. Lamb, Paul L. Kanjo, Godfrey Tangwa, Supo Laosebikan, and Judith S. Amsel. My very special thanks go to Michael E. Lamb who helped with the conceptualization of the book. An initial draft of the manuscript was completed when I was a Fogarty (post-doctoral) Fellow, under the mentorship of Dr. Lamb, at the U.S. National Institute of Child Health and Human Development (NICHD), Bethesda, MD. I sincerely acknowledge the support of the entire staff (October 1987-May 1990) of the Section on Social and Emotional Development (NICHD) and the assistance of the staff of the NIH Interlibrary Loan Department who obtained materials from other sources for me. I also appreciate the stimulation and encouragement of Kathleen Sternberg, Robert Ketterilinus, Nancy Kimmerly, Heidi Keller, Hans-Georg Voss, Marinus van Ijzendoorn, and Robert Serpell.

Most of all, I am grateful to my family: Yeh, Diyla, Sheri, and Vitavi, who granted me leave of absence from the family.

The translation of excerpts from French texts are my own and done within the context of their usage; they may not be perfect translations. I bear responsibility for all errors in the book.

—A. Bame Nsamenang

PART I

Conceptual Framework

A common conceptual shortcoming in developmental research is the separation of the developing person from the milieu in which development takes place into person and environment entities. This kind of divergent thinking ignores the fact that the human person "is never concretely encountered independent of the situation through which he [or she] acts, nor is the environment ever encountered independent of the encountering individual. It is meaningless to speak of either as existing apart from the situation in which it is encountered" (Ittelson, 1973, p. 19). The assumption of the existence of a clear and clean dichotomy between the biogenetic and ecocultural domains is thus erroneous because "the ability to profit and learn from the environment the way we do depends on human genes" (Grusec & Lytton, 1988, p. 117).

Although the primary focus of this book is on the ecoculture, we have devoted Part I to an appraisal of scientific psychology as a monocultural science (Chapter 1), as well as to an explanation of how genotype and the developmental environment interact and are interdependent (Chapter 2). Thus Part I is meant as a conceptual anchor for the book. We have also appraised the content-focus of scientific psychology and the current state of its theories and have expressed views informed by contemporary trends in the field.

1

BACKGROUND, CHALLENGES, AND PERSPECTIVES

BACKGROUND

In this book, I conceive of the human person as a biotic system developing under the priming influence of biogenetic, environmental, and evolutionary forces. The basic premise is that during ontogeny, ecocultural inputs induce, elaborate, and canalize biogenetic imperatives to produce developmental change. Once we accept that biology is as central to development as the environment in which it occurs, we simultaneously acknowledge and should become concernedly interested in human plasticity in varied ecocultures. But despite the potential impact of diverse developmental environments, the anchor-data for developmental literature has overwhelmingly been derived from the Western world (Curran, 1984) to the unfortunate exclusion of the Third World.

The lopsidedness of developmental knowledge in favor of the West clearly provides the primary rationale for the focus of this book on the Third World ecology. Second, although non-Western ecologies present a wider range of biological and ecological factors that influence development than do industrialized societies (E. Werner, 1988), they have yet to be represented in the scientific literature. They therefore deserve scientific attention as they are likely to offer broad theoretical leverage and novel research approaches. This could provide data to fill gaps or complement our knowledge of development. The exclusion of Third World ecologies from the biobehavioral science certainly limits the evolution of "a truly international psychology" (Ardila, 1982, p. 328). Third, misguided assumptions and lack of awareness that in non-Western societies psychology is practiced under different conditions than those in Western cultures further justify the book. Fourth, "contemporary psychology shares all the characteristics of Anglo-Saxon culture" (Ardila, 1982, p. 323). As a result, most theories of development, having been formulated in Europe or North America (and the former Soviet Union and Japan to some extent), have unwittingly been imported into and applied inappropriately in Third World contexts. That developmental theories reflect the worldviews of their origins may be illustrated by the fact that most Western developmental theories implicitly confer personhood on the human offspring from early in life and stress human dominance over nature. In contrast, Third World ontogeny, as represented by West Africa in Chapter 4, posits the age-wise accretion of personhood and emphasizes human kinship with the universe (Erny, 1987).

The central purpose of the book is to present the ecology of human development in a Third World context. This would provide a broader conceptual base on which to think about the development of *Homo sapiens* as a global species. In so doing, I wish to take the following route: (a) to articulate theoretical guidelines and chart a "road" map for theory development in Third World contexts, (b) to propose the ecocultural framework as a useful and relevant model for conceptualizing developmental research in the Third World, and (c) to present West Africa's ecology as an exemplary case study of a Third World developmental ecology. My intention is to stir up interest and systematic exploration of distinctly indigenous patterns of development (Serpell, 1984) so that developmental research in Third World contexts may fertilize and expand the visions, methods, and knowledge of psychology beyond current (Western) molds.

Part 1 of the book underscores the importance of differences in developmental ecologies and places ecological thinking within the context of current theorizing in psychology. While the need for psychologists to broaden their conception of the human species is emphasized, issues related to the monocultural nature of scientific psychology are raised. Consideration of the sources of development prompts examination of the modes by which genetic codes and ecocultures impinge on development. Thus Chapter 2 looks at genetic endowment and the developmental process, developmental ecology, biology-environment interface, evolutionary behavioral ecology, environmental experience, and a paradigm—the ecocultural perspective—that converges the nature-versus-nurture modes of thinking about development.

Clearly, history, habitats, and the conditions of life affect not only how we survive, live, and perceive the world and ourselves, but also how we develop. Hence Part 2 presents an illustrative case study—West Africa—of a Third World ecology with which I am more familiar. Like other Third World ecologies, West Africa is relatively unknown in the scientific community, especially with regard to developmental research. The key points of the two chapters of Part 2, are, respectively, the relative harshness of the West African ecology, and the centrality of the sense of community and the apparent similarity and coherence of indigenous West African worldviews.

Because history is a crucial factor in human life, I have adopted an historical approach to exploring the present (West) African developmental scenario shaped by Africa's triple heritage of religious imperialism and the superimposition of alien cultural fragments on endogenous systems. Whereas Chapter 5 traces the alien component of the triple heritage, Chapter 6 examines parenthood and the child-care situation in West Africa. Chapter 7 focuses on childhood and the life cycle in West Africa, with an attempt to describe how West Africans endeavor to socialize children and to satisfy their needs.

Finally, Part 4 deals with contextual research, emphasizing the need for developmental research to reflect the universal human condition, and—more importantly—for it to be sensitive to *development in ecocultural context.* It thus stresses the need for researchers in Third World societies to develop and use theories attuned to developmental paths in their research niches rather than depending excessively on models imported from other cultures. The main point of the section is theory building *in context;* we propose the ecocultural paradigm as a relevant model to guide the generation of endogenous developmental knowledge. The ecocultural paradigm appears more relevant for Third World societies than for the Western world because populations in non-Western cultures interact with a more naked terrestrial environment and their activities are relatively less abusive of the environment than those of populations in Western societies who deal with a more "carpentered" ecology. Furthermore, the worldviews of Third World cultures more forcefully point to the intimacy between the human person and the universe than Western viewpoints admit or actively foster.

Chapter 8 traces the evolution of contextual thinking in psychology and suggests guidelines for theory building and contextualizing developmental research in Third World cultures. Because cross-cultural psychology is done in the Third World and inevitably takes researchers (mainly Westerners) away from their home turf into contact with "strange" peoples, it seems expedient to devote Chapter 9 to a fresh look at cross-cultural developmental research at issue. Having done this, it becomes necessary, in Chapter 10, to outline possible future research directions for consideration by the scientific community. A logical end to the book, in Chapter 11, is a brief concluding statement about the global human condition and scientific psychology.

CHALLENGES TO SCIENTIFIC PSYCHOLOGY

Having sketched a road map to the book, the rest of this introductory chapter now shifts to examining the extent to which current theories, research methods, and orientations succeed or fail to capture the entire spectrum of human variation. This includes an appraisal of psychology's subject matter, the global psychology scene, and the need for relevant psychology. In the discussion, I take short glances at some theoretical, empirical, and moral challenges that psychology faces and that limit the evolution of universally applicable developmental norms.

PSYCHOLOGY:
THE SCIENCE OF WHOSE BEHAVIOR?

Psychology is regarded as "the science of human behavior." A direct implication of this definition "is that human behavior in all parts of the world must be investigated, not just those aspects of behavior conveniently available to investigators in highly industrialized nations with a history of scientific endeavor" (Triandis & Brislin, 1984, p. 1006). In this light, psychology should involve some four billion members of the human species worldwide. Despite the similarity in basic human strivings, variability in psychology's subject matter begins with genotype and physiognomy and extends beyond the content, structure, resources, and dynamics of human ecologies.

It is increasingly being realized that differences among human beings reflect differences in the ways competencies are socialized and channeled (see, e.g., Curran, 1984; Ogbu, 1988) to serve biological and eco-cultural demands. In fact, it is now "understood that cultures vary in the salience attached to certain skills, in the combination of basic cognitive processes that are called upon in any given context, or in the order in which specific skills are acquired" (Segall, Dasen, Berry, & Poortinga, 1990, p. 94; see also Cole & Scribner, 1974; Irvine & Berry, 1988). Unfortunately, the current psychological literature accords specific orientations and competencies to a subset of the human species (typically Euramerican middle classes) that, when juxtaposed with the experiences of humankind worldwide, teaches us that psychology has yet to portray the rich variety in humanity. Zukow (1989, p. 2), for instance, reported that children from the Third World and underprivileged classes in Western nations "comprise 95% of the world's children," but developmental data from these groups of children are severely underrepresented in the literature. Furthermore, Curran (1984, p. 2) pointed out that developmental psychology texts are generally "based on the behaviour of Western children in very contrived situations which bear little relation to those children's familiar environments." With this in mind, Serpell (1990) reminded us that the exclusive limitation of psychology's data bases to research in Western populations is responsible for certain inadequacies in the current developmental theories and literature.

The extant corpus of psychological literature, based largely on the study of accessible, privileged portions of the human race, has been presented as if it reflected and epitomized the universal condition of humankind. Failure to study the entire spectrum, or at least a representative sample, of the human species can rarely be regarded as a positive trait of a science of human behavior, properly defined. The witting or unwitting exclusion of the behavioral patterns of the bulk of humanity from a purported science of human behavior undoubtedly renders psychology an insular science—a science of exclusion. This implies that developmental psychology merely masquerades as a global science of behavioral development. It is therefore essential to open up to new scientific vistas. In this vein, Wright's (1984, p. xiv) instructive submission is that:

> We must begin to look for alternatives to the traditional views, not so that those views may be necessarily displaced, but so that we may come to wider, fuller understanding of man *qua* man. We must be willing to look at all views, no matter how diverse, and learn what we may from them; even if we learn that a certain view is worthless, we have learned something important.

We need to see the opening of new perspectives as an exciting scientific event rather than as a threat. Researchers who do not venture beyond their own research niches miss the "exciting and intellectually challenging experiences" (W. Russell, 1984, p. 1017) that come from trying to understand the viewpoints of persons who are not like themselves, even if the views are not to be internalized.

In light of Wright's (1984, p. ix) wisdom, "we can no longer allow [myopic] . . . views to dominate honest attempts to understand African" or other Third World viewpoints. We need to explore all sources of developmental data. We therefore ought to cease behaving as if the current sources of data and research models represented "the last word" in psychological functioning, theorizing, or modes of knowing. "Our work may require something akin to the Copernican revolution; if that is necessary, so be it" (Wright, 1984, p. ix).

Having mused over the bigotry and myopia in contemporary psychology, it becomes necessary to review the current status of psychological research, especially as it affects the field in the Third World.

GLOBAL PSYCHOLOGY AND THE THIRD WORLD

This section examines orientations and trends in psychology and their implications for the state of the field in the Third World. The appraisal focuses on classifications of psychology and the differences between psychology communities. It blames the inability of Third World countries to influence the field of psychology on material and personal poverty; the domination of the field by Western Europe and North America, especially the United States; and the irrelevance of contemporary research orientations and theorizing for Third World communities.

Categories of Psychology

Psychology may be categorized in a number of different ways. Kimble's (1984) classification, based on value orientations in psychology, reported fundamental rifts between scientific and humanistic issues in the discipline. On the basis of "power groups" in social psychology, some scholars (e.g., Lubek, 1974; Morawski, 1979) identified two main groups: an elite group that exerts considerable influence and a nonelite group that has little power to shape mainstream psychology. Moghaddam (1987) shifted focus from the characteristics of the discipline to the extent to which societies are "psychologized" (notions derived from scientific psychology). He identified three communities in which psychologists research and practice and the degree to which each community can influence mainstream psychology.

The Three Worlds of Psychology

According to Moghaddam (1987), psychology's "first" world is North America, particularly the United States; its "second" world comprises mainly Western Europe and the Soviet Union; while its "third" world consists of Africa, Asia, and Latin America.

Moghaddam's division was premised on the number of academic psychologists in the field, the availability of resources and facilities for psychological research and services, the quantity of psychological work already done, and the relative impact of the community in the global psychology scene. The three worlds have vastly differential capacities for generating and disseminating psychological knowledge or technology, and for shaping mainstream psychology and national policies.

Psychology's first world is the major producer and marketer of psychological knowledge and technology to both its second and third worlds— more so to the third than the second world. The second world rivals the first in some spheres, but its influence tends to be greater in the second and third worlds than in the first world. Psychology's third world is a net importer of psychological knowledge and technology because its capacity to generate psychological knowledge and technology through research is virtually nonexistent.

Although some of the most important concepts in contemporary psychology "originated elsewhere" they have been nurtured to fruition largely in the United States (Moghaddam, 1987), which itself has made significant contributions to the discipline and has established a unique but domineering identity.

The plausibility of this claim lies in Murphy and Kovach's (1972, p. 484) assertion that "the major psychological ideas of today . . . arose in Europe between the time of Darwin and World War II" and gained ascendant currency among North American authors. This perhaps explains the widespread, albeit misguided, acceptance of Anglo-Saxon worldviews as the intellectual frame of reference for the translation of psychological phenomena.

Need for Internationalism in Developmental Psychology

Cross-exchange of developmental knowledge and experiences, "especially in the form of theoretical concepts" (Moghaddam & Taylor, 1985, p. 1144) and normative principles, can help evaluate the state of global psychology and permit research in the Third World to enter into and enrich mainstream psychology. Internationalism in psychology can thus enhance scientific progress and facilitate psychology's portrayal of a more universalistic "range of human variation" (Serpell, 1990, p. 100). Unfortunately, however, the monocultural status of contemporary psychology is not in doubt (see, e.g., Kennedy, Scheirer, & Rogers,

1984; Moghaddam, 1987; E. Werner, 1988). This clearly points to the lack of cross-fertilization of psychological, particularly developmental, data.

Given the wealth of psychologists in some Western countries and their scarcity in international agencies and the Third World, it is surprising that efforts have not been taken to bridge the gap. Wagner (1986, p. 299), for example, found "very few American child development researchers who have maintained longterm professional contact with either international development organizations or Third World countries and who are committed to applied policy-driven research" in cultures other than their own. In reaction, Wagner (1986, p. 298) signified the need for child development researchers "to become more active in the application of child development research in an international and cross-cultural perspective." We need to continue to follow Plato's suggestion, in the Theateatus (168A) and engage in "[psychological] dialogue, no matter where that takes us, no matter what we have to explore to do so, because, in the end, only that will allow us to 'escape from [our] former [ignorant] selves and become different men' " (Wright, 1984, pp. xiv-xv).

Internationalism in developmental psychology is as limited as the circumscribed applicability of developmental laws and principles. The limited universality of developmental norms is perhaps due to isolationism and excessive segregation of the discipline by "stigmatizing" various peoples and ecologies with variants of the discipline. As long as psychology is regarded as a universal science, there is and there ought to be no such thing as "Third World psychology" in the same sense that there should be no Asian, American, or European psychology. Nsamenang (1989b) pointed out that the fragmentation of psychology with such designations as "African" or "American" psychology, "black" or "white" (if ever there is such) psychology, and so on, is not in the long-term best interest of the science because it is inimical to the evolution of a coherent body of universally applicable psychological laws—the essence of a scientific discipline. A viewpoint worth promoting is that of psychology in a particular context, meaning the scientific study of behavioral development or the provision of psychological services in a specific milieu.

We need to follow Mallory Wober (1975), whose review of psychological research in Africa is appropriately designated *Psychology in Africa*.

The apparent lack of a consensus about the content area for psychology or absence of a global view of psychology's legitimate subject matter is also responsible for the limited universality of psychological precepts. For instance, are the Pygmies of the southeastern forest of Cameroon the content area for anthropology as well as psychology? Do minority and middle-class children in New York City, for example, have "equal" chances as subjects for developmental research? In addition, the scale of scientific interest in the quality of life, the scope of research funding, the extent of advanced training of human development experts, and the perceived value of developmental research is much smaller in the developing than the industrialized world where, paradoxically, research has peaked at a time of declining child population.

Although academic freedom implies free choice of research topics and settings, E. Werner (1988) has highlighted a curious phenomenon in contemporary psychology, suggesting that scientists muse over the following three trends in developmental research. First, why has the developmental research enterprise peaked in the Western world at a time when Western birthrates reached an all-time low while birthrates in the Third World were at an all-time high? Second, why have behavioral scientists focused their research mainly on the middle-class segments of their respective communities while presenting their findings as though they addressed the global human condition? Finally, why have the overwhelming majority of developmental studies been carried out in milieus that are unfamiliar to most children around the world?

Domination in Psychology

"Interest in psychology is worldwide, but as long as the discipline is so much influenced by one culture (and it does not matter which culture)" (Ardila, 1982, p. 328), it will always exclude important phenomena in other cultures. That the West, especially the United States, dominates contemporary psychology is not in doubt. The Americanization of psychology probably derives from the fact that "most of the psychologists who have lived and are now living can be found in the United States. . . . The rest of the world has only about 20 percent of the psychologists that are now or have ever been alive" (Triandis, 1980).

Regarding West Africa, Nigeria, with an estimated population of 116 million (Paxton, 1987) people, had only about 58 academic psychologists (Commonwealth Universities Yearbook, 1985). With this small number, the psychologist-population ratio in Nigeria still exceeded that of most African nations. By comparison, the United Kingdom, whose mid-year population in 1984 was 56 million, had about 602 academic psychologists (Moghaddam, 1987). But the combined number of psychologists in the 22 largest commonwealth countries, including the United Kingdom, Canada, and Australia, was only the equivalent of 19.7% of psychologists in the United States alone (Moghaddam, 1987). In 1973, the number of academic personnel in psychology in North America was

45,686 (American Psychological Association, 1973). But in mid-1983 the American Psychological Association estimated that 102,101 psychological personnel worked in the United States alone (Stapp, Tucker, & VandenBos, 1985). Moghaddam (1987, p. 914) calls this number "a veritable 'army' supported by the world's most extensive research infrastructure." Sexton and Misiak (1984, p. 1027), however, "believe that the average American psychologist, in spite of having the greatest resources and possibly the highest levels of technical training, may be much more ethnocentric and parochial than" psychologists elsewhere.

Western domination of psychology even extends to the realm of cross-cultural research, where it might have been anticipated that the demands of the discipline for a universal understanding of humankind would have created and permitted more opportunities for disadvantaged psychologists attuned to cultures of Third World societies. Of course, the majority of Western psychologists are aware of the limitations and the price of a monocultural science, yet the myopia persists and remains a major heuristic and theoretical challenge inhibiting a science of human development, truly defined and universally studied. If this Eurocentric slant "were not so recurrently fashionable and if it were not reasserted by otherwise competent and respected scholars, it could have been dismissed as ludicrous. But, it is, sadly tenacious" (Segall et al., 1990, p. 98).

Contemporary psychology is more or less a science of the white middle class in the sense that it largely excludes other white classes and non-Western populations. Perhaps the exclusion is due to the fact that a model of white middle-class personality has been "utilized as a measuring stick against which all other psychological development is assessed" (Sinha, 1983, p. 7); "the standard against which others must measure up" (Segall et al., 1990, p. 93). Native Americans or African Americans, for instance, are not merely minorities; first, they are members of the human species with unique frames of mind before they, like whites, are ascribed a minority or majority status in the American Empire. Psychological research with Afro-Americans would be the study of people for whom the reminiscences of the forceful relocation of their ancestors to another continent where they were "designated . . . as property" (Liebenow, 1986, p. 63) are vivid and certainly not psychosocially innocuous. How the consequences of this kind of history compare with those of voluntary immigration is at the core of the psychological frames of orientation that determine how Americans live up to the "American dream." It constitutes, so it seems, the basis for understanding psychosocial differences among racial and/or ethnic groups in the United States.

THE NEED FOR RELEVANT PSYCHOLOGY

The need for relevant psychology is growing (Moghaddam, 1987). The call for the indigenization of psychology does not contradict the remark that variants of psychology should not be identified by geographic, racial, or ethnic source. To regard psychology as a science that can study behavioral development in all human societies is not to deny the remarkable variability in the ecocultures that shape and elaborate worldviews and basic personality attributes in diverse directions and channels. The emphasis should be on employing sound scientific methodology to explore, understand, and describe developmental and behavioral phenomena *in context*. This can unpackage contextual phenomena and help to establish the data bases that constitute the baseline for educated comparative cross-contextual research.

The Western worldview, within which scientific psychology evolved and became established as a professional discipline, is but one of diverse worldviews that have yet to find their niches in the field. The Japanese worldview has recently captured world attention; other worldviews too merit attention and incorporation into mainstream psychology. This is especially important because psychoanalysis, behaviorism, and humanistic thought, the three Western philosophico-political ideologies that underpin psychology, cannot "lay claim to universality" (Diaz-Guerrero, 1977, p. 937). Moreover, the issue of who decides which worldview is right or wrong is a critical, polemic question that modern humankind, especially psychologists, have yet to address objectively.

The notion of relevant psychology connotes the focus of research attention on indigenous realities and precepts. It is to this topic that we now turn, intending in the discussion to identify the major constraints hampering the growth of endogenous developmental knowledge and technology in Third World societies.

Generation of Indigenous Psychological Knowledge

Although progress in scientific psychology in the Third World is slow, human psychology is gradually being established as a professional discipline, a fledgling profession at best.

Psychology in the Third World largely involves populations who are attempting to preserve their sense of identity by defending indigenous behaviors and developmental agendas from the modifying influence of alien ideologies and life cycles. The common heritages that Third World countries share are easily discernible. For instance, West African nations with a largely Negroid population share deep-seated traditions and historical scars, the most impactful and insidious of which are slavery and the colonial encounter. The slave trade and colonization are largely responsible for the world's perceptions of Africa as well as the overall negative self-perceptions of Africans. Further, research in Third World countries is both nascent and inchoate.

In Africa, systematic research beyond the level of fulfilling the requirements for a university degree (Serpell, 1984) is noticeable by its absence and much of it is unpublished. Another category of research, much of it published in foreign publication outlets, has been conducted by itinerant Westerners (rarely committed to the systematic study of human development in those cultures) whose mission has usually been to test Western theories on strange populations or to explore exotic cultures. In this way, the authorship of developmental knowledge in non-Western cultures is dominated by nonindigenes. Thus the portrayed images of Africans contain the expertise as well as the vested "interests, prejudices, . . . and cultural background" the expatriates bring to the issues they study and the literature they produce (Wober, 1975, p. x). All this underscores the need for the institutionalization and systematization of developmental research in African countries. The sooner this is done, the sooner psychology can begin to serve Africa's multiple needs.

One explanation for the poor state of psychological research on the African continent is the embryonic nature of research institutions and facilities and the lack of personnel. Second is the unawareness in most African nations of psychology's potential role in shaping national policy and fostering understanding of national character. For instance, in the University of Yaoundé psychology is offered in the department of philosophy, while child psychology in Cameroon's Institute of Human Sciences is but a unit in the educational research branch. Support that the fate of psychology may not be different in other African nations comes from Serpell (1984) who claimed, then, that in sub-Saharan Africa "only a few of the African universities contain a psychology department: probably not more than 20 in all, and less than 10 with a history of research going back more than 10 years."

A researcher's greatest wish is for his or her work to be published. Unfortunately, publication outlets in the Third World are few and underdeveloped. In West Africa, publication problems are hellish and herculean. The poor condition of facilities and inadequate incentives for scholarship are further exacerbated by destructive student protests. For instance, protesting students in Nigeria's Kwara Polytechnic destroyed office and laboratory equipment ("Students," 1988). Although the large number of personnel dispensing psychological services may, in one sense, be symptomatic of how "sick" a society is to require psychological services, the low number of psychologists in West Africa cannot optimize the development of the discipline.

Constraints on the Growth of Indigenous Psychological Knowledge

The bulk of Third World psychologists "have a multi-cultural cognitive repertoire by virtue" (Serpell, 1990, p. 102; 1978) of their Eurocentric training, exposure to Western literature, and the dualism of their social systems. In this sense, they are likely to hold broader views of humanity than their Western peers. The constraints highlighted above, however, stifle their ability to develop and present these viewpoints to the scientific world. This shortcoming has often been attributed to deficient intellectual capacity or lack of scholarly ability among Third World researchers, especially with reference to Africa. African psychologists like myself counter thus: Back up scholarly efforts in Africa with the kind of resources and technology in Western academia and watch what Africans may do. Some unacknowledged evidence for this assertion is the fact that some African high school graduates, fresh from their purportedly "impoverished" home backgrounds, enter reputable universities in Europe and North America, encounter the most modern educational gadgets for the first time, and still achieve at the level of "straight 'A's."

There are other factors that further reduce the capacity of the Third World to generate indigenous developmental knowledge. First, in Third World societies there is the "tendency to undertake research that might confirm or disconfirm Western theories" (Wagner, 1986, p. 298). Petzold (1984) pointed out that, with few exceptions, little research has been undertaken with the explicit goal of being applicable to the Third World settings from which the data were gathered. The unspoken professional ideal seems to be for Third World researchers to identify with what characterizes Western psychology (W. Russell, 1984). This means that scarce resources and valuable research efforts are expended trying to slot Third World behavior patterns into preexisting Western casts instead of testing and trying to understand indigenous precepts and behavior patterns on their own merits. As Moscovici (1972) suggests, researchers should endeavor to derive their research hunches from the maxims that are indigenous to their research contexts.

Second, Third World nations inherited research traditions "ready-made from the West rather than having participated actively in its development" (Kagitcibasi, 1984, p. 164). The nonindigenes who initiated research traditions in psychology in the Third World inaugurated deficit models for the conceptualization and investigation of psychological phenomena. In addition, the research posture is being consolidated by researchers who were trained in Western societies or have been trained in their own nations in conformity to Western standards and today continue to function within those molds. Indeed, most of them are in great pain matching their acquired skills with the ecoculture in which they are expected to apply them (Moghaddam, 1987). They have thus found it difficult, if not impossible, to conceive and conduct research from the viewpoints of their own cultures. The irrelevance of Western models stems from the fact that the Western worldviews and social reality that organize and inform research differ markedly from those of Third World cultures.

Third, the psychology imported into the Third World is generally confined to the modern sectors and has not yet permeated traditional milieus that house the bulk of the people and—to some extent—constitute authentic laboratories for indigenous behavior. Furthermore, the few psychology centers in the Third World tend to affiliate and cooperate more with centers and institutions in Europe and North America than with sister facilities in other Third World nations. Finally, the absence of scientific ethos as an indigenous cultural value means a lack of extensive indigenous efforts systematically to explore and present a view of humanity in non-Western ecologies to the world.

The outcome of all this is that research orientations in the Third World have remained essentially Western in outlook. There is therefore urgent need to heed Wagner's (1986, p. 301) advice that attempts should be made in the Third World "to go beyond the Western paradigms typically used in cross-cultural research," and that there should be "an openness to new ideas and ways of investigation." Openness to new ideas and research approaches should compel psychologists to abandon their myopic frameworks in order to develop more universalistic views of human nature. There is therefore need to broaden theoretical and empirical models to incorporate the modes of behavior and developmental paths of representative segments of research niches—and in the long run to consider how the data we obtain reflect or fit the universal condition of *Homo sapiens*.

An unappreciated scientific reality is that the duality of contemporary Third World conditions makes the cultures more complex, at least from a theoretical standpoint, than Western cultures. Third World societies thus present more conceptual challenges and require cautious and more sophisticated theoretical thought and formulations than has hitherto been recognized. But the tendency has been to label non-Western communities "simple" societies, with implications for the prescription of simpleminded theories or simplistic intervention remedies, which have largely failed or are inappropriate.

In sum, developmental psychology in the Third World is "underdeveloped" in terms of the research infrastructure, the quantity and quality of trained personnel, and the availability and quality of publication outlets. It is severely deficient in its role in clarifying policy decisions, aiding the understanding of national character and the multiple problems of underdevelopment, and in providing human services. Its irrelevance is due to outright inadequacy or inappropriateness of imported models, ill-advised application of imported laws and technology, and the fact that it has largely been adorned with Western theoretical garbs. This suggests an urgent need to undertake psychological research from the perspective of developmental settings. This book represents a modest effort to sketch the framework to guide developmental research in this direction.

DEVELOPMENTAL RESEARCH IN GLOBAL PERSPECTIVE

It is essential to think of human development in global terms. The metaphor of the developmental niche (C. M. Super & Harkness, 1986) encourages the conception of the child in its context as the unit of analysis (Segall et al., 1990) in developmental research. Awareness of the role of this metaphor in shaping contextual research is growing.

The Developmental Niche

Homo sapiens is a species whose biogenetic systems require external booster cues. We know, of course, that such stimuli vary enormously in content and complexity from one ecoculture to another. Thus ecologies may differ in the extent and direction to which they affect development.

The idea that the environment influences human development is as old as the concept of development itself (C. M. Super & Harkness, 1986). Although the notion of environmental influence connotes the differential impact of different ecologies on development, developmental psychology has until recently idealized the individual as the primary source of data and "sought universal laws" (C. M. Super & Harkness, 1986, p. 549) with data obtained from decontextualized individuals. Because ecocultural considerations have not fully entered research conceptualization, a clear picture of the developmental niche and the place of context in shaping theoretical formulations are still emergent.

The developmental niche is meant "to expand both the methods and vision of psychology beyond the individual as an exclusive focus of analysis" (C. M. Super & Harkness, 1986, p. 550). It "is an open system where each component is linked with other aspects of the more general environment" (Segall et al., 1990, p. 115). This implies that developmental research should not be restricted to the developing target person in a proximate setting because

> the contextual boundaries of psychological phenomena do not always reside in the observable features of settings or in the demographic characteristics of their occupants. Instead, the effective context of certain phenomena may be better represented in terms of more covert, abstract dimensions of the relationships between people and their surroundings. (Stokols, 1987, p. 56)

The historical fact of slavery, for instance, haunts people of African descent everywhere today.

What surrounds us is tangible and intangible, physical and metaphysical, and for good or bad it impinges on us regardless of our wishes or knowledge of it. It therefore seems plausible to think of humans as niched organisms, embedded in a rich web of interactions among interdependent sets of ecocultural components. However, just as the meanings attached to natural or physical settings are culture-bound, so too are developmental niches culturally constructed and defined.

The cultural construction of developmental niches flows from worldviews, subsumed by the cultural history, cosmology, social reality, psychophilosophy, religion, and the resources of a particular polity or human group. C. M. Super and Harkness (1986, p. 552) rightly pointed out that the cultural construction of the developmental environment "may be the most important aspect of human ecology." Culture colors not only the values we ascribe to nature but also the manner in which we represent the universe (Knopf, 1987). Researchers like Marcus (1974), More (1977), and Aiello, Gordon, and Farrell (1974) attempted to demonstrate the extent to which adult value-characterizations of the physical world filter onto children. Thus it is not such things as the trees, animals, houses, clothing, books, marks on sand, or food, per se, that we perceive; it is the symbols and values we learn and hang on them during ontogeny.

Our cultures antedate our birth and contain values and modus vivendi most of us unquestioningly assume to be the best (Segall et al., 1990). Despite the deterministic impact of culture, "recent models of the environment of development . . . do not generally acknowledge its cultural structuring" (C. M. Super & Harkness, 1986, p. 552), particularly the underpinning psycho-philosophical ethos.

Worldviews or the belief systems people hold about the universe and their place in it, elaborated and encoded in cultural traditions during evolutionary history, prime human social action in a manner analogous to how genes undergird biology.

Worldview is thus a cultural blueprint for social functioning. Worldviews generate and sustain overarching ethos that permeate the social and cultural institutions through which they find expression. They pervade and prime all facets of life, orienting and guiding occupants of developmental niches in how to picture, relate to, and deal with the world, as well as how to organize life in order to maximize not just inclusive fitness but also human welfare. Because every culture has a worldview, prescriptions for social action and relation to the world tend to differ from culture to culture.

In terms of cultural evolution, worldviews represent "a past that is culturally present as tradition" and that has been "encoded in customs rather than in genes and transmitted socially rather than biologically" (R. LeVine, 1974, p. 227). Caretakers and caregiving institutions are forceful in transmitting to the next generation the ethos engendered by the worldviews of their developmental niches (R. LeVine, 1977). Being integral to personality, worldviews orient parents and careproviders, shaping parenting, socialization, and educational agendas.

The developmental niche can therefore be construed as the total scenario comprising the physical and social environments, the psychocultural climate that enmeshes the developing person, and the worldview that primes social life. The developmental niche is dynamic, not static. As explained in Chapter 6, Third World developmental niches, especially in Africa, are restive milieus, pervasively assaulted by the modifying effects of exterior influences, particularly religious imperialism and Westernization.

All components of the developmental niche modulate the developmental experiences of their occupants. Because we attempt to present such components in a conceptual framework in Chapter 2, it suffices here simply to state that the subsystems of developmental niches are interdependent and dynamically nested together (e.g., Bronfenbrenner, 1979) to constitute inescapable elements of the "environment of evolutionary adaptedness" (Bowlby, 1969). In real terms, the developmental niche surrounds children from conception, "enveloping them like the air they breathe and without which they could not grow into viable human beings" (Sharan, 1988, p. 1).

2

THE BIOECOLOGY OF
HUMAN DEVELOPMENT

Historically, biobehavioral research has been riddled with a persistent debate: whether human development is shaped by nature or nurture. This chapter tries to avoid such divergent thinking about the source of development. Nature and nurture may involve different processes and give rise to differentiable developmental outcomes, but they are parallel rather than competing forces (Segall et al., 1990). The central point of the chapter, then, is to highlight the bioecological roots of development. That is, developmental change is produced by biogenetic transmission as well as ecocultural influences. Thus, in acknowledging the complementary role of nature and nurture in human development, we attempt to explain how biology interplays with the environment during millennia of evolutionary history to shape development.

The chapter focuses on five key interrelated topics. First, I describe the nature of the developmental environment, attempt to identify its core components, and illustrate its diversity by describing two household scenarios. Next, I examine how biology interfaces with the environment to produce developmental change. In the third section, I consider the role of evolutionary forces on biobehavioral development. Fourth, I discuss how we experience the environment and how environmental inputs are incorporated into biological programs. Finally, I sketch the ecocultural framework as a convergent conceptual viewpoint that tries to accommodate both nativist and empiricist thoughts about development. The chapter begins, however, with a brief statement on genetic endowment and the developmental process—the biogenetic bottom line that underpins the bioecology of developmental change.

GENETIC ENDOWMENT AND
THE DEVELOPMENTAL PROCESS

Each human being is endowed with a genome with "specific instructions honed by evolution" to regulate development (Plomin & DeFries, 1985) and environmental adaptation. Although a large portion of heredity is species specific, each human being is considered a unique genetic experiment that may never be replicated (Plomin, 1986). Human beings are thus marvelously diverse genetically. Ordinarily genetic variability enhances human adaptability to diverse ecologies, but genetic endowment sometimes causes adaptive difficulties as well as predisposes some people to physical and psychiatric abnormality. In reality, genetic transmission sometimes goes awry, giving rise to various genetic anomalies and diseases that adversely affect the inclusive fitness or wholesome development of some 3%-5% of the population worldwide (World Health Organization, 1982, p. 186).

In crude terms, each of us is half each of his or her parents—genetically speaking, that is. The determination of the sex of the offspring, a biogenetic fact that is often taken for granted, has high social significance in West Africa where heirdom and inheritance are generally reckoned on gender. Some West African men are known to have resorted to divorce or polygyny because their wives could not "give them male children." Reproductive technology may eventually resolve such issues.

Developmental psychology is as concerned today with the identification and description of the determinants of development and how they influence the life course as it was a century ago. Sometimes psychologists undertake intervention research either to foster development or to promote environmental adaptation and human welfare. However, *human development* refers to any morphological or functional change from the moment of conception until death. *Developmental change* implies the emergence of more complex and sophisticated patterns of behavior and levels of functioning. In one sense, the study of human development involves the study of change that takes place within individuals from conception and throughout the entire span of life. In another, development is the process by which the genotype is transformed into the phenotype. It is the "interaction between genotype and environment that produces what we recognize as an individual" (Williams, 1966, p. 23). Virtually every aspect of what develops is intricately affected by heredity, environment, history, and learning (Hall, Lamb, & Perlmutter, 1986). Developmental change is generally inferred from the phenomena engendered by the psychomotor, cognitive, social, and conative dimensions of human personality. Psychologists endeavor to identify, measure, and explain such phenomena.

The debate about the source of development is not a silly affair; its basic issues are pivotal in the study of human development. As researchers are compelled to investigate the forces thought to underlie developmental change, they inevitably address these issues. This obliges theorizing about the impact of heredity and the environment on development. The crucial point is not to dichotomize these two potential forces, but to theorize in terms of their complementarity in instigating developmental change and influencing each other. Discussion in the rest of this chapter revolves on how this may happen.

The next section begins this discussion by looking at the nature of the environments in which human development occurs.

THE DEVELOPMENTAL ENVIRONMENT

Two decades ago, Little (1972, p. 113) remarked that: "Were an alien being to attempt to draw a picture of man's environment from the information contained [in the literature], it would appear as a set of disembodied significant others floating in a sea of abstractions." This critical remark is still true today, perhaps because most developmental theories have yet to represent humans as contextual organisms or have yet fully to incorporate ecological considerations into the research agendas they inspire. The *developmental environment* is any developmental influence that is not encoded in the DNA (Plomin, 1986). Williams (1966) identified three levels of the developmental environment: genetic, somatic, and ecological. The *genetic environment* is the locus at which gene selection takes place, that is, other genes at the same genic locus. The *somatic environment* is the product of the interaction of the genetic and the ecological environments and includes the *milieu interieur*. The *ecological environment* comprises the geographic, socio-demographic, and psychophilosophical factors that impinge on human organisms.

Literally, the ecological environment is "that which surrounds . . . something else"—the human person (Ittelson, Franck, & O'Hanlon, 1976). What surrounds us is physical, social, and psycho-philosophical— what Gump (1987) has called "in-the-head" environment; Kuippers (1982) labeled it "Map in the Head" or the "mind's eye." The in-the-head environment seems to exert an overarching impact on all other facets of the ecology. It not only ordains human social action but orients and guides how humans perceive themselves as well as conceive, relate to, and deal with the universe. The human ecology also possesses historical and metaphysical dimensions, for example, cultural history and cosmology.

Ecological contexts may be divided into shared and individual environments. Shared settings such as the home, school, and societal norms ordinarily tend to foster similarity among members, whereas individual environments like personal space or principles and friendship pairs tend to magnify individual differences. Developmental environments usually consist of behavioral settings that are niches or "entities within the ecological environment" (Barker, 1987, p. 1420). As the "hybrid of eco-behavioral phenomena," behavioral niches "are bounded patterns of human and nonhuman activity with integrated systems of forces and controls" (Barker, 1987, p. 1420). Behavior tends to vary by environment (Norris-Barker, Stephens, & Willems, 1982). Because human behavior is plastic and responsive to changing contexts (MacDonald, 1988), people tend to adjust and adapt their behavior to contextual demands as they move from one setting to another. Adaptation is necessary because behavior that occurs in one place could be inappropriate or decompensating elsewhere. "This place-specificity of behavior is the fundamental fact" of the ecological paradigm (J. Russell & Ward, 1982, p. 652).

Behavioral Ecology

Human behavioral ecology involves the study of how human beings survive and adapt to their environment of evolutionary adaptedness (Bowlby, 1969). Tinbergen (1963, p. 113) suggested that attempts to explain behavioral development should revolve on four legitimate types of *"why"* questions, namely: "questions about ultimate *function* (survival and reproductive value); questions about *causation* (internal and external proximate factors); questions about ontogenetic *development;* and questions about *evolutionary history."* Behavioral ecology is thus an essential domain of developmental research because the "way in which behaviour contributes to survival and reproduction depends on ecology" (Krebs & Davies, 1981, p. 1). The mechanisms by which this may be effected are the focus of this section.

Human interaction with the world not only depends on the soundness of the psycho-biological systems alone, but also on ecocultural inputs. The nature of environmental inputs varies by developmental niche and their impact depends on reaction range and experiential thresholds. Unfortunately, ecological thinking has rarely gained favor with all theorists and researchers. This is regrettable because the genetic code is as central to the developmental process as the ecoculture in which development occurs. The extent to which ecocultures influence biobehavioral development is addressed in greater detail later. The focus of attention in the rest of this section is on the wide variety of caregiving niches and the uniqueness of the programs cultures implement to foster inclusive fitness.

Human societies replenish their members by reproducing and rearing offspring to reproductive age and beyond. Typically, every culture defines, devises, and implements programs of social organization, governance, mode of life, view of the universe, and so forth. Because we characteristically face life with the mundane strategies and competencies that flow from our cultural heritage, different cultures value and transmit differing repertoires of knowledge and competencies as well as cultural modus vivendi. Diversity in ecocultures implies that "what is adaptive in one environment may be maladaptive in another, and hence, actions that are intelligent in one culture may be unintelligent in another" (Sternberg, 1984, p. 314). The wide variation in cultural orientations, tasks, skills, and contextual experiences is best illustrated with a description of two household scenarios in which all parents are active and in their late twenties or early thirties.

The first household consists of a marital pair, their two offspring, and a pet. The pet is usually referred to as "he" or "she." Both parents spend much of their working life in full-time employment in business and government bureaucracy. Their 9-year-old daughter is in elementary school; their 2-year-old son attends a day-care center half a mile from their urban home in an exclusive neighborhood. The family procures its food through weekly grocery shopping. Not only is the pet's food included in every shopping list, but the pet's veterinary appointment is an important family affair. Relationships among family members are conditioned by the concepts of individuality and equality. The socialization of children is inspired by notions of academic achievement and an unspoken dream that envisions career success. After school the elder child uses a public library to study or do her homework, the younger one is placed in the care of a paid baby-sitter. A large portion of the children's vacation is spent in a vacation camp. The family generally talks of career as if it constituted the definitive core of personality. The family's health and other social services are either covered by insurance or provided for by the social security system. Television or tending the lawn almost always occupies most members' free time.

The second household comprises a marital couple, their five offspring, two foster children, and an adult kin. The two parents spend almost all their working life in agricultural work. The husband cultivates and prepares industrial produce for sale but spends much "free" time in idle talk with peers or performing nonspecific functions. Literally, the wife "permanently" preoccupies herself with family food cultivation and preparation, and market gardening. The adult kin has no specific agenda, but sometimes is of assistance to the wife, husband, children, and neighbors. The 23-year-old first child has just been sent away from college for lack of school fees; the second and third children, together with a foster child, walk five miles to and from elementary school daily. The 13-year-old son, the fourth child, is a school dropout and runaway to an urban center 20 miles away from the village. During the day, the 3-year-old fifth child is placed in the care of a 9-year-old foster child, an out-of-wedlock cousin; the duet are members of a neighborhood peer-caretaking team.

The school children devote their out-of-school time to domestic work or school assignments. Often, the performance of domestic chores takes precedence over schoolwork and leaves the children little, if any, time to study. Current theorizing in psychology, however, does not seem to have a satisfactory explanation for the adeptness with which the children combine school- and domestic work and still excel in school. Much of the children's vacation is spent helping parents or relatives with farm and household work. Social relationships are conditioned by a nonspecific cautionary apprehension and a social ethos that fosters social living. Socialization is based on a moral code that emphasizes filial piety and service. The family tends to talk of maintaining a good face with relatives and the community as if this constituted the distinctive hallmark for wholesome personality. Access to health care is difficult, not only because health manpower is scarce, social services are underdeveloped or health insurance nonexistent, but more so because the family cannot even afford the high cost of traveling over long distances to obtain "free" biomedical health care. As a result, the family depends a great deal on the mutuality of kin and community and frequently seeks solace from endogenous health practitioners. Interaction in neighborhood age, gender, or agnatic groups occupies everyone's free time.

Few readers would have difficulty determining which of the two family scenarios sketched above involves a family either in the Third World or the industrialized world. Variability between households or developmental niches can be multiplied extensively, but the noteworthy point is that various niches are located in diverse neighborhoods and obviously present varied ecological conditions. For example, households vary greatly in physical structure, contents, composition, social controls, patterns of economic production, and psychosocial climate. These may foster different experiences that extort differential developmental demands and consequences. Whether the behavioral setting is the household context, the home, the classroom, the initiation site, the laboratory, the workplace, the farm, the factory, or the hunting ground or game reserve, they are culturally defined. They exert specific contextual demands on their occupants.

Although human beings possess unique genetic codes and may be subjected to varied ecological conditions and experiences, they are not mere aggregates of their genotypes and experiences but the product of a transaction among them. How the transaction might occur is the focus of the next section.

AREAS OF BIOLOGY-ENVIRONMENT INTERFACE

Genotype is no more than a biotic master plan that permits organismic sensitivity and responsiveness to environmental opportunities. As potentialities, genes are capable of nudging development in one direction or another (Plomin & DeFries, 1985), depending, of course, on the quality of impinging environmental inputs, experiential threshold, and reaction range. Genes are thus biogenetic blueprints that facilitate or impair the incorporation of ecological inputs into biological timetables. Inborn human forces are quite simple, yet pivotal in directing development; they circumscribe the potential for behavior change through experience (Lamb & Bornstein, 1987). The plasticity of genes is plausible because a novel environmental influence may substantially alter the behavior for which a genetic component has been known to be strong (Plomin & DeFries, 1985).

Contemporary theoretical frameworks on development see the interplay of biogenetic and ecological forces as essential for biobehavioral development (Susman, 1989). Hence the acceptance of the role of heredity and the view of the environment as one of the "factors involved in unravelling the biology of behavior" (Lamb, Pleck, Charnov, & Levine, 1987, p. 113). Biology and the environment, therefore, do not dominate each other; rather they concert in complex ways to influence behavioral development. Within the limits of reaction range and experiential threshold, genes function within the facilitative, restorative, or constrictive influence of ecological opportunities. The state of the *milieu interieur* within which genes function or are selected, for instance, depends on the coded experiences and the substances we have had or ingested since conception, particularly food nutrients and substance abuse.

The two major areas that "provide evidence—perhaps the best available evidence—for the importance of environmental influences on behavioral development" (Plomin, 1986, p. 5) are developmental behavioral endocrinology and developmental behavioral genetics.

Developmental Behavioral Endocrinology

Advances in technology now permit reliable and noninvasive assays of the levels of hormones that are causally linked to individual differences or changes in behavior. Susman (1989), for example, reports that developmental endocrinologists have documented developmental changes in the structure and function of the physiological systems responsible for the secretion of hormones from the prenatal to the later stages of the life span. Interest in linking these two sets of causal factors is rooted in observations that in the life span, periods of rapid development such as puberty, characterized by hormonal spurts, coincide with increases in psychological problems, primarily increases in negative affect.

Further, awareness of gender differences in hormone levels, magnified during the early gestation period, can lead to a more sensitive and differentiated approach to understanding sex differences in behavior. The current theoretical position regarding research linking changes in hormones of gonadal origin (e.g., testosterone) is that hormonal changes may be one process by which environmental conditions, primarily those characterized by stressful circumstances, may exert long-term influences on behavioral development (Susman, 1989). Thus, as discussed later in the chapter, stressful or hazardous environmental inputs have serious implications for behavioral development.

Developmental Behavioral Genetics

The best way to study environmental effects on behavior is through the study of genetic influences (Plomin, 1986). The "role of the genotype in determining not only which environments are experienced by individuals but also which environments individuals seek for themselves" is particularly important in developmental research (Scarr & McCarthney, 1983, p. 424). At any point during ontogeny, each of us is the product of the genes we inherited from our parents, the experiences our parents and our developmental environments have provided from the moment of our conception, and the path of our development as mediated by our ideals and the numerous substances and meals we have ingested throughout our life span (Williams, 1966). In brief, development is genotypic expression within the conditions under which that development occurs.

Contemporary research in behavioral genetics endeavors to partition phenotypic variance into genetic and environmental components as an effort toward identifying environmental as well as genetic sources of individual differences in behavior (Plomin & Rende, 1991). The current theoretical position in behavioral genetics research approximates the view that "an individual consists of genotypic information and information recorded since conception" (Williams, 1966, p. 23). The main theoretical thrust in behavioral genetics research seems to focus on nurture as it affects nature and the stability of behavior (Plomin & Rende, 1991). In this sense, variation in phenotypes is considered to be nourished. This accords with Eveleth and Tanner's (1976, p. 241) finding that "a considerable portion of the mean differences in body size between the [worldwide] populations we have been examining is due to the effects of environmental conditions." This means that phenotypes depend partly on the quality of the environmental inputs received during ontogeny. Different genotypes can thus produce similar phenotypes in diverse environments. Similarly, similar genotypes may produce different phenotypes in the same milieu (Scarr & Kidd, 1983). As Susman (1989, pp. 2-3) clearly elucidates, "environmental factors may contribute to make two children in one family as dissimilar from one another as two children picked at random from a population." Thus the source of stability of behavior may not be genetic. Environmental conditions may be solely responsible for fostering the stability of a behavior (Susman, 1989).

The one-to-one causal notion of genetic influence has been discounted and replaced by the concept of polygeny. "As yet, no single-gene effect has been found to account for a significant portion of variance for any normally distributed psychological characteristic" (Plomin, 1986, p. 13). Genic effect on development involves the cumulative effects of many genes (Plomin & DeFries, 1985). For instance, many genes together will determine the color of a moth and its preference for settling on some, but not other, backgrounds (Krebs & Davies, 1981). In this respect, the phrase *genes for* a particular trait or behavior is shorthand for alluding to several different genes functioning in concert to bring about differences or similarities in function or behavior. A useful analogy is in cooking: a difference in the measure of one spice for a particular dish may alter the flavor of the dish, but this in no way means that the one spice is responsible for the entire flavor of the dish.

The concept of *pleiotropy* refers to indirect genetic influence on development through regulating the coding function of polypeptides that are responsible for regulating the development of structural and functional systems. According to Krebs and Davies (1981, p. 11), genes "determine the behavior of an animal by coding for the chemicals (proteins) that are made in its body." Developmental change may thus be regarded as a series of nervous impulses initiated by environmental inputs and coded for by proteins that are genetically predisposed to respond to experiential cues. The proteins so coded activate physiologic and anatomic systems and structures. In other terms, behavior is "not . . . precoded in the genes." Rather, genotype is "the discriminator of what environments are actually experienced" (Scarr & McCarthney, 1983, p. 425). Because genotype merely modulates phenotypic responsiveness to environmental opportunities, the developmental strength of genotype is its inherent potential to code environmental experiences. Thus it is more accurate to view genotype not as a set of traits waiting to blossom, but as a complex biotic tendency to develop in certain ways in certain environments (Moshman, Glover, & Bruning, 1987). All this implies that the environmental inputs an organism codes during evolutionary time determine long-term developmental changes.

Although the short-term process for genetic effect is the coding of environmental experiences, in the long run, genetic influence is mediated through natural selection—the essence of evolutionary biology.

EVOLUTIONARY BEHAVIORAL ECOLOGY

From an evolutionary perspective, the story of development stretches over millennia and indicates how the human genome evolved through natural selection in diverse ecologies to program development. The current genetic pool of the human species is therefore the tip of an evolutionary iceberg, representing only one of the tens of thousands of the genetic signposts along evolution's highway.

The centerpiece of evolutionary theory is natural selection and genotypic variance. A modern statement on natural selection is in terms of genetic variability (Krebs & Davies, 1981). "Human variability is not merely imprecision in a process that, if perfect, would generate unvarying representatives of the species type" (Plomin, 1986, p. 6). Genetic variation is purposeful; it is one of nature's grand designs to enhance human adaptability to widely diverse ecologies. Genotypic variability connotes differential rates of survival and reproductive success, otherwise termed *inclusive fitness.*

Inclusive fitness means that "whatever gene is favorably selected is better adapted than its unfavored alternatives. . . . The selection of such genes of course is mediated by the phenotype" (Williams, 1966, p. 25).

The most successful genes are those that most effectively augment individual survival and reproductive success (Krebs & Davies, 1981). Ordinarily, "our identity is a direct function of those characteristics in our ancestors that were best suited for survival" (Moshman et al., 1987, p. 109). But exceptions sometimes occur because of unfavorable genetic recombinations that are further fragmented or destroyed during meiosis in subsequent generations.

We expect people to endeavor to maximize their inclusive fitness. This fundamental principle of human existence appears to find its fullest application in some cultures, the Nso of Cameroon for example, where people want children to "represent my (parent's) blood when I die." They argue: "If we do not at least repeat the reproductive cycles of our parents, what would become the fate of our species?" Nevertheless, not everyone who survives to maturity actually reproduces. Some people compromise their inclusive fitness by opting for voluntary childlessness; the reproductive capacity of others may be compromised by biological anomalies or interference with procreation and the birthing process via contraception, abortion, or genetic engineering.

Depending on how we use contraception, genetic counseling, and genetic engineering, the destiny of our species may somehow depend on our own choices, not those bestowed on us by natural selection. Contraception and genetic engineering are emotive topics that provoke profound ethical questions and moral dilemmas that society has yet to address fully (see Tangwa, 1988). Catholic theology, for instance, posits an absolute "respect for life from conception" and because it views God as the author of life, advocates noninterference in procreation (Vatican City, 1987). Nevertheless, regardless of the ethical overtones of such polemics, each human generation will always transmit its traits to the offspring. Human interference with evolutionary processes is crucial to the extent that, for good or for bad, it may lead to the disappearance, appearance, or multiplication of copies of some genes in the gene pool.

Mayr (1954) introduced the term *genetic environment* to emphasize the "genetic composition of the population as an aspect of the environment in which the selection of a gene takes place" (Williams, 1966, p. 59). When people die, their phenotypes and personal copies of genes are extinct, but their gene survival and representation in future generations (the gene pool) depend on the number of surviving members of the population who possess copies of their genes. Kin selection and altruism are the two mechanisms that enhance this kind of inclusive fitness. Selection for behavior that lowers an individual's own chances of survival and reproductive success but fosters that of relatives, has been designated *kin selection* (Maynard-Smith, 1964). Krebs and

Davies (1981, p. 18) define *altruism* as "acting in the interest of others at a cost to oneself." Altruism illustrates how gene survival in the population can occur through "benevolent self-sacrifice among genetically different individuals" (Williams, 1966, p. 195). The reciprocity of kin fellowship and the readiness with which kin exchange nurturing roles in West African cultures (Nsamenang, 1989a) doubtlessly promote kin selection.

Human beings endeavor to maximize their inclusive fitness through the caretaking and socialization of their offspring to reproductive maturity and beyond.

Child Rearing and Inclusive Fitness Considerations

Caretaking ensures offspring survival and socialization fosters inclusive fitness because those who are acceptably socialized become integrated into their group and enjoy physical, economic, and psychosocial rewards and benefits, whereas those who are inadequately socialized may suffer "ostracism, exile, imprisonment, institutionalization, or even death" (Leiderman, Tulkin, & Rosenfeld, 1977, p. 1). Child care permits examination of how caregivers contemplate and implement care-giving roles in accord with fitness considerations (Lamb et al., 1987).

The notion of fitness consideration implies that parents strive to strike a balance between the need for own survival and well-being and the investment to maximize offspring survival and welfare (Charnov & Krebs, 1974). In so doing, they endeavor to care for the entire brood rather than indulging a single offspring, because the survival of more offspring will ascertain the parent's gene survival (Dawkins, 1978) and gene frequency (Krebs & Davies, 1981) in more members of future generations. For instance, fathers who raise their offspring in health to reproductive maturity and beyond and who invest their time, effort, and resources on more offspring—"regarding whose paternity there is some confidence" (Lamb et al., 1987)—are more likely to increase their inclusive fitness than fathers who invest in the survival of a single offspring.

There are, however, trade-offs in caregiving. This means that the "best interests" of parents and their offspring sometimes conflict (e.g., Trivers, 1974). Thus natural selection sometimes fosters parental rejection. Fortunately, there are far more accepting than rejecting parents. Parental rejection or situations in which parental fitness considerations obstruct care are analogous, at least temporarily, to conditions that compromise inclusive fitness. Hinde (1983) hinted that infants may be adapted to cope with mothers who reject them. If this is true, it implies that human infants are innately predisposed to adapt to rejection. This might be the case if research on child abuse revealed that children survive and indeed thrive at varying levels of psychosocial functioning and adjustment under various degrees of rejection and abuse. Rejection may be regarded as an example of an environmental "mutagen."

Thus far the discussion clearly indicates that development does not occur in a vacuum; it occurs in behavioral settings or caregiving niches. Although contextual factors—including nurturance—influence development, their effect depends on the perception of the environmental cues that impinge on the experiential or perceptual mode. Thus the quality of ecological inputs and their perception are themes worth research consideration.

The focus of the next section, therefore, is on human experience of the ecoculture. In it I try to describe the biological bases of environmental experience, its nature, the behavioral effects of the natural environment, and the experience of the environment as hazard.

EXPERIENCING THE ENVIRONMENT

A common conceptual shortcoming in research is the view of the human person and the environment as separate entities. Such distinction is a common mode of human perception, consistent with the dualistic nature of our language, whose inflexibility only permits the definition of the developmental environment as "that" which surrounds the human person. Since, as part of nature, we are somehow "mere extensions of our environment" (Leff, 1978, p. 7), it is specious to emphasize the person-environment dichotomy. In other words, the experiencing person is an integral part of what he or she experiences (Ittelson et al., 1976).

"Experience is conscious awareness" (Leff, 1978, p. 4). In a more global sense, experience connotes apprehension or feeling; a conception that includes intuition. Experience arises and operates within an interdependent complex of biological, behavioral, sociocultural, psychological, and environmental inputs. In one sense, "the quality of your life over the long haul may be conceived of as a weighted composite of all your experiences" (Leff, 1978, p. 4). We, however, weight experiences differently.

If it is incorrect to dichotomize person and environment, what then is the link between human organisms and the inputs they receive from their developmental environments?

Biogenetic Bases of Environmental Experience

Human beings are innately "wired" to react to environmental opportunities in certain ways. They are "saddled with senses and psyche genetically programmed" for "sensing and preferring nature" (Knopf, 1987, p. 807). The mind also "has the capacity to create its own environmental experience" because "much of our knowing, particularly as we gain experience, is shaped by forces that have little to do with the character of nature itself" (Knopf, 1987, p. 807). Knopf's remarks contain three seminal points worthy of note: an innate program for experiencing and preferring environments; the mind's capacity to create its own experience; and the developmental impact of experience as shaped by other than inherent forces.

Scholars like Driver and Greene (1977) and Dubos (1965) also think that innately wired human rhythms are synchronized with environmental rhythms. In this respect, genes are collaborators in a highly complex and synchronous system that holds the key for the organism's experience of its environment. Genes circumscribe the organism's reaction range to environmental opportunities (Plomin, 1986; Scarr & McCarthney, 1983), pushing or restraining ecological forces from influencing the organism. For proper development, the human organism requires a sensitive environment in which the genetic program can find expression over development (Scarr & Weinberg, 1983).

The Nature of Environmental Experience

In a positive sense, environmental experience is an active process in which individuals deploy their cognitive, affective, and valuational resources to perceive environmental opportunities and to maximize the satisfaction they derive from the experience of the conditions so perceived. Thus environmental experience is an individual affair; we can only infer or assume its occurrence in others from their physiology, mood, behavior, or actions. Perhaps the best way to conceive environmental experience is to view it as encompassing all that we apprehend or perceive through intuition and the sensory modalities.

Developing a frame of reference is a critical developmental task. Because it constitutes the psychological baseline for environmental experience, frame of orientation is essential for relating to the physical and social worlds as well as to time, space, and events. People manifest two primary dispositions—person-orientation and thing-orientation—that link the personality domain with the environmental domain (Little, 1976, 1987). In practical terms, frame of orientation translates into being gregarious or asocial and adopting a supportive or competitive posture in social relationships. Consequently, people's entrée into social relationships is determined either by an orientation toward persons or things.

Modes of Environmental Experience

People's experience of environmental settings may depend on whether the dominant mode of experiencing them is as an external physical place, as the self, as a social system, as an emotional territory, or as a setting for action (Ittelson et al., 1976).

The differentiation of self from the environment is an essential developmental task in the process of individuation. A merging of the self and environment, however, is always present in adult life, to the extent that, for some people, the strict environment-self boundary vanishes and the "environment becomes self, and self, environment" (Ittelson et al., 1976, p. 202). Place attachment (Brown, 1987) or identification with objects can be so engrossing that separation from them brings severe grief and self-doubt. In support of the concept of place attachment is Preston, Taylor, and Hodge's (1983, p. 163) report that "despite their pessimism and acute awareness" of the severity of hazards in their residential community, "only a small number of people were committed to moving from the area." As a place with an intense sense of personal identity, the home is "a model of the cosmos as perceived by a people" (Cunningham, 1973, p. 235). In point of fact, "families project cultural identities in the ways they design, decorate, and live within their homes" (Weisner & Weibel, 1981, p. 417). Most of us can give testimonies of how a change in our familiar environments or loss of cherished objects (e.g., artifact, pet) was experienced as a dramatic change in the self (e.g., Bryant, 1985).

A conclusion emerging from the issue of place attachment is that "the mature adult, having made the distinction between self and environment, now regains a sense of identity with the world around him and breaks down the barriers he so painfully constructed" (Ittelson et al., 1976, p. 203). Attachment to homes, kin, territories, or nations, for instance, produces a sense of physical, social, and autobiographical "insideness" (Brown, 1987; Rowles, 1980). The deepest sense of place attachment is auto-biographical insideness—a scenario in which inhabitants make a "heavy historical investment in this place." Over time, the place becomes "laden with personal meaning and life history" and "becomes an auto-biography—literally an extension of the self" (Rowles, 1980, p. 162). This is the sense in which West Africans virtually are prisoners of their ancestral lands. Indeed, "a sense of place is closely related to a sense of personal identity" such that "we are, in an important sense, the places we inhabit" (Little, 1987, p. 221).

Some people value and experience the environment almost exclusively as a network of other people. For such people, places and objects imperceptibly drop out of awareness and social networks become the reality, the kernel, or perhaps the sole element of environmental experience.

Sometimes affect overwhelms our experiences to the extent that certain settings or objects are perceived, reacted to, or remembered mainly in terms of emotive associations. Most of us have milieus for which the dominant experiential mode is emotive. The reminiscences of the alma mater or childhood developmental niche, for example, often rekindle deep sentiments, bringing to mind entire years of collective affective experiences. Artists and poets are among the professional groups for whom the affective mode of experiencing environments is both a literary theme and the principal source of professional inspiration.

Although cognition, affect, and valuation are inseparable components of environmental experience, the affective quality is the bottom line for environmental experience. For instance, prior to entering a place we often visualize its nature, what it will possibly offer us, what it signifies, and how we shall behave in it. Afterwards, we often remember little more about places than their affective quality. In this sense, the affective mode perhaps is "a key factor in accounting for the cumulative influence of the environment on mood, health, and subjective well-being" (J. Russell & Snodgrass, 1987, p. 246).

When the environment is experienced as a setting for action, it is approximated to a stage on which different actors enact their roles. Role relationships become the primary vehicles for social networks and interpersonal encounters.

Researchers' own modes of environmental experience certainly influence the questions they choose to investigate and the ways they design and conduct their research. If researchers assume knowledge of their research settings on the basis of their own experiences, they would unwittingly insert answers, at least partially, into their research questions long before they ever pose them. Because scientists are not neutral fact finders, it is important that researchers be aware of their own modes of experience as well as their frequently disguised beliefs and value orientations that always influence research.

Behavioral Effects of the Physical (Natural) Environment

We are not neutral experiencers of environments. We do not simply internalize or react to environmental opportunities; we filter them through a complex biocultural sieve. As explained in Chapter 1, our relations with nature are culture-bound (Tuan, 1971). Culture colors not only the values we hold about the universe, but also the manner in which we represent it. This implies that we, like our research subjects, do not ordinarily respond to objective environmental elements or research tasks, but to storehouses of ontogenetic experiences and cultural repositories of accumulated emotive and symbolic meanings associated with them (Ittelson, 1973; Jacques, 1980). The potential developmental impact of environmental features are therefore their valuations and symbolic implications (Gibson, 1982; Wohlwill & Heft, 1987). Put differently, nature and its contents are meaningful and influential in human life. For instance, the nutritional value of cattle may be obvious, but in most nomadic pastoral societies cattle are cherished more for their social prestige value than as a regular food source.

Environmental resources represent a broad spectrum of meanings—from devices for self-gratification and social memory to enduring values and traditions. Because the impact of our daily environments is in terms of what they offer or signify to us, different people may find different things in the same environment. Accordingly, while some people may find full opportunities in a particular environment, others may find the same environment completely bereft of opportunities. Ecological objects can "affect what a person can do, either by expanding or restricting the scope of that person's actions and thoughts . . . objects have a deterministic effect on the development of self, which is why understanding the type of relationship that exists between people and things is so crucial" (Csikszentmihalyi & Rochberg-Halton, 1981, p. 53). In other terms, environments are channels for social action and social intercourse. They play an important role in creating a sense of meaning in human life (Little, 1987).

While some environments are sociopetal, pulling people together and promoting a sense of community (Little, 1987), others are sociofugal, pushing people away from each other, thus fostering social isolation and alienation (Altman, 1975; Osmond, 1957; Sommer, 1969). Social support networks are known to sustain and promote physical health and well-being (Little & Ryan, 1979; Moos, 1976; Tolsdorf, 1976). But Henderson, Byrne, and Duncan-Jones (1981) provide evidence that challenges the promotive role of social support on well-being. They argue that it is not so much the availability of social supports as it is the perception of their usefulness that seems to foster health. Their observation is consistent with the definition of environmental resources in terms of their perceived salience. While the environment may provide the possibility for social support, it cannot extort a sense of community from those who, out of confusion or conviction, either choose to unavail themselves of it or to settle for a life of solitude (Henderson et al., 1981).

Cities are thought to be stressful environments because they generate and overload occupants with information and stimuli beyond the threshold of many people to handle and process. Milgram (1970) explored the insidious effects of stimulus surfeit in the incidence of urban pathology and explained that the evolution of an impersonal social ethos in city life is a reactive response to stimulus or information overload. He reasoned that in an attempt to reduce stimulus overload urban residents create a set of adaptive responses, including reduction of the intensity and quantity of social encounters, the setting up of preference hierarchies guiding the choice of with whom and when to interact, and the concession of certain roles to professional persons and groups (Little, 1987). In order to test the hunch that nature enhances psychological well-being, Ulrich (1981, p. 548) explored the differential effect of three different environments (slides of nature with water, nature dominated by green vegetation, and urban scenes without water or vegetation) and found that "compared to the influences of the urban slides, exposures to the two nature categories—especially water—had more beneficial influences on psychological states." One inference from this finding is that some environments may exert hazardous effects.

Experiencing the Environment as Hazard

Most environmental features do not by themselves constitute stressors; their stressful status emanates mainly from our perceptions (Baum, Singer, & Baum, 1982; Magnusson, 1982). In this light, Preston et al. (1983, pp. 143-144) reported "growing recognition that technological hazards are rapidly replacing natural hazards as major environmental threats to human life and property." But to what extent are Third World citizens aware of the massive export of expired and trial drugs to and the dumping of nuclear waste in their countries? It is uncommon to find people who are totally unaware of the risks or dangers in their environments. Kates (1976) claims, however, that most people cannot extend their imagination beyond commonplace experiences since many people see order in random events whereas others are blissfully ignorant. Kates further states that people tend to label and perceive stress or hazard either as originating from natural sources (Act of God or Nature) or as intentional or accidental human acts. The evaluation of the source of hazards is therefore quite critical in the remedial or coping process.

Individuals and societies differ in the ways they react to and cope with what they perceive as hazard. The effects of hazards on human beings must be placed within the context of the wide adaptability of the human species to stress (Suedfeld, 1987). The degree of severity to which hazardous conditions affect the health and sense of security of individuals or groups depends largely upon biological response, perception, and the perceived efficacy of personal and collective coping resources. However, Sorensen (1983, p. 456) did not find awareness of potential hazard "to be a good predictor of knowledge of adaptive behavior." Previous experience with hazard may either facilitate or stifle current coping reactions. Hence Kates (1976) introduced the phrase "prisoners of their experience" to refer to the scenario wherein previous experience with or exposure to hazardous conditions affect the appraisal of and reaction to subsequent hazard events. Despite the negative connotation of hazards, individuals and groups sometimes gain from them.

Some people survive and indeed prosper in the face of hazards because individuals and groups deploy differential adaptive and adjustive strategies for coping with hazards. Similar populations tend to share some common physiological coping mechanisms that are presumed to have been enhanced through generations of biological selection (Suedfeld, 1987). Similarly, people from similar cultural backgrounds tend to manifest similar psychological coping mechanisms that are the outcome of centuries of sociocultural inheritance. Although individual and community responses to hazardous events tend to vary by type of hazard and the technological status of the society, Kates (1976, p. 144) referred to "the enormous ingenuity that is employed to develop and adapt adjustments to natural hazards" in less industrialized societies.

Having examined the nature of developmental environments, how ecological influences may enter biogenetic timetables, and the effect of hazardous environments, it is but necessary to outline a perspective, an ecocultural framework, that attempts to incorporate both innate and external determinants of human development into a single conceptual picture.

CONCEPTUALIZATION OF HUMAN
DEVELOPMENT IN GLOBAL PERSPECTIVE:
AN ECOCULTURAL FRAMEWORK

Our thinking on the determinants of development is presented in a conceptual framework in Figure 2.1. The model is anchored on the point that, for every human culture, a particular worldview guides and directs human life toward this or that direction, justifying their mode of life (Erny, 1972). The framework, inspired and refined by Berry's (e.g., 1966, 1971, 1975, 1976, 1986) laborious research over the years, is excerpted from Segall et al. (1990, p. 17). It comprises population-wide and individual-level variables, which include background variables, process variables, and psychological outcome variables.

Our habitats are both physical and political in nature, hence background variables include two kinds of contexts, ecological and sociopolitical. Ecological variables are natural conditions such as climate, terrain, soil conditions, vegetation, water supply, or natural resources. Adaptive or process variables consist of both biological adaptation and cultural adaptation, that are, in turn, organismic and sociocultural characteristics of populations (Segall et al., 1990). Whereas biological adaptations include any genetic or physiological response a population makes over evolutionary time, cultural adaptations are collective elaborations of survival experiences and strategies during cultural history that subsume all interventions that are adaptive to the demands of the ecoculture. Psychological outcome variables include observable personal behaviors as well as inferred or presumed-to-exist personal characteristics or traits.

"All of us, everywhere, adapt to the world around us in ways that our cultural ancestors have found to be functional" (Segall et al., 1990, p. 184). With this in mind, Erny (1987) advocated the necessity, in studying children in Africa, of considering the conditions under which the African child lives, especially those of the child's usual or familiar environment. Within this framework, ecocultural forces are viewed as influencing human development either directly or through the intervening adaptive variables, both sociocultural and biogenetic. It is thus a feedback system or a network of relationships in which ecocultures and individuals exert reciprocal influences. Its heuristic value lies in its ability to inspire the "discovery" of relationships among any combination of ecological, adaptive, and psychological variables (Segall et al., 1990), especially its potential to inspire contextual research. Although ours is an ecocultural model, innate variables enter the framework as genotypically based process variables that modulate and permit incorporation

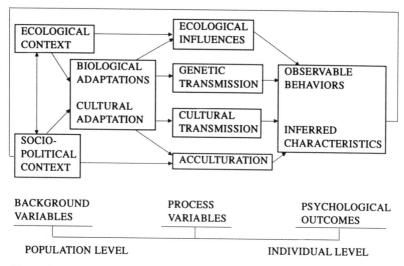

Figure 2.1. An Ecocultural Conceptual Framework for Cross-Cultural Research
SOURCE: Excerpted from Segall et al. 1990, p. 90. Reprinted with permission from Segal et al. Copyright 1990. Pergamon Press PLC.

of ecocultural opportunities into developmental agendas. The human genotype primes humans to experience the environment; genes push or restrain ecocultural forces from entering into developmental programs. In other words, coded-for environmental cues interplay and collaborate with genes to effect or impair developmental change.

Ecocultures influence development, first, by ensuring the physical survival of the offspring (R. LeVine, 1974) through the provision of protective and nurturant environments—secure and conducive developmental niches in which children live, learn, and develop. Second, human cultures provide the formulas, which predate the birth of children (Ogbu, 1991), by which adaptive skills and competencies are transmitted to and acquired by the offspring (Ogbu, 1988). Third, diverse ecocultural cues compete for (genotypic) "recognition" and incorporation into biological timetables by being coded for by genes.

En route to maturity at various life stations (infancy, childhood, adolescence, adulthood, marriage, retirement, etc.), developing persons enter diverse microniches with differential role demands and simultaneously confront global changes in the macroniche (e.g., climate, folkways, social policy, labor market, political ideology). "The developmental niche thus changes itself in the course of ontogenesis" (Segall et al., 1990, p. 115). It is in this way that "the modes of knowing toward which development proceeds in any setting are those produced by the socialization practices that are emphasized there" (Segall et al., 1990, p. 184). Consequently, to better understand development in context, it is essential to know how a given cultural context molds personality (Erny, 1987). With reference to intelligence, Sternberg (1984, p. 308) holds that the "environment shapes what constitutes intelligent behaviour."

At the core of each life stage is a developmental task, adequately identified by Freud (1956), Erikson (1950), Piaget (1970), and other theorists—at least for Western cultures. Existing theories, however, overlook culturally specific themes that transcend conventional stages (C. M. Super & Harkness, 1986). In reality, specific developmental tasks such as object permanence, basic trust, or the Oedipal conflict may be important but do not ordinarily preoccupy ontogeny in Third World cultures. Most Third World societies seem to be primarily concerned with transcendent themes such as obeisance, consideration for others, responsibility, social competence, and social living. The agendas for biobehavioral development in most Third World contexts seem to stress socio-affective rather than cognitive themes. Folk modes of fostering cognitive development in non-Western cultures thus seem to differ remarkably from Western, dominantly school-oriented techniques of cognitive stimulation. Indeed, "cultural differences in cognition reside more in the situations to which particular cognitive processes are applied than in the existence of a process in one cultural group and its absence in another" (Cole, Gay, Glick, & Sharp, 1971, p. 233). In this vein Ochs (1986, pp. 9-10) submits that on serious scrutiny of cross-cultural behavioral data, "most cross-cultural differences turn out to be differences in context and/or frequency of occurrence" of the phenomenon under investigation.

PART II

Developmental Roots

The concept of human "niche-ness" in an ecoculture implies that human development is sensitive to its context (Pellegrini, 1987). In this sense, "what is happening in the subsistence base" of Third World ecologies "must be taken into account in explaining their behavior" (Bernal, 1988, p. 91).

Although the primary purpose of this part is to familiarize social scientists with broad features of developmental contexts in the Third World about which little is known, I have, within the constraints of space, opted to devote it to the West African ecology (with special reference to Cameroon) with which I am more familiar. This is only intended to serve as an illustrative case study of a Third World developmental ecology. The main rationale for my decision is that embeddedness in *any* developmental niche is of critical importance regardless of its locus. The section focuses only on West Africa's physical and sociocultural ecologies; its historical experience is presented in Part III.

Physical and social environments provide culturally meaningful experiences to their members. In addition, the sociocultural system offers the agents, institutions, and the scripts that permit and facilitate the humanization of offspring and their social integration in some, but not other, ways.

3

DEVELOPMENTAL ROOTS
A Brief Perspective on West Africa's Geography

Human habitats are territorially organized and structured in accordance with the cultural meaning systems of the people who inhabit them (Valsiner, 1988). In Chapter 1 we referred to the centrality of the developmental niche in human life, and stressed the essential kinship between people and their environments in Chapter 2. Since place identity is integral to self-identity, developmental niches play a major role in organizing memory and providing expressive opportunities (Brown, 1987). Nowhere else does the environment so powerfully shape and sharpen orientations and attitudes as in Africa where "geography is the mother of [African] history" (Mazrui, 1986b, p. 41).

The purpose of this chapter is to outline the physical, historical, demographic, and economic conditions that surround human life in (West) Africa. This includes a brief look at environmental hazards, why geography is considered to be a strong factor in Africa's history, and the implications of population explosion and rapid urbanization. The chapter ends with a discussion of the implications of current economic trends.

PHYSICAL GEOGRAPHY

Africa, the second largest continent, "has an area of about 12 million square miles, nearly one fourth of the earth's land surface" that equals "the combined areas of the United States, Western Europe, and India" ("African economy," 1964, p. 72). Although the image of Africa that readily comes to non-African minds is that of a "jungle," "about two fifths of the

(African) continent is desert; two fifths grassland, and the remainder tropical land and other forest land" ("African economy," 1964, p. 72).[1]

West Africa is one of the five major geographical regions of the continent of Africa, located entirely within the tropics between the 2nd and 25th parallels and between longitudes 16 degrees East and 17 degrees West of the Greenwich Meridian. It stretches from the Gulf of Guinea in the south to the southern borders of Morocco, Algeria, and Libya, that is, the northern borders of Mauritania, Mali, and Niger. It is bounded on the south and west by the Atlantic Ocean and on the east by Lake Chad and the Adamawa Highlands. Its total land area of 6.2 million square kilometers (about 2.5 million square miles), shared by 17 states, is about two thirds the size of the United States (Udo, 1982).

Geomorphologically, West Africa consists of the world's oldest Precambrian rocks—outcrops of the parent rock that underlies the African continent. Physiographically, West Africa is a vast tableland with a narrow continental shelf and coastal lowlands, several interior plateaus, and varying undulating landscapes and sedimentary valleys and basins. The Cameroon Mountain, an active volcano, rises 4,070 meters (13,350 ft.) above sea level and is the highest peak in the region. Volcanic cones with crater lakes are found in the Cameroon Highland Range and the Jos Plateau. Inselbergs or erosional survivals appear here and there throughout the interior plains; they provided protective refugee outposts for settlement during the period of Islamic jihads (Islamic holy wars), slave raids, and internecine ethnic wars. West Africa's soils are generally poor, shallow, and leached. The coastline is swampy, straight, and free from the indentations that make for good natural harbors.

There are two seasons in West Africa, the wet and the dry, determined respectively by the southwest monsoon over the Atlantic Ocean and the harmattan over the Sahara. Annual temperatures and humidity are, on average, higher than in temperate climates. Many West African waterways have impermanent regimes; smaller rivers and streams usually dry up completely during the dry season. Part of West Africa's persistent drought problem is thus due to the seasonality of its rivers. Rainfall is either too abundant, causing destructive floods and erosion, or too scarce, causing aridity and drought. "Under torrential rainfall conditions characteristic of the area, gullying along water courses and sheetwash on flatter land is active, particularly at the onset of the rains when little protective vegetation exists" (Riddell & Campbell, 1986, p. 100; see also A. Campbell, 1981). The torrential rains of August 1988, thought to be the heaviest in a century, followed a long spell of drought and were responsible for the loss of human life, livestock, and crops, and extensive property damage. The heavy rainfall along the coast drops off rather rapidly as one approaches the Sahel and Sahara Desert.

"Much of sub-Saharan Africa lies in marginal rainfall areas, where drought is recurrent. Countries in the Sahel region have experienced the lowest normal rainfall over the past 15 years. Rainfall in 1983 and 1984 was the lowest in a century" (Schultheis, 1989b, p. 11). Rainfall has decreased so steadily that vast areas on the edge of the Sahel are being overwhelmed by desertification (Barrett, 1988). Timberlake (quoted in Schultheis, 1989b, p. 11) "estimates that in subSaharan Africa nearly seven million square kilometers of land, an area twice the size of India, is under direct threat of desertification, a process by which human mismanagement converts productive land into wasteland."

West African vegetation ranges from that of the scorchingly dry desert in the far north through savanna in the middle-belt to the rain forest and palm groves that lean over, nodding their crested heads to the rhythm of the Atlantic breeze. Each vegetation hesitantly but gradually yields to the next, until at the fringes of the Sahara desert, the Sahel (i.e., Mauritania, Senegal, Mali, Burkina Faso, Niger, Chad, Sudan, Ethiopia, Somalia, and the northern parts of Nigeria and Cameroon [Tchanou, 1976]) falls easy prey to arid conditions. The open savanna is vulnerable to annual dry season brush fires deliberately set by cattle rearers to encourage the sprouting of a healthier flush of pasture at the onset of the rains in March. Cut or burned to free land for agriculture and other purposes, or subjected to intense timber exploitation, the once dense forests have either assumed an aerated facade or are rapidly going out of existence, thereby relegating to history West Africa's jungle status. "Africa is losing forests at the rate of 1.3 million hectares a year" (Schultheis, 1989b, p. 11). This exacerbates the drought situation and threatens extinction of the rich fauna and flora.

Deserts and jungle forests are exotic environments that can be as stimulating as they are oppressive. For instance, heat in the arid north cracks lips and skins and deprives both humans and beasts of water and vegetation and a means of livelihood. The harmattan is so dry that it scorches crops and vegetation, blinds people, and is said to be responsible for annual epidemics of cerebrospinal meningitis along the Sahel and Sahara desert during the dry season. Where vegetation is abundant, there too breed pests and vectors that are responsible for the endemicity of several diseases. Disease and drought, rather than earthquakes and hurricanes, which are common in other continents, seem to be nature's major woes in West Africa. Nevertheless, West African ecologies can also be sources of wealth and panoramas of beauty. The luxuriant grass and woodlands of the open savanna, for instance, present the picturesque beauty of the undulating plains and plateau surfaces that the cattle rearers cherish and tourists admire.

Despite wide ecological diversity, as one travels through West Africa similar scenes recur. Along the coast and rivers, dugout canoes and ferries appear here and there, children are fishing or swimming and splashing one another, peasants take an evening bath after a hard day's toil in the farmfields. In the open savanna, peasants carpet the countryside with cultivated fields from which smoke rises into the sky as if from Abraham's sacrifice, wine tapers or hunters disappear into the bushes, herders and their animals come down to the valley for a drink of water, multiage "gangs" of children play about the neighborhoods. West African children thus live and grow in a variety of physical settings that obviously provide diverse ecological opportunities and doubtlessly exert varying developmental demands.

Food geography is a significant factor in human health and national development in West Africa. Although subregional and national variations exist, almost everywhere diets are defective in both quality and quantity, giving rise to many nutritional diseases like kwashiorkor and avitaminosis. The nutritional advantages accorded men in most communities condemn women and children to a slow—sometimes not-so-slow—insidious starvation and death. Further, the slum-related pattern of deficiency diseases in the sprawling cities is closely linked to the neglect of food farming and attempts by families and individuals to survive in a money economy without sufficient money (May, 1968).

The Role of Geography in African History

Although geography is a potent factor in African history, in no part of the continent is this as vividly evident as in West Africa. Evidence for this assertion comes from several sources. First, the desert and the presence of the tsetse fly checked the advance of Islam to West Africa in its early history, while the ubiquitous mosquito struck terror in whites. The "tiny insects of the west coast and central Africa . . . made Europeans nervous" (Mazrui, 1986b, p. 58) and prevented their settlement in West Africa. Second, the environmental damage that has been inflicted on renewable resources in the drier belt of tropical Africa will take a long time to repair. Rather than ameliorating the situation, the colonialists instead exacerbated the process in such a way that the natural resources of this part of the continent continue to be exploited without any hope of renewal (Tchanou, 1976). Third, this region is further subjected to unfavorable weather conditions that make long-term planning difficult

(Tchanou, 1976). Fourth, the random factor in the distribution of Africa's mineral wealth seems rather interesting. Much of Africa's petroleum is produced by north African nations that are predominantly Muslim, claiming closer affinities with the Arab world than with Africa south of the Sahara. Then, by an act of nature, Nigeria, the only West African country that possesses large quantities of petroleum, has a substantial Muslim population that has produced more Nigerian leaders than the non-Islamized population. Incidentally, apartheid South Africa is in control of much of the continent's solid mineral resources. Fifth, the extent to which Western multinationals stealthily export expired and trial drugs into and dump nuclear wastes in Africa poses the possibility that Africa may yet experience an ecological disaster worse than the greatest tragedy of human history, the diabolical Atlantic Slave Trade (Cummings, 1986).

Comparatively, few habitable environments appear to be as harshly hostile as are those of West Africa. In the next section, we consider the inhabitants of these seemingly hostile environments.

DEMOGRAPHIC PROFILE
AND POPULATION DYNAMICS

Africa is not the continent where *Homo sapiens* has multiplied the most. Throughout history, however, Africans—descendants of *Zinjanthropus, Homo habilis,* and *Homo erectus*—"were able to solve every major survival problem which confronted them, so that their populations could and did expand in measure with the slow but steady expansion of their productive capacity" (Davidson, 1985, p. 6). Paradoxical and worthy of deep reflection is the fact that it was not until the 20th century, when Africa came under the full pejorative grip of the West, that it was to be faced with any great crisis of overpopulation. The population problem exists despite the fact that Africa's 30.2 million square kilometers—22% of the earth's surface—is much greater than its population, which is only 10.5% of the world's total (Udo, 1982). This implies that although Africa has the world's fastest rate of population growth, it is still a sparsely inhabited continent. Africa's population problem therefore stems mainly from a worsening inability to feed itself. Population distribution, like food geography, varies widely by nation and region. That history is crucial to explaining the current population map of Africa is shown in the next sections.

A Historical Perspective

A historical perspective of the (West) African population focuses on Africa as home of the earliest humans, ancient population clusters, ancient civilizations, ethnic variety in West Africa, and Africa's early contacts with external cultures.

Home of the Earliest Humans. The remotest ancestors of humankind are said to have appeared in Africa during the Lower Pleistocene Age, some 2 to 3 million years ago, having evolved from Hominidae of the Late Miocene. "It is possible—on present evidence even probable—that they were the earliest types of mankind to appear anywhere" (Davidson, 1985, p. 3). Evidence for this comes from East Africa (M. Leakey, 1979; R. Leakey & Lewin, 1979). In 1931 on Rusinga Island in Lake Victoria, Louis Leakey excavated a creature in the ape line called *Proconsul.* In 1959 in the Olduvai Gorge (East Africa), Leakey and his wife, Mary, excavated a more advanced creature called *Zinjanthropus.* Further archaeological evidence to suggest that humankind "originated in East Africa" (M. Leakey, 1979) came in 1984, when Kamoya, Kimeu, and Richard Leakey recovered the skeletal remains of a 12-year-old boy in a swamp on the western shore of Lake Turkana (formerly Lake Rudolf). The boy was an example of *Homo erectus,* one step along the evolutionary scale between *Homo habilis* and *Homo sapiens.* These archaeological findings increase the probability "that if there was a Garden of Eden where the first man and woman lived that garden was in Africa" (Mazrui, 1986b, p. 42).

Remnants of Pygmies, considered more direct descendants of early humankind, are found in the southeastern forest of Cameroon and in the Central African Republic, Congo, and Zaire. They are similar in many ways to the !Kung San of Southern Africa (see Lee, 1979). The Pygmies are bonded in an exchange relation with settled populations on the fringes of their hunting fields. Social programs to entice them out of their isolated existence are minimally successful because, like humans everywhere, they are in no hurry to abandon their ancestral mode of life.

Ancient Population Clusters. Paleodemographic studies locate Negroid, Capoid, and Caucasoid population clusters as follows: (a) West, central, and parts of east Africa show closest affinity to the Negroid; (b) The south of the continent shows closest affinity to the Khoisan populations (!Kung San, Bushmen, Hottentots); (c) The far north of Africa shows more affinity to Caucasoid forms, but the Sahara and extreme northeastern end of the continent are also Negroid. In terms of numbers, about one third of Africa's population belongs to the Mediterranean world; linguistically defined as dominantly Hamites and Semites, but racially identified as the Mediterranean branch of the Caucasiform population (Trevor, 1955). The other two thirds of the population, predominantly Negroid, belong to sub-Saharan Africa. Despite the presence of these racial "roots" from prehistory, the mainstream history of human development and population growth in Africa "has long been concerned with the growth and evolution of the 'Negroes' " (Davidson (1985, p. 3).

Negroes seemed to have flourished at a number of growth points during the Late Stone Age and were responsible for peopling much of Africa south of the Sahara. For example, "a great South-North movement brought the African peoples of the Great Lakes region into the Nile Basin. They lived there in clusters for millennia . . . it was they who created the Nilotic Sudanese civilization and what we know as Egypt" (Diop, 1987, p. 3). Negroes are also considered to have inhabited the Saharan region before it began to desiccate around 2000 B.C. (Davidson, 1985). As they fanned out from various "growth points" over the continent, they mingled with pockets of other infiltrations descended from Paleolithic or Neolithic populations. These population movements eventually culminated in the so-called Bantu Spread. Later migrations precipitated by the Islamic jihads and the slaving raids are discussed further in Chapter 5.

Ancient Civilizations. Africa is not merely the probable cradle of humankind, it is also the "Nursery of Civilization" (Mazrui, 1986b, p. 41). Although East Africa is the birthplace of humanity and initial culture, several foci in the continent made major contributions to settled civilizations. Northern Africa, specifically Egypt, initiated grand civilization and produced an unprecedented scale of innovation and construction that still astonishes the world today. As Diop (1987, p. 3) explains, "these first Black civilizations were the first civilizations in the world, the development of Europe having been held back by the last Ice Age." A similar pattern of civilizations developed in a number of foci in West and East Africa: Ghana, Mali, Nok-Ife, Songhay, Kanem-Bornu, Zimbabwe, and others. The Nok civilization, for example, "has been traced back to the first millennium BC" and "the *Tarikh es-Sudan* tells us that the city of Kukia, on the Niger . . . was contemporaneous with the time of the pharaohs" (Diop, 1987, p. 4). Toumboucktou, capital of the Songhay Empire, was reputed for its erudition center. Toward the Gulf of Guinea at about A.D. 1400, beyond the range of Islamic influence (Davidson, 1985), some "court" civilizations flourished. Among them were the Bamum, Benin, Dahomey, Ife, and Oyo kingdoms, which had known urban life from prehistoric times. However, the dismemberment of these and other African civilizations irreversibly began with the slave raids and intensified in the 19th century with the European partition and occupation of Africa.

Ethnic Variety in (West) Africa. The Negroes who inhabit much of Africa evolved "a thousand languages and cultural variants over the past several thousand years" (Davidson, 1985, p. 3). The two major linguistic components, located respectively north and south of the Gulf of Guinea parallel, have Sudanic and Bantu roots (Andah, 1979).

As Negroes dispersed from ancient population centers, their differing ecologies constituted natural laboratories in which they tested and elaborated the series of routine activities and strategies they devised to ensure their inclusive fitness. The diverse ecologies thus evoked and molded "a bewildering variety of socio-structural responses, and nourished the evolution of a correspondingly wide variety of cultures" (Davidson, 1985, p. 6). This gave birth to the immense variety of ethnic polities that have survived to the present day. July's (1974) claim that West African languages and customs suggest a common ancestry far into the remote past therefore has historical merit and is consistent with Andah's (1979) statement that studies of early settlements in Africa before A.D. 1000 "reveal much conformity, rather than discontinuity in the continent's population history." Andah (1979) has further pointed out that if Arab and European sources are accurate, then the ethnic groups in West Africa have existed from some time in the first millennium A.D.

"No area of the earth has a greater concentration of ethnic groups than Africa" (Cummings, 1986, p. 2). Every (West) African nation contains a great variety of ethnic stocks with different tongues. For example, Nigeria has more than 200 ethnic units (Udo, 1982), whereas Cameroon with only 10% of Nigeria's population comprises more than 239 ethnic groupings (Che, 1985). The proliferation of ethnic polities and languages on the African continent is thus unparalleled in human history. It is therefore safe to assert that Africa is not only the birthplace of humankind, "but it is the very site where the biblical Tower of Babel was [is] located" (Cummings, 1986, p. 2). Given the historical evolution and deep roots of ethnic polities, it is not at all surprising that in West Africa today, as elsewhere in Africa, ethnicity is a more passionate concept than nationalism. One commonality among several African ethnics today is the English, French, or Portuguese language, a colonial bequest adopted for convenience of communication among peoples of otherwise diverse dialects in spite of "old linguistic unities" (Diop,

1987, p. 7). The need "to synthesize ideas, thoughts, values and beliefs common among the diverse and multiple people of Africa is sufficient justification for the study of traditional African thought" (Ojiaku, 1974, p. 214) and institutions.

In spite of her checkered but largely oral history, Africa's contributions to global human civilization is generally unacknowledged, hence unappreciated. This topic is taken up in Chapter 5.

Africa's Contact with External Cultures. Contemporary Africa is under the yoke of a triple heritage, a culmination of centuries of healthy, and later not so healthy, blending of indigenous and exterior values and lifestyles that stretches further into the remote past than is generally acknowledged. The roots of external contacts go to Ancient Egypt, which established mutual interactions via trade, religion, and erudition with ancient Babylon, Mesopotamia, Persia, and the Greco-Roman Empires. Other population clusters in the Horn of Africa and East Africa had similar external contacts. West African early contacts with the external world came mainly by way of long-distance trade through the trans-Saharan route.

African history somehow took a different, albeit traumatic, course when Arab and European slave merchants began to buy and ship Africans into slavery in Asia, the Americas, and Europe. The slave trade resulted in the purchase and forceful relocation of "between 14.6 and 20 million" (Oyebola, 1976, p. 11) Africans, predominantly to European plantations in the Americas. No people in history have ever been marketed and exported into slavery on such a massive scale. That created the Black Diaspora and wrought irreversible changes in Africa's demographic landscape, particularly West Africa's from where the bulk of slaves were taken. The Atlantic Slave Trade began in the 1440s and vastly expanded after the early European settlement of the Americas, ending only in the 1880s. The human cargo to Asia and Europe began much earlier and persisted even longer, but its general impact on Africa's fate was far smaller than that of the trans-Atlantic. "How profoundly the Atlantic trade influenced African society remains a modern controversy. There was much suffering. . . . Africans were landed in the Americas, not counting all those who died before embarkation or during the 'Middle Passage' of the ocean" (Davidson, 1985, p. 11). In certain areas, the "ravages of slavers . . . entirely ruined a number of polities and their peoples" (Davidson, 1985, p. 11). Thus it is but obvious that

when Africans read about the slave trade they wonder in astonishment about what happened to their clansmen whose descendants were dissolved in the vast ocean of human faces and names now called America. When Euro-Americans study the slave trade, they remember the excesses of their ancestors and the divisive nature of slavery in their own society. (Cummings, 1986, p. 4)

The African Population Profile

How history has played a role in determining the African population profile can be gauged from the fact that today about one out of every five people of Black African ancestry lives in the Americas (Mazrui, 1986b).

About 51% of Africa's population is in West and East Africa on 41% of the total land area of the continent. Central Africa has a larger land area (24.53%) than West Africa, but its population of 66 million is less than half that of West Africa (Udo, 1982). West Africa's estimated population of 169 million in 1985 compares with 264 million for North America in the same year (United Nations, 1986). Every other West African is said to live in Nigeria since Nigeria's estimated population of 116.2 million (Paxton, 1987) is more than half that of West Africa's.

The uneven distribution of the population in West Africa is obvious from the fact that less than 5% of the population lives on two thirds of the total land area (Udo, 1982). Areas with fewer than 4 persons per square kilometer coexist with population densities of more than 230 persons per square kilometer (600 per square mile). The most densely populated areas, southeastern Nigeria and the Mossi district of Burkina Faso (Udo, 1982), are among the world's most densely peopled rural districts. Population pressure on the land in such densely settled areas has given rise to acute shortages of farmland, resulting in land overuse and soil erosion. But aridity is the most critical element that accounts for differential population densities. For example, all settled areas have at least 750 mm of annual rainfall.

Arid conditions in the northern parts of Niger, Mali, and Mauritania account for the sparse population. The sparseness of the population throughout the West African Middle Belt is due partly to the ravages of river blindness and sleeping sickness, as well as the large-scale depopulation of the region during slave raids and Islamic jihads. Entire villages were exterminated, captured as slaves, or driven to refugee outposts in inaccessible or defensible mountain sites—for example, the montagnards of the Mandara Mountains of north Cameroon (Riddell & Campbell, 1986).

Demographic Parameters. The African population is characterized by rapid growth and by migratory movements of many kinds. "The fertility rate, which varies substantially from one country and one habitat to another, lies between 160 and 204 per thousand" (Touré, 1983, p. 2). Ware (1983, p. 18) observed total fertility rates in West Africa to "vary from just over 4.5 in Cameroun to something close to 7.0 in most countries of the region." The divergent trends in birthrates and general mortality and infant mortality rates, which have been brought about by progress in health practice, are undergoing drastic changes caused by the combined effects of drought, famine, and war in a number of African countries, particularly the Sahel zone and southern Africa. Ungar (1986) cites Africa's rate of population growth as 3.2%; in Cameroon it was estimated at 3.1% in 1986 (Ministry of Plan and Regional Development [Ministry], 1986). The highest crude birthrate has been observed in East and West Africa where the rate per 1,000 population in 1980-1985 was 49. This is an overwhelming figure when contrasted with 16 for North America (United Nations, 1986). In general, the mortality rate in Africa varies from 8 to 30 per 1,000 population, being higher on average than on other continents (United Nations, 1986). Life expectancy at birth is short; it is still as low as 40-50 years, compared to 70 years in developed countries (United Nations, 1986; World Bank, 1980). That is, on average, children born in Western nations live at least 20 years longer than African children.

In the majority of African countries females (World Health Organization [WHO], 1976) and youth outnumber the rest of the demographic cohort. A few countries, such as the Gambia and Mauritania, however, have a sex ratio in favor of men (Udo, 1982). Age structure determines people's needs, work status, the dependency ratio, and patterns of personal and public expenditure. With national and regional variations, in 1975 children below 15 years of age constituted more than 43% of the total population of Africa (WHO, 1976), compared to 25% in developed countries (Udo, 1982). In fact, Africa's population "is a very young population, with half under 15 years of age, and growing by three percent or more annually. The proportion of young people places a heavy burden on the resource base of governments and on the present adult population" (Schultheis, 1989b, p. 10). This implies that the productive portion of the total population is less than about 40%.

Marital status also varies, and as an index of age at first marriage and a determinant of fertility and illegitimacy it is an important demographic parameter. Although it seems that most West African women (71% in Cameroon [Ministry, 1986]) tend to contract their first marriage prior to their 20th birthday, there seems to be a tendency to postpone marriage in order to become economically viable before assuming the challenging demands of marriage and parenthood. In this direction, Nsamenang

(1981) reported the preferred age for marriage among a group of Cameroonians pursuing higher education as 28 years for men and 26 years for women.

Africa is marked by multiple religious faiths, dominated by indigenous religions, Islam, and Christianity. Although the picture is certainly different today, of 130 million black sub-Saharan Africans in 1960, there were 28 million Muslims, 13 million Catholics, 4 million Protestants, and 85 million who professed indigenous religions (Mazrui, 1986b). The heartland of Islam south of the Sahara is West Africa.

The Labor Situation in West Africa. By ILO (International Labor Organization) definition, the portions of the population accorded dependency status (children under 15 years of age and old people 65 years and older) are excluded from the labor force. West African countries exhibit a high dependency ratio, implying that their small labor forces are overburdened with a large dependent population. With few exceptions (e.g., Benin, Burkina Faso, Mauritania [Udo, 1982]), the labor force in West Africa is less than 50%; for Cameroon it is 40% (Ministry of Plan and Regional Development, 1986). The comparable figure for developed nations is in excess of 60%; it is 65% for the United States (Udo, 1982). Female economic labor force participation (with a general disregard of West African market women's economic and social power; see, e.g., Bernal, 1988; Turrittin, 1988) varies from 63% in Guinea Bissau, and 52% in Benin, to 5% in Niger (United Nations, 1975). However, Peil (1977) reported rates of female economic involvement in the southern parts of Cameroon, Ghana, and Nigeria to be high by world standards. Boserup (1970) found that Cameroonian women in Bamenda contributed about 44% of the family's income. Women's contribution to the family income has perhaps increased in recent years because the slump in cash crops is contemporaneous with increases in the marketing of food crops and the participation of women in paid employment.

The labor situation is one in which there exists serious unemployment and underemployment in urban centers, whereas the rural areas suffer from an acute shortage of agricultural labor because a large portion of the able-bodied men and women have migrated to the cities. There seems to be excessive and wasteful dependence on foreign expertise in fields where qualified nationals are available.

Migration and Urbanization in West Africa. Migration is not a recent phenomenon in Africa; "Africans have always been 'on the move,' long before any regular contact with Europe" (Schultheis, 1989b, p. 3). In fact, the origins of migratory flows in Africa are lost in history. The prehistoric North-South movement into the Nile Basin, the Bantu Spread, and the movement of people during the Islamic jihads and the slave raids are some pertinent examples of major migratory flows in Africa. Globally, migration is either voluntary (in search of work or for religious reasons), or because of disasters of natural origin (famine, floods, droughts, etc.) or those caused by human agencies (the slave trade, wars, expulsions, failures of rural development policies, etc.) (Touré, 1983).

> An estimated 15 million or more Africans are uprooted from their homes, nearly half displaced by conflict and armed violence; the rest reluctantly left their homes to search for food. They are silent witnesses to a global political-economic crisis, manifest in Africa by political conflict, declining standards of living and widespread hunger. (Schultheis, 1989b, p. 3)

The destinations of most migrants today are centers of learning, areas of employment opportunity, usually urban centers, areas of better economic or food security and favorable political climate.

A universally acknowledged problem in (West) Africa today is the dizzying pace of urbanization. Africa has the distinction of being the most sparsely populated and least urbanized continent, but the continent with the fastest urban growth rate. The growth rate of the urban population in Africa is even greater than the natural rate of population increase. This is due to rural exodus and a huge refugee population, which explain the phenomenal rise in urban populations and the number of urban centers (Udo, 1982) within a short time in a predominantly rural continent. In 1980 rural-urban migration was responsible for 3.4 million migrants to the towns in Africa south of the Sahara. "This exodus, which is steadily increasing, will in the long term contribute to a stagnation, or even a decline, in the growth of the rural population in a number of countries, including Cameroon, Benin, Mauritania, Botswana, Mauritius and Gabon" (Touré, 1983, p. 9).

CONSEQUENCES OF POPULATION EXPLOSION AND RAPID URBANIZATION

Almost everywhere in (West) Africa, labor supply has outgrown the capacity of national economies to generate productive and gainful employment. Per capita food production has declined so precariously that most countries have been obliged to import basic food items they themselves could produce, given proper planning and harnessing of local resources. In 1970, Africa was producing enough food to feed itself; in 1982, the equivalent of the entire urban population was totally dependent on food imports (World Bank, 1984, pp. 10-14). "Food shortages should be an anomaly in a continent where more than seventy percent of the population works in the rural sector" (Riddell & Campbell, 1986, p. 89). The hungry and the unemployed are a restive population, a potential sociopolitical time bomb requiring timely diffusion to avert social chaos. It has already exploded in some African countries. Not only does unemployment represent personal or family, indeed, national tragedy, it is also a waste of human resources involving a delayed or "denied" return on huge investments in education by families and governments. In spite of the low literacy rate in most nations, the school population has exceeded developments in educational infrastructure and the per capita cost of education is rising faster than the per capita income. Because resources are so scarce and rural development policies have almost failed everywhere, governments and families find it awesome to satisfy even basic needs. As a result, the number of relatives who depend on fellow kin, themselves with meager means, is alarming.

> Intense demographic pressure on living space, lack of economic and social infrastructure in low-income neighborhoods, the haphazard maintenance of existing infrastructures, lack of employment and the high cost of living in African cities are largely responsible for the deterioration in urban living standards and the increase in delinquency and in strife between different urban communities. (Touré, 1983, p. 11)

In such depraved conditions, children are usually the worst victims. "What modern city life offers more is health, education and welfare services, often hard and costly to come by, but better than those of the countryside—an indication of the essentially unequal, unfair and unjust distribution of services" (Southall, 1988, p. 4). In this sense, the living conditions (health, work, habitat) of rural residents are deteriorating like those of city-dwellers (Touré, 1983).

WEST AFRICA'S ECONOMIC GEOGRAPHY

West Africans are still more dependent on the food they grow themselves and the animals they herd than on the goods they manufacture (Nsamenang, 1987), hence their sentimental attachment to the ancestral land (Udo, 1982). About 80% of the African population, with national variation, survives by peasant agriculture (WHO, 1976) and depends on it for industrial raw materials and foreign exchange. "Twenty-three of the world's 30 poorest countries are in sub-Saharan Africa. Their annual per capita income is below $220. Per capita output declined by 11 percent from 1980 to 1983" (Schultheis, 1989b, p. 11). In a largely rural continent, "what is happening in the subsistence base of rural life must be taken into account in explaining their behavior" (Bernal, 1988, p. 91).

Thus this section highlights West Africa's economic behavior: resources, agricultural practices, productivity, and the implications of current economic and industrial trends.

West Africa's Economic Resources

In West Africa the principal economic resources are agricultural produce, the major export crops being cocoa, palm products, coffee, tea, cotton, peanuts, tobacco, and rubber. Maize, millet, sorghum, rice, yams, cassava, potatoes, bananas, plantains, and assorted vegetables and fruits are the main food crops. Mining of petroleum, diamonds, bauxite, and the exploitation of timber and other forest products provides employment opportunities and inlets for foreign exchange. Whereas in most parts of the world the bulk of industrial crops are cultivated in large commercial plantations, in West Africa they are produced mainly in small peasant holdings (Udo, 1982). Livestock, found mainly in savanna and Sahel vegetations north of the tsetse fly belt, is largely in the hands of nomadic populations. The tsetse fly is inimical to cattle because it causes sleeping sickness (trypanosomiasis), a deadly disease for both cattle and humans.

The mining sector also plays a key role in the development of infrastructures. Amenities like railways, roads, ports, schools, hospitals, and electricity built to serve the mining areas are/were often extended to non-mining communities. Minerals are a significant source of revenue in the economies of some countries, especially Mauritania and Liberia (iron ore), Togo (copper), Ghana (gold), Guinea (bauxite), Nigeria (tin and petroleum), Cameroon (petroleum), and Sierra Leone (diamonds). Most top management and technical positions in mining are still held by expatriates. Coal, petroleum, natural gas, and hydroelectricity are the major sources of industrial power, although Nigeria is the only country with coal in commercial quantities. Nigeria is the leading producer of crude petroleum in sub-Saharan Africa, but Cameroon, the Ivory Coast, and Senegal produce modest amounts of petroleum. Natural gas exists in commercial amounts in Cameroon and Nigeria but is not yet being exploited for lack of capital equipment and accessible markets. The supply of electricity is largely limited to urban centers.

Industrialization of West African economies started much later than in the underdeveloped nations of Asia and Latin America (Logli, 1985) because colonial policies shaped industries and the productive sectors of African economies according to European needs for raw materials, rather than stimulating and promoting local industries and productive capacity. This pattern of production has persisted until today and West African economies have stagnated at the stage of processing primary products and extracting mineral concentrates for export. Thus far, policy initiatives for African industries "flow mainly from a single source, the international lending community, and within it, from the IMF and the World Bank, which have become its guiding spirits" (Mytelka, 1989, p. 77). Of course, this constitutes a tacit acceptance of the paradigms that have given to African industry its current stagnation and fragility.

Three decades after independence, few would dispute that African industry is in crisis.

> In a recent survey of 343 factories in over 16 countries, spanning sectors as diverse as beverages, textiles, pulp and paper, flour milling, sugar refining and cement, fully 23 percent of the companies were found to have ceased production by mid-1980 and a further 57 percent were found functioning at less than 70 percent of nominal capacity—well below their break-even point. (Mytelka, 1989, p. 77)

No sub-African country has been spared, including those that, like Ivory Coast, had been regarded as economic miracles in the first two postindependence decades. Whereas a dozen examples of semi-industrialized nations can be cited in Asia and Latin America, Nigeria is the only West African country that has truly started industrialization.

Nevertheless, indigenous industries like iron smelting, household utensils, cloth-making, leather and wood work, and perfumery in Islamized communities flourish as family enterprises, alongside faltering industrial production. Treasured examples of indigenous industries are craft production and artworks such as the Benin and Ife (Nigeria) brass figurines and the Oku and Bamum masks (Cameroon), among which Maquet (1972, p. 146) claimed "are found smiling masks, probably the only ones in Africa."

In West Africa, the bulk of commercial exchanges takes place in daily or weekly markets, not in malls or shopping centers although some exist in urban centers. The marketplace is thus one of the unique features of

West African life where people meet for social and economic exchanges (Udo, 1982). Women and children play the most visible role within the market system. There is, however, some separation of men's and women's economic spheres. For example, "traditional Bambara [Mali] beliefs prescribe a strict differentiation with respect to marketing activity" (Turrittin, 1988, p. 586). Women's activities are related to selling products of the land and petty trade, men's activities to buying for resale, negotiating commercial transactions, and long-distance trade. "These distinctions are not strictly observed in practice, however" (Turrittin, 1988, p. 586). Women and men engage in the distribution chain for some food and imported commodities and in some countries some women participate in long-distance trade. The market's social organization illustrates the degree to which men's and women's economic domains are separate. Men and women from the same village or region with similar goods sit at known but different open sites or shaded stalls, with their wares displayed in front of them.

Almost every village has its own market day when practically the whole village and some nonvillagers come together to the marketplace, for buying and selling, for meeting friends and relatives, for drinking and exchange of news, gossip, and gifts. Young men and women also use markets for dating and courtship, while everybody has the opportunity of discussing community affairs. Bamenda Grassfields markets are also used to make public announcements and to admonish criminals (Chilver, 1962; Ritzenthaler, 1962). Furthermore, because nocturnal spirits are believed to use marketplaces as habitats, markets carry important religious and ritual significance.

Agricultural Patterns and Economic Activities

In most African cosmologies, an important natural endowment such as land does not have a marketable value. Most indigenous African land tenure systems vest land rights in a corporate group that has overriding rights over those of the individual. Land belongs to the living and to the unborn, as well as to the dead (Cheater, 1990; Udo, 1982). However, a chief, family (lineage) head, or a designated representative holds the land in trust for the community. The land itself is never regarded as individual property—individuals possess land they till by right of occupation only. Generally, a person has use rights to a plot for a predetermined period of time. In some communities, such as the Mandara of north Cameroon, some "trees can be sold, loaned, given, or inherited independently of the terrace on which they are found" (Riddell & Campbell, 1986, p. 98).

In other words, because land is regarded as communal property, title to land is purely usufructuary (Udo, 1978). When a holder abandons his or her field permanently, it reverts to the headman for relocation (Cheater, 1990). Outright sale of land or its permanent alienation, as in East Africa where 1,300 square kilometers of "European land supported 385 Europeans," whereas only 1,500 square kilometers of native reserves supported a total population of 143,924 natives (Thomas, 1988), is thus avoided. In precolonial Africa, most "families had free access to land and subsistence resources sufficient for sustenance and reproduction" (Southall, 1988, p. 5).

Far-reaching changes have, however, occurred in land tenure and land use systems in almost all African countries to the extent that today, three categories of land exist, namely, communal land, freehold, and state land. "For each of these categories there are vast discrepancies between the ideologized models and the very different realities of both holding and use" (Cheater, 1990, p. 188). For instance, land in urban centers is increasingly becoming a saleable commodity (Lawrence & Livingstone, 1985). Most of the changes were initiated by land-grabbing colonizers and Islamic influence and exacerbated by land reform policies, population pressure, agricultural capitalism, and extensive socioeconomic changes. Some of the changes have deprived some populations of pasturage and the best farmlands, giving rise to thinner herds, land overuse, and poor harvests.

Because West African soils are relatively poor, the people developed intensive land-use systems in which soil-building strategies through shifting cultivation and mix farming were, and continue to be, integral components (Boulet, 1975). "The importance of the variety of activities which promote soil conservation and fertility is fully recognized by the montagnards" of north Cameroon (Riddell & Campbell, 1986, p. 94). Almost everywhere in Africa, peasant agriculture involves shifting cultivation and mixed cropping. Among the Mafa of north Cameroon, for example:

> Crop rotation and intercropping also play an important role in maintaining sustained yields. (D. Campbell, Lev, & Holtzman, 1980)

> Many Mafa farmers participate in a two-year sorghum rotation cycle with millet, the point being that each farmer in an area follow the same system. This not only rotates the demands on the soils, but also alters the breeding habitat for pests. The cereals are also interplanted with nitrogen-fixing legumes. These are the main defense against *Striga hermonthica* (witch-

weed), the most intractable weed problem facing the mountain farmers. (Riddell & Campbell, 1986, p. 94)

Although mixed cropping may result in decreased yield per acre, it nonetheless serves as insurance against the failure of any one crop (Udo, 1982). Because various crops mature at different times, it provides variety to the diet and ensures harvest during different periods of the year. This prevents excessive food shortages, since traditional food storage techniques can barely preserve food until the next harvest of the same crop.

West African agriculture is characterized by a low level of technology (farming implements consist of hoes, machetes, scythes or sickles, and the spade). The preparation of new farmfields involves traditional slash-and-burn techniques (July, 1974), a technique that adds nutrients like sulphates to the soil. Farm sizes are small (0.8-4.0 hectares or 2-10 acres) and located about 2-11 km (1-7 miles) from the homestead (Udo, 1982). African farmers vary in their access to the basic resources of agricultural production: land, labor, capital (D. Koenig, 1986). For instance, access to the labor of the opposite sex is crucial because a gender-based division of agricultural responsibility is by crops and the right to mobilize resources (Nsamenang, 1987). Polygyny facilitated, and still facilitates albeit to a limited extent, mobilization of female labor since "another wife" meant additional hands for agricultural and domestic work (Guyer, 1980; Nsamenang, 1987). The primary motive for polygyny is thus economic, rather than men's promiscuity as some writers have intimated. Men, women, and older children, each according to ability, participated in the food production chain. The extent to which the introduction of industrial crops, taxes, and schooling altered the subsistence base of peasant life is considered more fully in Chapter 6.

While socioeconomic life among settled populations is organized around agriculture, pastoral societies—especially Sahel people (Tchanou, 1976)—organize theirs on herding different combinations of animals. Nomadism, transhumance, and settled pastoralism are the three kinds of cattle-rearing (Tchanou, 1976). Nomadic pastoralism involves movement with livestock from one pasture to another, without permanent homes. Transhumance entails seasonal movements of livestock and herders to different grazing grounds, often across national borders. But for nomads, international boundaries do not represent any reality; they go across borders at will (Tchanou, 1976). Usually, women and old people remain in permanent homes, while those who engage in transhumance are young men and adolescent males. During the dry season, they move from open savanna or Sahel to valleys that preserve their green pasture and in the wet or rainy season when valleys become marshy, they move upland to savanna plains and plateaus. In settled pastoral societies herding is undertaken by cultivators, whose children tether goats and sheep, tend poultry, and act as herdboys and dairymaids to cattle.

African agriculture relies extensively on nature. The success or failure of agriculture or pasturage usually depends on the amount, distribution, and reliability of the rainfall, which frequently delays or fails to bring relief to scorched seeds or animals and plants parched by aridity or long months of harsh sunshine. Even with normal climatic conditions, the chronic insufficiency of energy intake threatens farming efficiency. This is especially acute during the cropping season when the people undertake labor-intensive activities in the fields, with exhausted granaries and empty stomachs (Nsamenang, 1987). Although the use of high yielding crops and livestock are already giving positive results in many countries, the contribution of machinery, fertilizers, and highbred varieties of crops and livestock to agricultural productivity is perhaps the lowest in the world (Food and Agricultural Organization, 1982).

Hunter (1962) remarked that agricultural methods in Africa are often well adapted to the soils and climates. In this light, the fact that some African communities have sustained high density agricultural production for centuries in areas of very poor soils and unfavorable climate is evidence of the evolution of an indigenous "production system in which environmental management, social institutions, and agricultural practices are intimately linked" (Riddell & Campbell, 1986, p. 90). For instance, Burkina Faso, a Sahel country with a land surface equivalent to that of Gabon in the equatorial belt, supports a population of 5,500,000 inhabitants, but Gabon's population is only 1,000,000 inhabitants (Tchanou, 1976). If, to this paradox, one adds the fact that Sahel peoples are big-time cattle-rearers and that humans and animals depend considerably on vegetation, one can begin to understand the great danger posed on ecological balance in the Sahel. We can also appreciate the extent to which Sahel peoples endeavor to survive in a harsher ecology. It is thus unreasonable "to fail to appreciate, even with a certain admiration, the complexity of a culture so intricately adapted to its limitations" (Hunter, 1962, p. 101).

Agricultural Growth and Productivity

In the 1960s the production of crops and livestock in Africa grew in volume by 2.3% per annum, or roughly at the same rate as population growth. In the 1970s, however, increase in agricultural output dropped to a dangerous low of about 1.3% a year, while population grew at 2.7% (World Bank, 1981). Of course, this is an indicator of the poor performance of African governments. Most African countries have yet to realize that social and economic development depend on a healthy, resourceful population, which cannot come into existence if the population, particularly children, are not adequately socialized and nourished at the time of greatest need—childhood. Countries like Cameroon have found out that "infections due to malnutrition affect the delicate groups of our population (pregnant women and children)" (Ministry, 1986, p. 51). But in much of Africa the extent to which problem awareness is backed up by appropriate policies and intervention programs is doubtful.

Shaped by nineteenth-century colonialism and a Euramerican world order, sub-African economies were drawn into the international division of labor essentially as junior partners: producers of raw materials and consumers of manufactured goods. Thus some of the multiple factors that lie behind the economic crisis in Africa are alien in origin. "Some are ecological and are due to a combination of unfavorable climatic conditions, human mismanagement and population pressure. Others arise from the dependent nature of African economies, the policy failures of African governments, and the nature of the relationship to the international marketing systems" (Schultheis, 1989b, p. 11). With the self-sufficiency of their households already destroyed by capitalist relations and bureaucratic control, Africans are submerged in a system in which "the weak and the poor bear the burden of policies and institutions imposed and maintained by the powerful and the rich" (Schultheis, 1989b, p. 13). African nations thus remain poor because they are forced to operate as if they were equals in a world dominated by the rich (Nyerere, 1977).

In sum, the present economic difficulties and food shortages in African countries are a combination of the neglect of peasant agriculture, misdirected development programs, shifts in the international economy, and Africa's limited ability to adjust to those shifts.

> Whatever the causal interactions and relative importance of these factors, the results are evident in several areas: 1) hunger and economic hardship for most people and rural communities; 2) increased corruption among government officials and bureaucrats; 3) growing unrest across the population; and 4) increased militarization, as governments attempt to control an uneasy population. (Schultheis, 1989b, pp. 12-13)

This scenario of want and despair has for some time not only generated large-scale forced displacement in Africa, but has recently led to widespread agitation (sometimes violent) for more democratic political reforms and freer market forces for agricultural produce.

A host of remedial schemes ranging in scope from attempts to replace peasant practices or settle nomads through cooperative production to socialist transformations and state farms have been undertaken in most countries. Their common denominator, however, is the varying degrees of failure recorded across countries. The failure may be attributed to a number of tactical and logistical errors that persist to date. In the first instance, peasants were usually antagonized by the uncivil manner in which their land was seized. In the second place, the introduction of agricultural innovation meant an onslaught on existing indigenous knowledge base and technology, with the attendant consequences this engendered. In addition, agricultural policies and incentives tended and still tend to encourage export crop production and industrialization along Western lines to the neglect of food crop production.

There was also inadequate forward planning, further complicated by bureaucratic control and overcentralization. In many countries agricultural schemes are predicated on a certain amount of unpaid labor from household units that also produce much of their own subsistence. The state usually "receives all the benefits derived from controlling the farmers' labor, the production process, and the product without having to pay for the labor" (Bernal, 1988, p. 101). Most efforts so far have not built on nor have they utilized the indigenous "fund of agricultural knowledge of great historical depth" (Riddell & Campbell, 1986, p. 101). For example, in the Mandara Mountains of north Cameroon, the introduction of cotton and other exogenous crops and associated techniques, new types of land tenure and settlement, and other interventions neither provided viable options that could meet the demands of the rapidly growing population nor considered endogenous inputs (Riddell & Campbell, 1986).

Furthermore, the land does not usually have a high potential yield to cover the high running costs; and most projects suffer from inadequate technical inputs like the study of soils, rainfall regimes, and the possibilities for the use of fertilizers and mechanization. There have even been unfortunate situations in which fertilizers meant for temperate soils were imported and applied to tropical soils in West Africa. Finally, many of the projects are usually spurious imitations of similar projects successful elsewhere but imported with little, if any, consideration of contextual peculiarities. The success of agricultural innovation therefore depends not solely on its net benefits but much more on its perceived salience and cultural relevance to the peasantry.

Consequently, knowledge of the beneficiary's ecoculture and psychology is an essential fore-component of the package for innovation. Perhaps this fact explains why many agricultural schemes intended to have a "demonstration effect" on the peasantry failed (Udo, 1978). According to Riddell and Campbell (1986, p. 100),

> the production system of the Mandara Mountains provides an important example of intensive land use in Africa. It keeps land in production, it supports a population density equal to that found in worse-case scenarios predicted for other parts of the continent, all on inherently poor soils using indigenous technology.

This kind of well-adaptive technology certainly arises from the long-term interaction between social, economic, and environmental components of a rural system whose members have first-hand knowledge of their labor capacities and the limitations of their ecosystem. Given that peasants all over Africa possess such deeply ingrained agricultural knowledge, it might be advisable to entrust the prime responsibility for agricultural innovation and research to the local farm communities (Riddell & Campbell, 1986) rather than to elites, who in reality, are obstacles to agricultural development in Africa. This might reduce, if not eliminate, the conflict of interest between farmers and management that is inherent in an inefficient control of agriculture from the top-down.

ECONOMIC TRENDS AND THEIR IMPLICATIONS

Despite the nominal increase in the number of industries in Africa today, peasant households are still the main units of production. But rather than actively support and expand the productive capacity of peasants, African governments have set up systems in which peasants' decision-making power is circumscribed by their overdependence on corrupt elites. Hence peasants' power to maximize efforts and increase their efficiency and productivity is virtually nonexistent. The class interests of the powerful elites limit their assumed progressive role. While contemporary Africans are largely motivated by endogenous precepts, their governments have created, with eloquent but vain promises, socioeconomic programs without adequate ecocultural roots in Africa. Of course, the outcome has been so glaringly disastrous that today African economies are on a daily deterioration course.

A disturbing but noteworthy fact is that the decline in African economies occurred over a period when the various governments and international "helping" agencies focused more strongly on food production projects than ever before (World Bank, 1981, p. 47). Another largely ignored fact is that food production in the peasant sector actually increased with little or no expert assistance, but declined in the expert-staffed and publicly funded projects during the same period. Hubbard (1985, p. 57) substantiates thus: there has been "widespread failure of large-scale, government-operated estates launched in the first two decades of independence, with heavy capital investment in mechanization and irrigation." This should alert governments, foreign advisors, and international agencies that the relentless efforts to replace peasant practices that have the merit of building a firm, local economic base, offering more employment outlets, and requiring less foreign exchange are somewhat faulty.

> Whether in the Mandara Mountains or elsewhere, agricultural development by external agencies, no matter how well-intentioned, is never simply an effort of the rich to aid the poor. Projects may contribute some funds and expertise, but it is the local community that has to assume all the risks while investing their most prized capital: land and labor. (Riddell & Campbell, 1986, p. 101)

Ironical as it may seem, "American agriculture is rediscovering such technologies as minimal tillage, just at the time African farmers are being advised to give it up" (Riddell & Campbell, 1986, p. 101). And all this is in face of overwhelming evidence that "tremendous cost are involved if African agricultural systems were to be modernized along Euro-American lines" (Riddell & Campbell, 1986, p. 89). We must be concernedly aware that farming technology in temperate climates has not provided the answer to Africa's agricultural problems. Since no ready alternative has been found to replace the African small producer, the most rational and cost-effective use of Africa's limited development resources would be to facilitate production by realizing the full potential of the indigenous system (Riddell & Campbell, 1986). This is in fact a model that has proven effective elsewhere, Japan and Taiwan being excellent examples.

There is urgent need to take seriously the fact that African economies thrive on the productive capacities of peasant households. This calls for serious reflection and replanning of economic growth from the level of the peasantry. Because the economic salvation of Africa hangs on the peasants, economic programs that do not fully integrate them at their current levels of productivity are doomed to fail. Industrialization in Africa must therefore be on what Africans themselves produce and it is necessary to curb Africans' insatiable tastes for foreign goods.

SUMMARY AND CONCLUSION

West Africa, located entirely within the tropics, is one of the five geographic regions of the continent of Africa. Its dry and wet seasons are determined by the flow of the northeast (over the Sahara Desert) and the southwest (over the Atlantic Ocean) trade winds. The vegetation that ranges from the northern desert to the coastal rain forest and mangrove swamps grows on various degradations of the oldest Precambrian rocks. The region sometimes fluctuates between destructive floods and extensive droughts, dry heat and humid weather. Few environments are as overtly hostile as the West African in the sense that heat deprives humans and beasts of water and vegetation, and heavy rainfall sustains the vegetation that breeds a variety of predators, vectors, and pests. The overexploitation of the environment, especially the forest, has virtually deprived West Africa of its "jungle" status and threatened the extinction of a rich fauna and flora. Nature is not just the cause of human misery in West Africa, it is also a source of wealth and a panorama of beauty as represented by the scenic elegance of the luxuriant savanna and wooded grassfields.

Population history reveals that Africa had been home for Negroid, Capoid, and Caucasoid races from prehistory and that the Negroid race multiplied the most to people much of the continent. Africa has the distinction of being the most sparsely populated continent, but the continent with the fastest urban and natural growth rates. Population growth in Africa today is in excess of per capita food production. African economies are sustained by peasant agriculture, characterized by low agricultural inputs and dependence on the elements. So far, peasant modes of agricultural production seem to have been more successful than the so-called modern techniques, probably because the latter are frequently "imposed" without the active involvement of the peasants. Because West African economies are largely family based, it is expedient to plan economic development from the current level of the peasants rather than continue blindly to imitate inappropriate Western economic models.

To conclude, well-intentioned administrations throughout Africa have tried to improve the lot of African peasants. But "by failing to understand the complex interactions between society and environment, they have encouraged" policies and schemes "which may yield current users only short-term opportunities rather than alternatives providing time for long-term investment in the land" (Riddell & Campbell, 1986, p. 100). In order to correct the decline in the food production situation in Africa, we must examine four crucial factors (Bernal, 1988). First, the degree to which subsistence production has been undermined; that is, what is happening to the subsistence base of rural life. Second, the extent of control peasants (not elites and bureaucrats) have over production decisions. Third, the classes and institutions that shape conditions under which peasant production takes place play a major role in helping or hindering agricultural development. Finally, the degree to which women participate in agricultural production and are included in agricultural planning and intervention schemes is not clear.

The topics and issues raised or discussed in this chapter are central to developmental psychology not only because the human species is a contextual, gregarious animal, but more so because the environment in which development occurs determines human activities and survivability and the direction in which humans use their abilities. Human activities and demographic dynamics, in turn, determine the shape and path along which development and human personality proceed (Segall et al., 1990).

NOTE

1. Copyright © 1964 by The New York Times Company. Reprinted by permission.

4

DEVELOPMENTAL ROOTS
The West African Sociocultural Environment

This chapter is about "Africanity . . . the totality of cultural features common to the hundreds of societies of sub-Saharan Africa" (Maquet, 1972, p. 54), with special reference to West Africa. Contemporary Africa is a vast mosaic of variegated states, a direct result of the African's fierce but failed resistance to European colonialism. The ecological, ethnic, economic, sociocultural, and linguistic diversity in Africa was further exacerbated by the different policies and forms of administration set up by the different European colonial powers. Despite the wide variety, however, similarities are no less remarkable. But what justifies the notion of the cultural unity of Africa (Diop, 1960; Erny, 1987) in the midst of such diversity?

Africanity is based on a similar experience of a common world and on the dissemination of several culture traits (Maquet, 1972) from prehistory until our time. Three mechanisms interplayed to create Africa's cultural unity: the development of similar adaptations to the same conditions of life (Diop, 1987), indelible traumatic experiences, and the diffusion of culture traits through culture contact with similar patterns and contents of enculturation and acculturation. The depth and impact of this common cultural heritage makes it possible to "perceive a certain common quality" (Maquet, 1972) as one encounters and experiences the apparently diverse societies in Africa. According to Erny (1987, p. 29), *"Les meme elements se retrouvent dans la plupart des systemes, agences souvent de manniere identique. La diversite vient surtout de l'importance relative qu'on leur accorde, de manniere dont ils se trouvent accentues et valorises, du poids qui les marque"* (i.e., Similar elements are found in every system; institutions are often identical. The diversity emerges mainly from the relative importance given to them;

71

from the manner in which they are valued and weighted). Copet-Rougier (1987) confirms this by reporting that in spite of linguistic and historical differences among neighboring Gbaya and Mkako communities of East Cameroon, they share much similarity in social organization and cultural patterns. All this implies that "Africans experience and think about the person and the life cycle" (Riesman, 1986, p. 71) from a deep-seated common cultural base (Erny, 1987). West Africa's superficial diversity therefore seems to betray deep-seated commonalities across communities.

Our effort in this chapter to highlight the similarity and coherence in the West African social world is not meant to mask the overt, albeit superficial, diversity, but to draw attention to some of the common "sources of Africanity" (Maquet, 1972, p. 16). Our position is that early scientific efforts that emphasized diversity rather than commonalities were perhaps rationalizations for the colonization of a "divided" Africa. In point of fact, "as a direct result of the African encounters with Europe and, indeed, as a direct result of the African reluctance to accept colonial administration, Africa is today divided into more than fifty states" (Cummings, 1986, p. 13). Perhaps they were also intellectual justifications for the subjugation of people with "rejected [i.e., un-European] forms of wisdom" (Mudimbe, 1985, p. 150).

Furthermore, earlier scientific concerns—rather than exploring and presenting the intrinsic worth of the African universe—were largely directed at depicting its "illness" vis-à-vis the "health" of European civilization. Anyone who genuinely cares to glance beyond the surface diversity and chaos said to be the distinctive identity marks of (West) African life would be amazed at the insights of its worldview and the logic of the wisdom it engenders. African "knowledge" diverges from Western versions of epistemology and possesses "an intrinsic order that could be grasped even if the reality to which" it is oriented seems obscure. This justifies the need to study and record it (Riesman, 1986).

The purpose of this chapter, therefore, is to try to paint in broad strokes the constituent elements of a West African social ecology. The explication in the first part centers on the West African worldview, including concept of the universe, causal theory, embedment in a human community, notion of personhood, ontogeny, and view of death. The second section discusses kinship, the organizing principle of indigenous West African social systems. This leads to a brief examination of institutional rules and goals and the value of the community. As emotive concepts in West Africa, ethnicity and territoriality merit consideration as a prelude to focusing on the nature of indigenous governance. Because indigenous religion is integral to cultural life, its examination in the sixth section involves rituals and festivals. The chapter terminates with a brief overview of illness behavior and indigenous medicine.

WORLDVIEW:
A PSYCHOLOGICAL FRAME OF REFERENCE

Worldview is a culturally shared window through which we peer into the universe. Although worldview derives from the culture, it is a personal (psychological) frame of reference in the world. Being inseparable from what we perceive as reality, worldviews are conditioned by our intuition and experiences. A concept of the world answers a fundamental human need: a wish to understand the universe and one's place in it. Ecocultural inputs therefore play a key role in its development. For instance, a society with a high mortality rate and food scarcity would likely develop a different cosmic outlook than a well-fed society with a low mortality rate (Maquet, 1972). The (West) African worldview is a composite term comprising concept of the universe, causal theory, embedment in a human community, personhood, ontogeny, and the notion of death.

Concept of the Universe

A West African universe consists not only of "this" world, the world in which we live, but also of the "next" world, a three-tier spiritual world: the realm of proximate (recently dead) ancestral spirits and lesser deities; the realm of remote ancestral spirits and higher deities; and the home of a Supreme Being, the highest realm. That is, for Africans the universe is "a hierarchy of interconnected forces," with God at the apex (Riesman, 1986, p. 73). Ancestral spirits are viewed as powerful and are believed to be in contact with the living (Menkiti, 1984). Ritualists, some "gifted" persons, and kings are the principal intermediaries between the dead and the living, hence the notion of divine kingship. Although dead ancestors are in reality not alive, they are believed to exist in the world of the dead (Jahn, 1961). So vivid is the sense of the supernatural that its distinction is not always clearly present to the common awareness (Baeta, 1967). Dead ancestors are conceived of as continuing spiritual presences watching over and admonishing their living descendants (Ellis, 1978) to help keep them from faltering in life. We may designate ancestral spirits as the "living-dead" (Mbiti, 1970).

Since dead ancestors are intercessors in the transcendental world, the living frequently enlist their help through rituals and sacrifices (Onwuanibe, 1984; Menkiti, 1984). Dead ancestors intercede on behalf of the living kin because, having been human, they are thought to be knowledgeable about worldly affairs and to be able to represent them appropriately to God. With a lively faith in the "living-dead," Ghanaians, like most West Africans, "have shrines of their ancestors" to which they go "to ask the blessing of their ancestors in any important project they want to undertake" (Tetteh, 1967, p. 215). The recent dead are usually invoked by personalized identification (e.g., personal names) to indicate their closeness to the living. The remote dead are said to belong to a higher realm of the spiritual world and are invoked by generic ancestral names.

Causal Theory

The world is thought to be orderly; there are always cause-effect relationships. In other words, all events are said to be "caused" and potentially explicable, mainly in terms of the machinations of evil people and kindred spirits (Wiredu, 1984). But as scientists we rationalize our ignorance by attributing events to "chance." The African world is not inherently capricious, although humans, even the innocent, are vulnerable to evil influences of all sorts. God infused the universe with natural powers that humans may exploit in beneficial or malicious ways (Minkus, 1984). West Africans maintain an optimistic posture despite frequent encounters with tragedy and disaster because of their faith in cosmic justice and the Supreme One (Minkus, 1984). They tend to see current hardship and injustice as temporary, mundane conditions. The Supreme One retains ultimate dominion over the universe he created. Justice will prevail in the end: The righteous will be rewarded after death, the wicked will be punished (Oguah, 1984), and justice will be done or at least be perceived to have been done.

While individual dependence on fellow humans and spirits may seem crushing, humans are not thought to be pawns at the mercy of external forces. A person's actions are essential but insufficient determinants of his or her progress in life. Much of what happens to an individual is usually regarded as precipitated by his or her own acts (Minkus, 1984). For example, infertility is usually blamed on the individual's or couple's wickedness or on such tabooed acts as infidelity or the misguided forfeit of one's fertility for the sake of wealth. Although other causes of misfortune —like acts of God, or witchcraft—are acknowledged, the presumption of a personal input into one's predicament justifies the contemptuous treatment most people with certain types of misfortune sometimes receive. The four major sources of misfortune thus are the operation of malignant spiritual influences, activated by personal or collective wickedness; destiny; the wickedness of others; and acts of God or of unknown etiology.

Personal blame or blame of others for one's misfortune is acceptable, but to claim total credit for success or fortune is unacceptable (Minkus, 1984). Modesty demands acknowledgement of the spiritual component and others' goodwill. To do otherwise is to undermine and anger them—to court spiritual or ancestral wrath and loss of face with kin and the social network. This kind of causality provides satisfactory explanations for chaos and misfortune and simultaneously sustains faith in the benevolence of the universe as a whole. Because the ultimate source of all evils is the machinations of spiritual forces, mediated by means of known agents such as ancestors, humans, personal acts, and malicious agents, bafflement or events without apparent cause are typically referred to God for an explanation (Minkus, 1984). That is, if one cannot understand or locate the specific cause of an event or situation, then one must accept that it is in the nature of creation that it should be the way it is. Prior to such ascription, however, much effort and resources are always expended to understand and locate the etiologic agent.

Embedment in a Community of Other Humans

A frame of reference that focuses on the individual does not come to the West African readily. In the West African viewpoint "man is not man on his own; the individual gains significance from and through his relationships with others" (Ellis, 1978, p. 6). Menkiti (1984, pp. 171-172) captures the primacy of the "environing" community by asserting that

> it is in rootedness in an ongoing human community that the individual comes to see himself as a man, and it is by first knowing this community as a stubborn perduring fact of the psychological world that the individual also comes to know himself as a durable, more or less permanent, fact of this world.

The sense of self that we possess cannot therefore be attained without reference to the "community" of other humans. That is, the human "animal" becomes humane by virtue of incorporation—humanization via care and socialization—into the human community.

Without socialization or incorporation into "this" or "that" human community, individuals are considered mere "danglers" to whom the designation "person" does not appropriately and fully apply. It is perhaps on the potency of this recognition that West African social systems emphasize the rituals of social incorporation at various life stations (naming, puberty, marriage, funeral, etc.). It may also be on the merit of this social reality that every human society emphasizes the learning of the social code by which it functions. In this way, human neonates, original biological imperatives par excellence, come to attain social selfhood. It is in this light that Itard's account of *The Wild Boy of Averyon* becomes more meaningful and reinforces more strongly the critical importance of the human community in the development of the human offspring to wholesome personhood.

The Sense of Community

In West Africa "the individual exists in and for the community" (Atado, 1988, p. 7). Societal norms and status roles are in terms of individual obligations to the commonweal. Thus in the West African novel "individual sentiments and actions" tend to derive "force and logic from those of the community" (Obiechina, 1975, p. 36). The importance of the community is evident in the maxim: "Seek the good of the community, and you seek your own good. Seek your own good, and you seek your own destruction" (Oguah, 1984, p. 221).

In *Things Fall Apart,* Chinua Achebe (1958) depicts the strengths and rhythms of collective life and shows how individual interests must be subordinated for the public good. The usefulness of this kind of social system is exemplified by the ease with which the victims of the Nigerian civil war "just disappeared" into the households of the relatives who had obligations to them (Nwogugu, 1974). Until alternative systems of social security replace extended family networks, the primacy of kinship systems will remain paramount in West Africa, even where they conflict with the exigencies and demands of nation-states.

The Notion of Personhood

West Africa's concept of being is dynamic (Erny, 1987); personhood is not ascribed simply because one is born of human progeny. This notion of personhood can be inferred in almost every culture because uncivil attitudes and behaviors are almost always characterized as animalistic.

This explains the need in every culture to educate and "guide" children from the innocence and dependency of infancy to the wisdom and independence of adulthood (Erny, 1987, p. 31). In other words, person-hood is systematically achieved during ontogeny as one internalizes and enacts status roles commensurate with his or her developmental stage. Hence, the terms used to describe persons and the social posture adopted toward others vary according to developmental stage and social status (Erny, 1987). Personhood therefore is something at which individuals could be competent or better, fail, or be ineffective (Menkiti, 1984).

Thus full personhood is not perceived as an imperative of birth nor the onset of earthly existence, but is attained after one is well along in society. This clearly indicates that the older a child becomes the more of a person he or she becomes. This implies both a claim of a qualitative difference between the old and young and a claim of ontogenetic progression from birth to death. An Ibo proverb cogently expresses this idea: "What an old man can see sitting down, a young man cannot see standing up" (Menkiti, 1984, p. 173). This proverb applies not just to the incremental growth of knowledge or wisdom as one ages; it also applies to the maturation and organization of a complex mix of other attributes considered to be definitive of full personhood. This means that during ontogeny humans undergo progressive humanization and fundamental transformations in the core of their personalities until death.

West African Ontogeny

Viewed from the perspective of its social construction, the West African conception of *person* centers around the image of the "unfinished child" (D'Alessio, 1990, p. 70). In one sense, West Africans consider the newborn a "no-body" (Erny, 1968, p. 19) but with all the potentialities to become human in future. West Africans conceive of infant personhood and personality mainly in terms of their "becoming" (Erny, 1968, p. 12).

The idea of the "unfinishedness" of the human child or the ontogenetic acquisition of personhood is not unique to West Africa. It seems to be supported by a tendency in most languages of referring to the neonate as "it." Even a cursory overview of infant development literature will corroborate this assertion. While most languages freely refer to babies as "it," there is no such freedom when referring to older humans. In fact, there is usually dismay or outrage when an adult is addressed as "it."

Traditional West African cultures operate from the position that person-hood is attained not only as one ages but also in direct proportion to the enactment of one's status roles. The enactment of such roles gradually but progressively transforms the child from its it-ness status early in life into the person-ness status of later life. The it-ness status of the early stages of life are perhaps attributable to the amorality and ignorance that is assumed to characterize this phase of life and the uncertainty surrounding the survival of the human infant. To varying degrees, all cultures assume the amorality of early life, but the uncertainty of infant survival is more characteristic of some societies than of others. Later years of life are marked by greater confidence in human survivability and a wider maturity of moral consciousness—a moral maturity without which West Africans think that personhood would have eluded the individual.

Menkiti (1984) has pointed out that in West Africa the depersonalized reference marking the beginning of life also marks its end—the beginning of life in the spiritual world. The spirituality of the (West) African is perhaps rooted in a very strong belief in life after death and in reincarnation.

The West African View of Death

The conception of death as an integral part of the human condition is universal but shrouded in fear and mystery because it is not fully understood, hence not usually wholly accepted. Death, however, has a redeeming feature. West Africans see it as a "passage" to the next world. Although the deceased is deeply mourned, it is believed that his or her spirit has gone, first, to the ancestral world, and later to higher spiritual realms. The West African thus sees himself or herself more modestly as part of the great stream of life that transcends his or her own self.

The mourning of the dead is somehow related to the level of personhood attained prior to death. For example, one notes the "relative absence of ritualized grief when the death of a young person occurs, whereas with the death of an older person, the burial ceremony becomes more elaborate and the grief process more ritualized—indicating a significant difference in the conferral" of ontogenetic status (Menkiti, 1984, p.174). Thus the funeral and mourning rites of famous people are usually more elaborate than those of children and ordinary folks.

It is believed that "there is something in the human being which is eternal and indestructible, and which continues to exist in the world of spirits" (Gyekye, 1984, p. 208) after it has been separated from its anatomical habitat. There is thus more to a human person than his or her biology. Personhood, therefore, is a manifestation or presence of a vital force through a body, though never completely identifiable with that body. Consequently, there is high regard for the human person in recognition of the presence of the force. In daily life, the high regard for this force is reflected in warm greetings (Onwuanibe, 1984) and intimate social relations. Nobody greets an anatomical unit, per se, but "what" is manifest through it. Because greetings signify the acceptance and acknowledgement of human-ness, it is quite offensive not to be greeted. Not to be greeted is regarded and felt as a mark of disregard; a form of dehumanization. Some people tend to regard the amount of time Africans devote to greetings as a waste of valuable time and effort, but its humane and socio-therapeutic value cannot be compensated by any other gains.

The high value of greetings in West African life denotes a high regard for the human organism. For instance, strangers are expected to be treated with cautious hospitality, especially if they are in difficulty. For lack of proper expression, the general mode is that "pure" strangers are God's emissaries, sent to assess human kindness and goodwill. When the "new" kinds of humans (Arabs and whites) first appeared in Africa, Africans extended (and still extend) their hospitality toward them. As Cummings (1986, p. 5) substantiates, "there is reference to the hospitality of the Ethiopian Negus (the Sea King) to the Muslim refugees from Mecca." Hunter (1962, p. 31) adds that some of "the first Europeans . . . came as lowly missionaries or explorers, often in need of help and hospitality, which they constantly received even among people of infinite poverty." Unfortunately, however, "African legendary hospitality" was abused and eventually became and still is the major source of her subjugation and ridicule.

The valuation of humanity in West Africa is rooted in kinship.

KINSHIP, ETHNICITY, AND TERRITORIALITY

The way human beings organize their social systems reflects their perception of the universe, life, social reality, and human destiny. The endogenous West African social field is punctuated by kinship ramifications (Ayisi, 1979) and, in general, common habitation with a tendency for the claim of territory, the ancestral land. This claim is deeply emotive because "where the ancestors are buried, there the soul of the clan resides, and there the prospects of the health of the next generation should be sought" (Mazrui, 1986b, p. 270).

No area of the earth has been more affected by various streams of population movement and none has "a greater concentration of ethnic

groups than Africa" (Cummings, 1986, p. 2). In almost every region of
Africa "people and communities relocated to maintain ecological balance, to seek a more secure environment and to achieve better conditions
of living" (Schultheis, 1989, p. 3). This brought into contact different
peoples and cultures that borrowed from each other; thus a common
African cultural inheritance was gradually built. The prehistoric meeting of different peoples perhaps introduced notions of rights and spheres
of influence and this might have precipitated intergroup conflict.

The roots of territorial claims may thus be embedded in the oldest
human survival activities: hunting and gathering. In historical time, hunting and gathering attained a competitive edge. Questions arose of who
had rights to hunt or of where to gather fruit, giving rise to the twin issues
of sphere of activity and territorial boundary. Questions about spheres
of control and locus of operation perhaps initiated the earliest versions
of the territorial imperative in human behavior and inaugurated, in grand
style, the distinction between "we" and "they."

In historical time, this culminated in the distinction of peoples and
might have constituted the precursors of ethno-racial differentiation. As
hunting grounds and fruit fields increasingly became scarce as the
population grew, competition intensified and probably ignited intergroup conflicts and violence. Ancestry and common residence thus
became the core identity criteria for people with a felt need for collective security to band together. As animosity and disputes about who had
the right to hunt game or gather fruit where it grew, they exacerbated
the strife among the nascent human collectivities. Group differentiation
and territorial claims became a matter of armed confrontations and
mutual injury. The vestiges of armed territorial conflicts have persisted
across millennia to our day.

In the course of time, the various human collectivities consolidated
into egalitarian or hierarchical societies with gathering, nomadic, or
settled life-styles and varied patterns of settlement. As people demonstrated varying levels of competence, some members of the group who
distinguished themselves by prestigious deeds or acts of bravery might
have been referred to with pride and were revered, accorded glory or
"royal" status. Such ancestors represent "the apex of a triangle with a
base that broadens with each [new] generation" (Maquet, 1972, p. 57).
This probably introduced the cult of the royal ancestors. Because the
tradition of such ancestors weighed and still weighs like a nightmare
on the brains of the living (Ouden, 1987), they actively conjured the
spirits of the past to claim legitimacy to power by inheritance. This
probably validated dynastic legitimacy as a traditional pattern in some,
indeed most, West African polities.

"For centuries slave raiding for sale to European trading stations as well as for internal use was an important source of domestic insecurity" (Ouden, 1987, p. 7) in West Africa. Polities indulged in mutual rivalries, sometimes to the point of civil war. This resulted not only in civil disorder but also in the weakening of political authority within some "states" (Law, 1987). Some states that had earlier exercised some degree of suzerainty over others were themselves captured, subjugated, and/or incorporated into the dominant or victorious polity.

Although most West Africans generally trace their pedigree to a common, usually remote ancestor or ancestress, their genealogies are more complex than claimed, if not uncertain. For instance, members of one clan claimed descent from the same ancestor but forgot his name (Copet-Rougier, 1987). Because "Africans have always been 'on the move' " (Schultheis, 1989b, p. 3) and there were streams of population distribution and redistribution over historical time, almost every African ethnic group came from "elsewhere" (Maquet, 1972, p. 23). This undoubtedly caused ethnic intermingling and sometimes the assimilation of other peoples; a critical factor for stability in West Africa. Since ethnicity connotes collective identity, the triangle referred to above constitutes all the descendants, that is, a line of persons who feel a close solidarity. But for some people, membership in the clan is by reason of social accretion rather than descent. In this sense, claim of a common descent may be fictitious "since again and again outsiders were assimilated by the clan" (Frank, 1990, p. 287). This may explain the sneers or whispers in many communities that some members of a lineage were descendants of slaves, for example, the Osu (an outcast clan) in Iboland.

Clans may follow patrilineal or matrilineal descent and, depending on size, are subdivided into various lineages and sublineages. The vast majority of West African societies are patrilineal. The Ashanti of Ghana and the Kom of Cameroon are two examples of matrilineal societies. Within each lineage there exist numerous kinship lines based mainly on birth and marriage (Nsamenang, 1989c). Kinship by birth extends to all those a person can identify or claim as "having the same blood," and this can extend over several generations. Kinship by affiliation extends to all traceable kin of either spouse. The marital couple then become kin to spousal affines in rather extensive relationships.

Whatever its norms, the kinship system is the primary social network in which each individual finds his or her own niche. The syntax in the terms used to express the values and expectations of kinship is not merely rhetorical but morally obligatory, instructing kinsmen so described to behave within the cultural scripts of the terms used (Ayisi, 1979). Inheritance and succession are either matrilineal or patrilineal, although some societies follow both. Matrilineal inheritance is becoming unpopular as such societies are under increasing pressure to reverse their rules of inheritance. Matrilineal inheritance makes relatively little difference where there is not much to inherit. But it can be quite hurtful if the children's father had built up a fortune whereas their maternal uncle had barely scratched a living. Children in matrilineal societies aptly argue: "Everyone has a father but not everyone has a maternal uncle" (Nsamenang, 1987, p. 290). With this kind of mind-set, children see no sense in working hard in their father's farm or enterprise if the result would go to others.

Because daughters are expected to be given out in marriage, they do not, as a general rule, own landed property in their families of origin. However, daughters can inherit transmittable goods like kitchenware (Ayisi, 1979), and in some communities widows may inherit their husband's property. Succession is often problematic where many beneficiaries, especially in polygynous homes, expect to inherit limited property. In such cases, inheritance sometimes become a disruptive and litigious affair.

INDIGENOUS GOVERNANCE

West African forms of indigenous government vary from small, single ethnic chiefdoms and stateless polities to empires or kingdoms with hegemony that extends over several viceroyalties. All these forms have certain common characteristics, the proportions of which vary considerably across different systems of government and societies. For example, the cult of royal ancestors was more highly developed in some but not in other polities. Large kingdoms were built by conquest, slow accretion of smaller units seeking protection from stronger polities, or agglomerations of migrating groups to conducive sites. The "genuinely innovative features" of the kingdom of Dahomey, for instance, "derived its legitimacy from the appropriation and manipulation of existing ideological traditions" (Law, 1987, p. 338).

Political power in stateless polities is diffused rather than centralized and vested in a sovereign as in state societies. Because the notion of equality is widely accepted, stateless societies rely more on consensus than on a centralized locus of political power, hence the reliance on the sanctity of custom and tradition rather than on coercion in stateless societies. But, in the course of time, some individuals in stateless societies strove for positions of "first among equals" (Henn, 1984) and the principle of equality became difficult to practice. Eventually, some people acquired serfs from whom they extracted allegiance, services, and tribute, thereby becoming more "powerful." It seems that the stateless societies in West Africa were built by nomadic pastoralists, while the chiefdoms and kingdoms were built by settled cultivators (Mazrui, 1986b).

In much of traditional West Africa, political power devolves around royal dynasty, but in almost all polities royal offspring of slave progeny are denied the right of succession. Kings wield ritual, political, and administrative powers and obligations (Busia, 1967). They rule not by whim but through permanent consultation with multiple functionaries and agencies that seek to preserve law and order as well as ascertain the observance of the right ritual measures necessary for the health and progress of the kingdoms (Fisiy, 1983). Monarchical rule is for life, on the proviso that the king is a good king (Oguah, 1984). It is therefore not uncommon for an impeachment suit to be initiated by kingmakers against a king who has become too transgressive or impervious to advice.

To ensure proper administration and prevent kings reigning as despots, monarchs are surrounded by various levels of power sharing and institutional checks and balances. First is the royal coterie, an authoritative source for advice and consensual decision making. Whenever the royal court meets to discuss community affairs, it deliberates until "unanimity" is attained (Busia, 1967). This African mode of governing by conciliation has entered contemporary African politics as a key principle in the Charter of the Organization of African Unity. In the second place, powerful regulatory societies exist to monitor the king's activities and can bring him to reason by declaring a curfew or placing him under palace arrest. Third, establishment of viceroyalties is effective because of a traditional belief in the delegation of royal authority. Fourth, kings are usually never permitted to receive foreign emissaries alone for fear that they might enter into secret pacts of betrayal. The most potent check on monarchy, however, is fear of ritualistic retribution. The fear that the transgression of the laws of the land would provoke ancestral wrath cautions monarchs. Kings incarnate their cultural heritage and are intermediaries between the living and the ancestral spirits and deities. As such they are not expected to transgress the taboos and customs they pledged to uphold during enthronement. It is believed that the ancestors and gods keep a watchful eye on the living through the mediation of the king. The perceived link between monarchy and the transcendental world is one example of how the West African worldview attempts to unify into a coherent framework apparently disparate phenomena and components of the universe. The link between monarchy and the spiritual world infuses religiosity and myth into government. In the authority structure of some West African polities, the paramount chiefs and some of their subchiefs have a female counterpart, the queen-mother, who wields great influence over women's affairs. In prophecy, divination, and indigenous medicine, both men and women are eligible for the same social positions and status (Nsamenang, 1987). But though political authority in much of West Africa is male-dominant, male-dominance may be a matter of appearance rather than reality. "Africa is the world region with the most extensive female solidarity organizations, an indication of the importance among women of ties outside the household boundaries" (Staudt, 1986, p. 199). In some cultures "women houses" come "together in public contexts to protest against what they feel are infringements of their economic and political prerogatives" (Dikuk, 1989, p. 339; Wipper, 1982). The Aba riots of 1929 and the Bamenda Grassfields protests of 1958 (Dikuk, 1989) are illustrative examples of how the combined force of women's houses can overwhelm even the most astute patriarch or state force.

A key ritual office like "Queen of Fertility" (*Ya-ah woong* in Nso, or literally "Queen of the Universe"), falls in the sphere of women's roles. Because women "give" life through birth, they should be responsible for the fertility of the fields (Erny, 1968). "Women's power thus derives from men's dependence on their child-bearing capacity and their services as domestic workers par excellence, as well as their agricultural labor" (Turrittin, 1988, p. 585).

Depending on type of political system, children play various roles: they may be pages, retainers, errand-runners, herdboys, dairymaids, and so forth. They also assist at rituals and perform useful services in the exclusive male or female societies to which they may gain access by right of birth or by outstanding achievement.

Marriage and Parenthood in West Africa

The most basic socially acceptable family unit is established by a man and woman in marriage (Nsamenang, 1988). Bachelorhood, spinsterhood, or single parenthood is not a normal, expected social status and is best avoided. An unmarried, childless person is never accorded full adult status, and marriage alone confers only proto-adult status. Full adulthood is therefore a matter of social definition rather than of chronological age (Nsamenang, 1988). For example, 14- or 15-year-old adolescents may become adults by virtue of marriage and parenthood while unmar-

ried, childless persons, 24 years of age or older, remain socially imma-
ture. Full adult status, thus requires that a person be "married with
children."

Marital arrangements are characterized by the exchange of gifts
and/or payments, usually in kind. The girl's kin receives "gifts" in compensation for "losing a member" whose fertility is crucial for the
reproductive success of the husband's lineage. The purported "sale" of
African women into marriage is both a misunderstanding and a misrep-
resentation of the facts of the mode of matrimonial arrangements in
West Africa. In accord with inclusive fitness considerations, the essence
of bride payment is compensation for the loss of fertility and its simultaneous transfer to another lineage. In principle, the matrimonial goods
or gifts received should be used in contracting another marriage. The
wife so acquired replaces the fertility of the daughter already married
out. This ensures the inclusive fitness of every lineage. In many communities, however, the self-regulating system of contracting marriages
has become corrupt. However, the epidemic rate of teenage pregnancy
(Nsamenang, 1988) and the difficulty of getting husbands is tempering
excessive abuse of the system.

The marriage rite confers sole access to sexual relations and establishes paternity rights (Maquet, 1972; Nsamenang, 1987). The offspring
of a woman whose matrimonial compensation has not been remitted
traditionally belong to her lineage, not the father's. According to Erny
(1968, p. 83), however, among the Toupouri of North Cameroon, if an
illegitimate child is a boy he belongs to his natural father, if a girl to
the mother's husband. Bride wealth confers certain rights and obligations on the marital pair as well as on their two families, even lineages
(Ayisi, 1979). A spouse must learn to distinguish those spousal kin to
treat with deference and those with whom to develop joking relations.

Marriage is regarded as "a seed to bear fruits" (Nsamenang, 1987).
Without children, marriage loses its significance (Erny, 1987, p. 42)
because parenthood is a primary reason for marriage. The slightest indication of infertility often precipitates a high degree of anxiety. Individuals, couples, and families spare neither effort nor resources to establish, restore, or prove fertility (Nsamenang, 1988). Infertility stirs up
the most disturbing emotions in a woman (Erny, 1968, p. 84).

The West African Family and Household

The marital couple comes in contact with spousal kin. Everyone
involved in the relationship becomes a "relative" and endeavors to treat

each other accordingly. Network members describe themselves in terms that by Western conception are used only for near relatives. *Brother,* for example, is freely used for almost all male members of the group in the same age cohort (Ayisi, 1979). Similarly, the terms *father* and *mother* apply to all kin of one's father's or mother's generation. From early in life children are introduced to adult kin as "other" fathers and mothers and to their children as brothers and sisters. They in turn regard and treat them accordingly (Maquet, 1972), even if the relationship is of the seventh order (Ohuche & Otaala, 1981).

Marital partners are usually not the only adult members of the household. Sometimes adult relatives and/or friends are members of the same household (Nsamenang, 1987) and together with the children, a picture of a large household begins to emerge (Hake, 1972). The West African family may therefore be viewed as the people who belong to the same line, at least in the proximate sense (Nsamenang, 1987). Within family and spousal networks, kin feel a strong obligation for supportive fellowship and reciprocal assistance in all their activities, including child rearing.

The literature tends to refer to West African families as extended, but the true nature of the "extendedness" still awaits empirical specification.

INSTITUTIONAL RULES AND GOALS

Although individuals, particularly children, are submerged in a network of social scripts and status rules that demand conformity and promote collectivism, they are not overly subdued by a herd mentality. From early in life, children come under the sphere of influence of several relatives and quickly learn how to relate and behave toward them. By the daily life of the family, lineage, and village, by precept and occasional remarks or snaps of adults and older siblings (Maquet, 1972), West African children at the threshold of adolescence are already firmly anchored in their niches and are expected to have imbibed the essential codes of the sociocultural milieu. Socialization seeks to discourage self-seeking and to encourage getting along with others rather than excessive competitiveness. When members of an age cohort reach socially recognizable stages (Nsamenang, 1988), they are sometimes initiated (where this is practiced) together. The custom of ritualizing ontogenetic changes helps gradually but progressively to mature children to adult roles without disruptive transitional crises.

The social system is characterized by deference to and locus of authority in elders, especially parents. Cultural traditions clearly define and strictly regulate social life and zones for certain relationships, especially those pertaining to children's welfare, sexual access, and marriage. For instance, the allocation of time, attention, and resources to children is often determined by gender and age of the child and laterality or the side of the lineage to which the child belongs. Furthermore, sexual intercourse between close kin is abhorred and strict incest inhibitions enjoin kinsmen to marry outside their consanguineous group (Nsamenang, 1988). Nevertheless, some nomadic pastoralist groups are endogamous (Ekpere, Oyedipe, & Adegboye, 1978). The value of dividing society into discrete categories not only establishes each person's place but may also define lines of responsibility and jural rights, the basis for inheritance and succession in West Africa. It may also help to distinguish between sociological paternity and biological paternity.

The principle of cosmic justice and the perception of divine omniscience are proxy enforcers of social conformity since both imply reward for good behavior and punishment for evildoing. The maintenance of good health requires the adoption of the right moral posture, the observance of taboos, and the avoidance of spiritual defilement or acts of disgrace.

RELIGION, RITUALS, AND FESTIVALS

European missionaries, like their colonial peers, fervently believed that prior to their arrival, (West) Africans were religious blank slates that had to be filled with their own religious texts. Perhaps this was the most erroneous colonial assumption. Long before the religion of the Crescent or the religion of the Cross arrived on the African continent, Africa was at worship, its daughters and sons were at prayer (Mazrui, 1986b) and treated their sick. Our task here is to attempt to sketch West Africa's concepts of theology and divinity and to examine the socio-medico-religious role of rituals and festivals.

The West African Concept of Theology

The seminal concept of the West African worldview is theocentric in outlook: A vital force inheres nature and pervades all facets of human existence. African theodicy [or natural religion] (Mudimbe, 1983) is not an evangelizing religion; it is integral to cultural life. It therefore did not, but may now, require zealots to propagate it. In the face of large-scale assault on African values and the apparent failure of alien religions to be genuinely and truly meaningful to the large majority of West Africans, it seems culturally and liturgically expedient to begin the process of systematization and evangelization of African religions. This seemingly startling proposal is made in light of Baeta's (1967, p. 240) illumination that in Africa both "Christians and Muslims . . . have recourse to the traditional sorcerer's magical help . . . while some Christians would pour libation to the ancestral spirits or be present at strictly animist ceremonies." The tenacity and potency of indigenous religious beliefs and values are therefore undeniable even to the most avowed Christian or Muslim fundamentalists. Christian and Muslim missionaries are greatly disturbed as they increasingly realize that the most assertive values in the lives of their African converts emanate more from African religious codes than from Christian or Islamic doctrine. To survive, alien religions "will have to share in the dynamic tension of African culture" (Okeke, 1988, p. ix).

West African theology posits two levels of the universe: a prosaic world for the living and a three-tier spiritual world for ancestral spirits, deities and gods, and the Supreme One. Everyone has a soul; the body is its "house." Belief in immortality is evident in the view of death as the separation of the soul from the body and its "passage" to a world beyond that in which we live. The dead remain in the memories of the living who solicit their assistance through sacrifices and rituals (Menkiti, 1984). The recent dead still retain their personhood until a certain period of time when they slide into a world of personal nonexistence and lose all that they once possessed by way of personal identity (Menkiti, 1984). The soul cannot enter the right realm without the appropriate ritual action by the living. The ritual of incorporation thus transforms the soul from its liminal condition into an ancestral spirit or prepares it for passage into a higher spiritual realm. Non-adoption of the right ritual posture means that the ancestral spirit, indeed ghost, lingers near its natal home and may torment its relatives, especially the heir. It is the duty and right of every ancestor to torment or punish the living, particularly heirs and kings, if they stray from the "true" ancestral path (Mendonsa, 1975; Minkus, 1984).

Although not universally held throughout Africa, the deceased—the ancestors—are believed to reincarnate as children (Erny, 1968, p. 88). In fact, some dying elderly persons often console and entreat their relatives that they would either reincarnate or send them a representative.

Neither Islam nor Christianity has solved "the theological problem of 'co-existence' with" African religions (Taylor, 1963, p. 8). As a result, there is an intense deistic dilemma in the African psyche. In this light, it does not at all seem whimsical to ask for a fundamental distinction between "holy" items and totems. Are totems not symbolic representations—familiar and commonplace objects with deistic significance imputed in them? Totemism in West Africa led people to identify with and adopt certain objects and animals as "totemic symbols which established a sense of continuity between nature and Man" (Mazrui, 1986b). They are "visible symbols of the invisible" God (Metuh, 1973, pp. 10-11). That is, totemism represents one human endeavor to reach a God who is so distant from the universe he created (Goody, 1975). The labels of a *deus incertus* (uncertain God) and a *deus remotus* (remote God) (Westerman, 1935, p. 74) tagged on the African God is in sharp contrast to the full "sense of divine presence and need for God's care and protection" in African greetings and daily life (Metuh, 1973, p. 2).

In LoDagaa, as in other West African cultures, the belief is that God "has no altar and there is no way of communicating with him" (Goody, 1975) except through his intermediaries. Many prayers are thus offered to God through ancestors and deities. Hence the elaborate attempts to bring God into human life by domesticating divinity. Ancestors and gods or deities are the mouthpieces of the Supreme Being (Busia, 1954). The hierarchies of totems and ancestral spirits in West African theological thought are not God, per se. Disregarding the "language of derision" and ridicule (Mudimbe, 1985, p. 157) thus far used to describe African theodicy, one may argue that the hierarchies of totems and ancestral spirits are earthly representations of the divine, probably at comparable conceptual levels as the holy objects and saints or their equivalents in other religions. For instance, ancestors intercede on behalf of their living kin; saints intercede on behalf of their living Christians. In African theology, deities and ancestral spirits are expected to intercede and supplicate on behalf of the living, "helping where they can and enlisting the assistance of the Supreme Being when they are incapable of helping" (Ayisi, 1979). When intercession is considered to be too complex and difficult for a single ancestral spirit or deity, the intervention of a cohort of spirits is usually solicited.

The thesis that the ancestor cult is an end in itself and that ancestor worship has as its sole objective an adulation may not only be specious, but naive ethnocentrism. In this respect, Mudimbe (1985, pp. 151-153) equated the expatriate missionary spirit with "cultural propaganda" and submitted that as "an agent of a political empire, a representative of a civilization, and an envoy of God," the missionary's objective was "the conversion of African minds and space."

Concept of Divinity

West African theology holds that humankind and the universe were created by the Supreme Being, the "Great One" (Busia, 1954) who is "high above all deities and who animates them all" (Ayisi, 1979). It does not see humans as extensions of God's image, although it acknowledges a primal human link to God. The link between humans and God is via filiation, hence the significance of children to West Africans. While some children are regarded as reincarnated ancestors, others are divine gifts—"children of God" (*woon-ah Nyuy* in Nso). The human link to God constitutes an important dimension of personhood and immortality. God (*Nyuy* in Nso; *Chineke* or *Chukwu* in Ibo) is immortal and confers immortality on humans (Onwuanibe, 1984). This explains why the soul, the life force, leaves its biological habitat, the body, for the "land" of the ancestors, en route to the Supreme One.

In real terms, God "is near and yet far" (Goody, 1975). Although God looms so large in African life and psychology (Metuh, 1973, p. 2), the belief is that human beings can only reach him through multiple intermediaries—ancestral spirits and various classes of deities associated with specific mundane objects, places, and phenomena. Hence the ancestor cult—an elaborate set of rituals of homage and supplication developed around ancestors (and deities) rather than around the Supreme Being. As previously hinted, the ancestor cult seems to be a universal religious phenomenon (Radcliffe-Brown, 1952). The plausibility of this contention rests on the tendency in funeral eulogies and burial speeches or sermons everywhere to request the deceased not to forget the living.

The ancestor cult prescribes appropriate rites for contact with ancestors and deities (Ayisi, 1979). It is a means by which ancestral spirits, having once been human and having possessed human attributes, are thought to be knowledgeable about mundane affairs. They are thus considered to be well placed to bring the world of spirits in contact with that of the living and to represent human needs properly to God.

Spiritual Health, Sin, and Punishment

Ideas of spiritual health and sin are rooted in a belief in "ancestral affliction" (Mendonsa, 1975, p. 69) and the capriciousness of spirits and deities if defiled. Belief in ancestral torment gives wide scope to causal explanations and plays a key role in divination and health care. Although the world is not inherently capricious, goodness and evil coexist as part of nature and the human's free will may harness the "power in nature" for good or evil (Minkus, 1984). The deity or ancestral spirit torments people (heirs or relatives) because of the need for their timely performance of the correct rites or sacrifices of propitiation. Spiritual contamination comes from evildoing, transgression of taboos, and failure to adopt the right ritual posture. Other sinful acts include murder, failure to follow the ancestral path, dissension among kin, and wickedness and lack of compassion for others, particularly strangers. The soul is fragile and very sensitive to defilement and often neglects or even deserts the individual if it is persistently assaulted. Spirits—even the most benevolent of them, like the ancestral spirits, who departed in peace—are also very sensitive to any acts of disrespect or disgrace by the living. Defilement and sin lower spiritual resistance and render an individual vulnerable to evil influences, especially capricious spirits, witches, and the "evil eye" (i.e., evil machinations of others).

Since spiritual defilement is sin, it is punishable and requires atonement or purification. This is necessary to cleanse and purge sinners and to appease the ancestors or the gods. Prayers and sacrifices of different descriptions are offered. "Sacrifice is the most common redressive rite" (Mendonsa, 1975, p. 69), however, to cleanse the effects of sin or spiritual contaminant. It may also be used to prevent any threatening or looming evil force from exerting its influence (Minkus, 1984). A closer look at the types of sacrifices offered in West African religious worship identifies four major types, namely, those offered to one's personal guiding spirit; those offered to ancestral spirits; those offered to lesser deities (goddess of fertility, rain god, etc.); and those offered to the High Being. The goal of the first three categories of sacrifice, most often but not exclusively, involve propitiation, expiation, and other related intentions to avert imminent danger. Offering a sacrifice to a "Supreme Being who is great and powerful" (Anderson, 1969, p. 97) is a major community affair, a public liturgical event, in thanksgiving for God's beneficence.

Rituals and Festivals

Festivals and rites are ubiquitous social acts with varied cross-cultural intentions and procedures. In West Africa, rituals and festivals surround ontogenetic transitions and other critical life events such as harvest, royal enthronement, and religious thanksgiving. Although separate, rituals and festivals almost always go together. Rituals generally precede festivals. Most rituals are shrouded in myth and secrecy; this scenario fosters unquestioning acceptance. Rituals may involve families and individuals or they may be a public affair involving an entire community or kingdom. Routine ritual practices are more characteristic of some societies or groups than others. For instance, Akan elders in Ghana are expected to leave a portion of whatever they have to consume on the ground for their ancestors before they themselves may eat (Ayisi, 1979); Catholic Christians and Muslims are expected to pray over their food prior to eating it.

Festivals and rituals have socio-medico-religious value. Not only are they psychologically therapeutic, their perceived potency and solemnity is often enough to reform and purify offenders (Oguah, 1984). Most religious festivals and rituals therefore serve as a form of catharsis, freeing the offender of pent-up feelings of guilt, since they are thought to extirpate offenders of the effects of sin or evildoing. They also help to eliminate the human sense of powerlessness. It is only through them that humankind can bring the profane world into contact with the spiritual without causing damage to the social fabric (Ayisi, 1979). Rituals thus serve as sanctifying institutions through which to approach an otherwise unreachable God.

ILLNESS BEHAVIOR AND INDIGENOUS MEDICINE

Disease is said to be an integral part of the West African sociocultural landscape (Udo, 1982). Although West Africans believe that good conduct promotes health and longevity, no presumption is made of a totally illness-free life (Minkus, 1984). How then do they avoid illness or react to it?

Health and Ill-Health Behavior

Ill-health is attributable to a variety of causes. Although every ethnic group has its own etiologic category, ill-health is usually attributed to: natural or unknown causes, human ill-will, punishment for wickedness, or spiritually induced illness (see, e.g., Minkus, 1984). The gap between the need of ancestors for propitiation by kinsmen "even though they have committed no breach of the moral code" "produces an explanation for the ubiquity of calamity, disease and illness" in West African cultures (Mendonsa, 1975, pp. 69-70). Life, like the very essence of the soul itself, is tenuous at best. The belief that "all wrong-doers, no matter how secret, are seen by God and never go unpunished; or if a wrongdoer does escape, his descendants will not" (Metuh, 1973, p. 4), implies that an individual's sins can be visited upon others. Breach of the moral code and lack of harmonious relations with others can also predispose people to certain diseases or misfortunes. All this presupposes a keen awareness of the physical, social, emotional, and spiritual components of health and illness.

Line of Treatment

Some "healthy" people occasionally consult diviners to find out if any harmful spell looms over them (Minkus, 1984). Once illness or misfortune strikes, the first line of action is to make a lay assessment of its gravity and etiologic source. When it is regarded as a minor ailment, home or lay remedies are first tried. If the condition persists or was initially identified as serious illness, the principal means of "determining the cause and cure of the affliction lies in the institution of divination" (Mendonsa, 1975, p. 69). Determining the cause of a disease or misfortune is critical because some diseases (infertility, mental disorders, convulsive seizures and "bad dreams," etc.), are not generally believed to be amenable to biomedicine. In such instances the appropriate indigenous specialist is preferred to the biomedical practitioner. Proficient indigenous practitioners as well as quacks and impostors exist. However, "when a West African is ill he is likely to make use of the traditional healer as well as the [biomedical] doctor" (Maclean, 1971). Dasen and his colleagues (Dasen, Inhelder, Lavallee, & Retschitzki, 1978, p. 56) further reveal that when Baoulé villagers became ill, they reverted either to traditional medicine or to the village health center—or in order to be more certain of treatment, to both.

The Art of Healing

The art of healing is said to be derived from three sources: heredity, divine gifting, and learning. Some people are thought to be born with the "gift" to heal. Many groups, among them the Nso of Cameroon, believe that twins and children born with the umbilical cord wrapped around the neck are genetically endowed to heal. Many societies also believe that some children or persons sometimes mysteriously disappear and reappear. Such people are said to have been "stolen" by God in order to confer on them "the gift of healing and performing extraordinary feats." On the other hand, some people undergo prolonged periods of apprenticeship in order to become proficient healers.

Systematic research to unravel what indigenous practitioners use and how they actually heal is still nascent. Nevertheless, indigenous practitioners have a very large clientele. This is perhaps due to the fact that endogenous medicine adopts a holistic therapeutic model and addresses questions about the person *in ecocultural context*. On the other hand, in its preoccupation with the right professional posture and insistence on accurate diagnosis and precise cure, modern medicine probably loses sight of or fails to attend to the patient in context.

SUMMARY

Early research focus on West Africa dealt mainly with the superficiality of the African world, emphasizing stereotypes and how Africans differed from Westerners. Objective scholarship aimed at understanding the value of the West African world on its own terms is at best emerging. There is an amazing similarity in West African worldviews and coherence in the wisdom they engender. The West African worldview posits a vital force that inheres nature and literally pervades all facets of human life. The West African universe consists of a physical world and a three-tier spiritual realm of ancestors, deities, and a Supreme God. Because dead ancestors have contact with both the physical and spiritual worlds, they intercede with God and higher deities on behalf of their living kin. West Africans believe in retributive justice or nemesis.

The close texture of family life and kinship support, the warmth and courtesies of interpersonal relationships, foster a high sense of community in which children are firmly anchored from early ages. Personhood is not acquired simply by being human progeny; personhood accretes in reference to ontogenetic status, from the amorality and ignorance of the neonate to the wisdom of the dying old sage. A great deal of emphasis is placed on social ethics rather than the ethics of the self. Ethnicity is intense and attachment to ancestral land is passionate. The indigenous political system is either an acephalous nomadic ethnic group or a composite kingdom with hegemony over several chiefdoms. Leadership is dynastic and monarchs reign for life, except that they may be dethroned for being too transgressive or impervious to advice.

African theodicy is not evangelical; its beliefs, precepts and practices are integral to cultural life. West Africans have a keen awareness of the physical, social, emotional, and spiritual aspects of health and illness, especially the spiritual component. In spite of the existence of biomedicine, there is widespread reliance on endogenous health practice for health care and treatment, perhaps because it deals with the patient in context.

Human beings are territorial and social organisms. Sociocultural imperatives foster a unique ethos and modus operandi. In this respect, the sociocultural environment, the focus of this chapter, is central to developmental research because all human cultures provide cultural formulas and the mechanisms for canalizing development in some but not other directions.

PART III

The Triple Heritage

Nowhere else is social history so potent a determinant of the shape of sociopolitical systems and human social destiny as in (West) Africa. History has not only shaped and sharpened the West African psyche, albeit with many negative consequences, but has perfectly marginalized indigenous West African traditions and behavioral patterns. For instance, the scars of slavery, the stigma of colonial bondage, and the coercive suppression of West Africa's cultural patterns and religious practices by Arab envoys of Allah and European emissaries of God and agents of imperialism provoked a "deep sense of inferiority and aggrievement" (Hunter, 1962, p. 6) in West Africans. This has remained a lively influence on West African attitudes and behavioral repertoires until today.

In this section, we attempt an explication of the triple heritage to which West Africa, like the rest of the colonized world, is heir. Whereas Chapter 5 focuses on the major historical events whose legacies largely determine the present socioeconomic and political condition, Chapter 6 represents a portrayal of continuities and discontinuities in parenthood and the child-care scene in West Africa. Chapter 7 is devoted to a discussion of the conditions of childhood and human development in West Africa. It also examines how, with limited resources, West Africans endeavor to satisfy children's needs.

5

HISTORICAL ROOTS
(West) Africa's Heritage

Chapters 1 and 2 provided a cognitive map for the book. The third and fourth chapters examined the ecocultural roots of human development in West Africa. The present chapter focuses on the major historical forces that have shaped the contemporary West African developmental ecology. This concerns an explication of dimensions of Africa's triple inheritance and its effects on the African psyche and heritage culture.

THE TRIPLE HERITAGE

The triple heritage (Mazrui, 1986b) addresses a contemporary African reality pertaining to a social scenario characterized by Africa's rich indigenous inheritance, Eastern traditions, and Western legacies. Indigenous institutions and traditions constituted the mediums and codes by which alien cultural fragments became "domesticated." The triple heritage then is the extent to which such things as religious imperialism, slave trade, colonialism, and exterior secular influences "set to work on the cultural raw materials of pre-existing, indigenous Africa" (Davis-Roberts, 1986, p. 1). The domesticated patterns of the external cultures, in a manner of speaking, have become inescapable components of the African experience and thus qualify as integral elements of the African condition.

Before delving into the main subject matter of this chapter, however, it is essential to identify Africa's impact on other cultures and the routes the externalization of African cultures took. Use of the term *externalization* in preference to the conventional *Westernization* is intentional:

Western influence is but one of several external influences on Africa. The main sources of the external influence, which is the focus of our attention in this section, include religious imperialism, the slave trade, colonialism, and Western and Eastern secularism.

CULTURE CONTACT AND
CULTURE INFLUENCE IN AFRICA

No part of the earth has been a greater recipient of alien influences and foreign invaders than Africa. But what often deceptively and simplemindedly "looks like an impact upon Africa may sometimes be an influence from Africa" (Mazrui, 1986a, p. 263). A passive view and interpretation of Africa depends on the degree of prejudice, ethnocentrism, and the angle of perception, especially the preceptor and his or her theoretical mission. A new wave of (Western) discourse is somehow emerging; within it, it is becoming "acceptable to recognize some wisdom in Africans" rather than absurdity, backwardness, and savagery (Mudimbe, 1983, p. 135). What is Africa's influence, if any, on other cultures?

Africa's Global Acculturative Impact

Balkanized into more than 50 states, "Africa's numerous political and socio-economic units provide many examples of political and social engineering for students of underdeveloped world societies" (Cummings, 1986, p. 1). This, of course, is not a very positive feature, at least from an Afrocentric viewpoint.

Davidson (1985, pp. 9-10) cites an unreferenced Dutch visitor who described Benin City (Nigeria) in A.D. 1600 as follows: "As you enter it, the town appears very great: you go into a great broad street, not paved, which seems to be seven or eight times broader than the Warmoes in Amsterdam. The houses in this town stand in good order . . . as the houses in Holland stand." Davidson (1985, p. 3) further explained that "during the fourth millennium BC one of the great civilizations of antiquity emerged in the delta of the Nile, and along its banks for some way to the south . . . these early populations of Egypt developed the astonishingly stable and often brilliantly innovating kingdoms of the Pharaohs." Mazrui (1986b, p. 43) characterized the Egyptian civilization as "the explosion of one of the most dazzling galaxies of cultures in human history." In his *Message to the Second Convention of Black Writers and Artists* in Rome in April 1959, Gurvitch remarked how:

> Black African culture set for the whole world an example of extraordinary vitality and vigor. All vitalist conceptions, religious as well as philosophic, I am convinced, came from that source. The civilization of ancient Egypt would not have been possible without the great example of Black African culture, and in all likelihood it was nothing but the sublimation thereoff. (quoted in Diop, 1987, p. 5)

"Even if Africa is not the honored locus of such a major biblical event" as the Garden of Eden, it remains a scientific fact that Africa is the continent "which prepared the diverse races of humankind to embark upon global human civilization" (Cummings, 1986, p. 2). Indeed, Africa is the land out of which the magnificent Egyptian civilization flourished as a primary locus for human habitation and civilization. Africa not only served as the birthplace of humankind—as M. Leakey (1979) and R. Leakey and Lewin (1979) would affirm—but also as a place (East Africa and the Nile Valley in particular) from where many cultural ideas and initial adaptive techniques diffused in all directions.

Further, African art forms, sounds, and movements have been plagiarized and incorporated as forms of Western cultural expression (Ungar, 1986, pp. 14, 23). How many Westerners, for example, recognize or are ready to accept that much of the music and dance steps they enjoy today is directly descended from traditional African sounds and rhythms? In point of fact, "when Westerners encountered the rich tradition of African sculpture, woodcuts, music, and other art, they sometimes incorporated its characteristics into their own work, but they could not accept it as an accomplishment in itself" (Ungar, 1986, p. 23). Thus the reluctance to acknowledge the inspiration of classical Western, especially Mediterranean European, artists by Africa's artistic genre. Nevertheless, half a decade ago, how many Westerners could dream that African carvings and other artistic creations would adorn Western museums and art galleries and become prized possessions in many a Western home? Many aspects of African arts, vitalist conceptions, and movements have been "absorbed by nearly everyone else" (Ungar, 1986, p. 14) but without any acknowledgement.

In a certain sense, the Horn of Africa saved Islam by providing "sanctuary to the Muslim Meccans fleeing from Arabia because of persecution" (Cummings, 1986, p. 5). Africans (slaves) also took Islam and Muslim culture to the Western Hemisphere (Bastide, 1967). In addition, slavery and apartheid, whose victims were/are Africans, have had a universally profound impact on human rights everywhere. The slave trade, humanity's greatest tragedy, though it exterminated or ruined many an African polity and civilization, was "the historical event that altered both African and American history" (Cummings, 1986, p. 4). The voluntary as well as forced coexistence of millions of European immigrants and Africans in the Americas and the Caribbean resulted in the emergence of a new center of civilization built on African slave labor, and the eventual birthplace for a new kind of scholarship, African studies. Unfortunately, there do not seem to be any active scholarly exchanges between Africans and African-Americans!

An African mode of settling disputes, conciliation, was the founding concept of the Nonaligned Movement.

THE EXTERNALIZATION OF AFRICAN CULTURES

Why and how did alien cultures render Africa a cultural prisoner? How did Africa become a flourishing common market for other cultures? Answers to these questions are embedded in six themes: Africa's (prehistoric) links with other cultures, African encounter with alien spiritual traditions, Africa's contact and experience with Europe, Colonialism, African-American connections, and African involvement in world affairs.

Africa's (Prehistoric) Links with Other Cultures

The roots of Africa's external contacts go beyond the ancient Egyptian civilization. From prehistoric times, Africa had mutually beneficial interactions via cultural and commodity exchanges and through erudition with the Arabian and Persian peoples and the Greco-Roman Empires. The cultural, linguistic, and racial ties between the South Arabians and the ancestries of the present inhabitants of the Horn of Africa are indisputable. "It is now known that many Ethiopians lived in the Arabian Peninsula long before Islam" (Cummings, 1986, p. 5).

The biblical "little boy" (i.e., Moses) who floated the Nile and became a key figure in the Judeo-Christian tradition clearly confirms Africa's long-standing relations with the external world (Mazrui, 1986b). The civilizations of Ancient Egypt, Phoenicia, Mesopotamia, Greece, and Rome were not local phenomena; they owed their extraordinary innovativeness to the creative melding of peoples and cultures from Africa, Arabia, and the Mediterranean littoral. Even Byzantium and the post-

Hellenic Christian civilizations were similar blends of African, Semitic, and Caucasian cultures (V. Levine, 1986). West Africa's initial contacts with the external world are generally believed to have come from across the Sahara about the 8th century A.D. when North African Berber Muslims were drawn by trade to West Africa (Davidson, 1985). The trade flourished for several centuries and through it Europe was supplied with gold and ivory. The "earliest gold currencies of the late medieval Europe, as for example, the *fiorentino* or florin of the 13th century, were almost certainly struck in West African gold" (Davidson, 1985, p. 8).

The commodities (salt, spices, leather, firearms, cloth, spirits, etc.) that West Africans acquired from Arabs, Berbers, and eventually Europeans in their trade exchanges probably whetted African appetites for un-African goods. Africa's penchant for luxury is today reflected in inordinate acquisition of wealth and conspicuous consumption in communities whose abject poverty marks their identity. It was perhaps the lust for foreign goods that blinded Africans into warring and bartering one another into slavery for a few European goods and "pieces of iron and silver frippery" (Ellis, 1978, p. 5). The trend does not seem to have stopped. If recent media reports ("Students," 1988) that nuclear wastes are being dumped in some West African countries by some industrialized nations with the shameless connivance of prominent Africans in exchange for a few "coins" or mere favors are correct, then Africa is in for incalculably more damage than the ignominious slave trade inflicted.

Africa's Encounter With Alien Spiritual Traditions

Africa's early contacts with the outside world were also spiritual. Christianity and Islam reached Africa from Palestine and Mecca in the first decades of their history.

Christendom in (West) Africa. The Christianity that arrived in Africa in its early history was riven with controversy over the nature of God. Because Africans saw God in the image of indigenous divinity, they emphasized his Monophysite nature (Skinner, 1986). The church was thus divided and persecution was rife. Converted North African Christians —from among whom later emerged such eminent theologians as Cyprian, bishop of Carthage and Saint Augustine, bishop of Hippo—coined the expression: "The blood of martyrs is the seed of the church" (Skinner, 1986, p. 69). Attempts to escape persecution and evil led to the establishment of the first-ever Christian monasteries in the desert. Christianity in North Africa was nearly extinguished with the advent of Islam in the 7th century A.D. Today Coptic Christianity still exists in Ethiopia as a state religion; in Egypt it was embattled with Islam from its introduction.

The Christianity that later arrived in West Africa in the 15th century allied with European imperialism, was sectarianized by the Protestant Reformation, conditioned by capitalism, and colored by Eurocentrism and nationalism. Indeed, it was not "the older, Catholic Europe which finally took hold of the heart of Africa, but the self-assured, Protestant, capitalist, industrial, scientific spirit, bred particularly in Europe's West and North" (Hunter, 1962, pp. 3-4). The Bible was used to pave the way for the capture of African minds and space (Mudimbe, 1985). In this sense, missionaries were accomplices in Europe's hegemonic exploitation of other lands and peoples.

Islamization and Arabization of (West) Africa. Accounts of the spread of Islam into Africa describe the dispatch of some of the Prophet Mohammed's disciples to Christian Ethiopia to seek sanctuary from fierce persecution in Mecca. In addition, Muslims appeared in Africa in A.D. 647 and waged a series of jihads that led to the permanent establishment of the "Faith" in North Africa and the Horn of Africa (Skinner, 1986). This served to isolate Christian Ethiopia from its Islamized neighbors. Early attempts to Islamize Africa south of the Sahara through jihads were defeated by armed resistance and the desert. Faced with defeat, Arabs, experts in long-distance trade, immediately embraced trans-Saharan trade, using the camel, with West Africa. They used North African Berbers who (despite initial fierce resistance) had accepted a sect of Islam whose egalitarian posture and alliance with indigenous religionists rendered it more appealing, hence acceptable, to Western Sudanese peoples (Davidson, 1985). In some communities today, belief in Allah has so coalesced with the High God of African theodicy that the African name for God is almost synonymous with Allah. Islam later took advantage of the weakened condition of West African polities by slave raids and the colonial situation to extend its outreach to the Gulf of Guinea coast.

The advent of Islam in Africa also resulted in Arabization, a linguistic assimilation into the language of the Arabs. Islam provided a convenient framework for the political integration and cohesion of North Africa as well as the replacement of local languages by Arabic. This created new Semites, the Arabs of north Africa, who began to identify more with Arabs than with Africans. The spread of Islam to sub-Saharan Africa created new monotheists but not new Semites. The Copts of Egypt and Ethiopia were Arabized and linguistically became Semites but they were not Muslims. On the other hand, the vast majority of such peoples as the Bamum, Hausa, and Wolof of West Africa were Islamized, but not Arabized.

The heartland of Islam south of the Sahara is West Africa. Although the bulk of the congregation in this part of the Islamic world does not understand Arabic, the Koran and Islamic prayers and sermons are still entirely in Arabic. It is as if Allah understood only one language, Arabic (Mazrui, 1986b).

Africa's Encounter and Experience with Europe

During their voyages of exploration, Europeans believed that Africans and Indians in the Americas began to exist only at the point when they were "discovered" by Portuguese, Spanish, British, or other European voyagers (Liebenow, 1986, p. 14). Besides imposing her concept of the universe on the rest of humanity in the 15th century, Europe also defined races, thereby inventing racism (Mazrui, 1986b). For instance, until Western Europeans reached Africa south of the Sahara, skin color was taken for granted, especially as the Arabs who arrived earlier had intermarried with black Africans without stressing skin pigmentation. Europe also institutionalized apartheid in South Africa. Purely for conjecture, would we have the contemporary orientation and system of logic had the voyages of "discovery" been undertaken by people with a worldview different than Europe's?

Africa's early contacts with Europe were less traumatic than later encounters. Hunter (1962, p. 7) stated how "the Portuguese in 1480-90 treated the King of the Congo . . . as a kingly colleague" and "accepted Congolese notables . . . as ambassadors to the Court of Lisbon." Later European interactions with Africans were different in both quality and intent. The period from 1500 to the abolition of the slave trade in 1807 is characterized by coastal trade contacts in human cargo, agricultural produce, rare minerals, and missionary activities. Has the essential intent of the relationship changed today?

The appearance of whites in West Africa meant a virulent confrontation with a new kind of people whose attitudes and life-styles differed sharply from those of Africans. Whereas the African worldview and religious orientation fostered, as pointed out in Chapter 4, hospitable reception of "the new people," both the colonizers and missionaries labeled Africans "savages," saw their culture and modes of life as barbaric, and sought to transform or replace them. Of course, Africans resisted fiercely. It is difficult to measure the damage this level of denigration left on the African psyche and self-esteem. As the suspicious and insidiously hostile relationship between Africans and imperialists persisted, Africans gradually but painfully noted the competition, controversy, discrimination, even hatred among their self-avowed saviors. How could Africans not be perplexed by the attitudes of missionaries who—ostensibly so deeply committed to religion—simultaneously so fervently believed in the superiority of the white race and European culture? Yet the same missionaries pretended to preach equality before a Creator God—the "Supreme One" of African divinity.

Everywhere European encounters with Africans were fiercely resisted. In fact, Europeans encountered confident, self-assertive African kings who resisted European penetration and subjugation. The story is repeatedly told of the blunt refusal of the *Fon* (king) of Nso to greet Queen Elizabeth II of England, during her maiden visit to Nigeria in the 1950s, by handshake in order not to violate a Nso custom that forbids *Fons* from greeting by handshake. He wondered how he would explain to his subjects and colleagues the violation of a customary tradition he vowed to uphold. *Fons* in the Bamenda Grassfields of Cameroon do not greet by handshake, particularly women. Everywhere Europe unhesitatingly responded to African resistance by military force. Thus the history of white encroachment into African communities includes armed combat. However, records of the resistance confirm that Europe eventually gained a foothold in Africa through a combination of forces. They depended on "the spirit of the missionary journeys of St. Paul, the expansive spirit of Protestant capitalism, the imperial spirit of the 19th century European states and the growing power of their economies to give both the moral impetus and the physical strength to grasp, to hold and to change" Africa (Hunter, 1962, p. 4). In other words, it could not have been "the trader alone, nor the missionary alone, nor government alone, but the three together, and the settler in their train . . . and these four, with their different yet interwoven interests" (Hunter, 1962, p. 4) were strong enough to assault and subjugate Africa.

For roughly 400 years Europe used Africa mainly as a victualing station en route to the more lucrative Far East. But Europe developed an abrupt interest in Africa after her domination of the Americas, Asia, and Australia. This was in order to obtain Africans as slaves for "European exploitation of the agricultural and mineral resources of the Americas from Virginia to Uruguay" (Liebenow, 1986, p. 15). European slave merchants did not venture inland because the African middlemen "had the military means to prevent such a situation" (Liebenow, 1986, p. 16). However, filled with Saint Paul's missionary spirit, European missionaries ventured inland to establish mission stations.

The quest for slaves created a warring scenario in which Africans fought, captured, and forced each other to coastal shipyards where they were sold to European slave merchants who exported them to European plantations in the New World. Vestiges of the animosity and hostility precipitated then still linger on and continue to plague many an African community today. Despite the unsettled debate about the exact number of Africans exported to the New World, there is "a unanimity of view that millions of Africans were lost to this holocaust whose magnitude was taken less seriously until recent times" (Cummings, 1986, p. 7; Liebenow, 1986, p. 16). This certainly wrought untold havoc in those African communities where large numbers of able-bodied men and women were taken into slavery. "If enslavement was an abomination— even by the standards of the day—the sea voyage, the so-called Middle Passage of six to ten weeks, was totally destructive" (Rotberg, 1986, p. 112). Tens of thousands of Africans died during the Middle Passage, some as a result of abortive rebellions or opposition to capture, and others as a result of illness or psychological decompensation.

"It was their relative resistance to disease that made Africans so valuable as slaves in the New World, where European labor was prone to tropical disease and American Indians rapidly succumbed to the most elementary of European diseases, like measles and chicken pox" (Posnansky, 1986, p. 42). That is, were it not for African labor, it would have been more costly, in fact impossible, to develop the agro-industrial base for American civilization (Rotberg, 1986).

Colonialism: The Epic of European Exploitation of Africa

In 1901 Samuel P. Verner, a missionary from Alabama, hinted that "the fact that Africa is to be a white man's land is now a foregone conclusion" (quoted in Ungar, 1986, p. 22). And indeed, by 1914, it was clear to Africans that white rule had become part of their unsolicited heritage.

"The absorption of three quarters of the globe into European imperial system began with the steady probing of the Western African littoral in the early 15th century by Portuguese mariners in search of a sea route to India" (Liebenow, 1986, p. 15). The incorporation of Africa into the European colonial nexus was systematic: the establishment of coastal victualing stations and trading posts, the traffic in human cargo, the use of missionaries "to soften the harshness" of imperialism, European explorations of Africa's hinterland, and the 1884-1885 Berlin Conference where Africa was shared among European imperialist nations. This Conference marked the end of informal empires and the beginning of formal colonial rule. In order to define their spheres of exploitation, the imperialists disregarded the boundaries of African ancestral lands (Asiwaju, 1984) and balkanized Africa into "arbitrary, untidy colonial aggregates of heterogenous territories" and ethnic composition (Rotberg, 1986, p. 118). "They adjusted boundaries, traded favors, and recognized each other's sphere of influence without much regard for the sensibilities or needs of the Africans" (Ungar, 1986, p. 44). But the United States watched from a distance as "the European powers continued to fill in the African colonial map" (Ungar, 1986, p. 44). The fragmentation of Africa in terms of artificial state borders—straddled by ancestral homelands—undoubtedly sowed the seeds for the political instability and bitter rivalry in Africa today. The arbitrariness of national boundaries is equally an exacerbating factor of the refugee problem in Africa.

The period between the partitioning of Africa and African independence was an era of Europe's "rather base, avaricious motives in bringing an unwilling people into the political orbit of those who possessed superior military or technological skills" (Liebenow, 1986, p. 18). Europeans vowed to satisfy their "sweeping hopes and purposes" (Hunter, 1962, p. 17) against the unanticipated resilience of unyielding Africans. Belgium, Britain, France, Germany, Holland, Italy, Portugal, and Spain are among the most notable imperialists that flourished on African colonies, but because by the mid-1870s the British and the French were the only significant European exploiters in Africa, the discussion will focus mainly on British and French colonialism.

British colonial involvement in Africa started in the 16th century and lasted up until the last quarter of the 19th century. The degree of "British influence and presence varied very greatly in different parts of the continent" (McCaskie, 1985, p. 16). Like all European imperial nations, Britain's overriding interests in Africa centered on profitable trade, including traffic in slaves, acquisition of colonies, cost-effective management of colonies, and strategy for imperial competition for African wealth and space. The unusual "burst of humanitarian zeal" (McCaskie, 1985, p. 16) in Britain to settle Sierra Leone in 1787 and Bathurst (Banjul) in the Gambia in 1817 with freed slaves and to grant independence to African colonies later was forced on her by circumstantial forces. The quest for colonies led Britain to a series of wars with and political control of various ethnic polities in West Africa, as elsewhere. Britain's deployment of her religious "opium" and imperial terror through troops of occupation into the hinterland eventually resulted in so-called British West Africa: the Gambia, Sierra Leone, Ghana, Nigeria, and (West) Cameroon (a United Nations Trust Territory). British imperialism in West Africa ended in 1965 with Gambia's autonomy.

French contact with West Africa began in 1659 when Caullier established St. Louis off the mouth of the River Senegal. France sometimes "owned" the island of Goree off Cape Verde, which was fought for by other European powers as an entrepôt for slaves and other valuables. The French conquest of West Africa, through the use of soldiers rather than civilians, was eased by and followed the direction of Afro-Islamic wars. The French eventually backed up their "reign of terror" with paramilitary forces. Today French "occupation" troops are still stationed in a number of Francophone African countries. The French use of soldiers led to their occupation of large tracts of commercially useless land, whereas the British, whose military expeditions were largely dictated by commercial considerations, occupied much smaller but commercially more valuable areas (Crowder, 1985, p. 25).

As the conquest proceeded, there were several cynical border revisions. For example, "Upper Volta [Burkina Faso] was created by 1920 through the excision of parts of Niger, Ivory Coast, and Soudan [Mali]; it was dismembered in 1932 and recreated in 1947" (Crowder, 1985). Further, after the First World War, "German" Cameroon was unequally shared (under the auspices of the League of Nations!) between Britain and France as Trust Territories. The French presence in what constitutes French West Africa was generally already firmly established by the end of the First World War. The principal French preoccupations in West Africa were judicious exploitation of the colonies, profitable trade, safeguard of colonies, assimilation of a handful of "natives" as French citizens, and conscription of Africans "on a compulsory basis for the Free French" campaign (Crowder, 1985, p. 27).

The most remarkable feature of colonialism in East Africa was the conducive climate that favored white settlement. Kenya, for example, was literally "a colony of white settlers and stateless indigenes" (McCaskie, 1985, p. 19). However, by 1929 the 2,000 settled European land-grabbers had become the "whiteman's burden" as the problems they posed to the colonial administration were out of proportion to their numbers. Ethiopia was free from imperial grip until from 1936 to 1941, during which period Italy governed it. The Portuguese gained possession of parts of Mozambique, Angola, and some portions of West Africa, while the Belgians consolidated their grip of the Congo (Ungar, 1986).

South Africa was, and remains, a unique colonial story with Britain holding the trump card. Although Britain entered South Africa late (17th century) after the Dutch (the Boers, in 1652), she is responsible for the entrenchment of apartheid there. The British defeat in 1881 by the Boers had intricate political ramifications for that region, which persist to date. It added fuel to South Africa's "time of troubles" and aggravated the intense animosity and violence between white invaders and Africans. Eventually, under the leadership of charismatic Shaka, the Zulus presented a solid front to the British and Afrikaners (descendants of Dutch and Protestant Huguenots) (McCaskie, 1985).

With the discovery of vast deposits of solid minerals in the hinterland, the interior of Southern Africa assumed a new importance. Following the Zulu defeat of the 1870s, the British moved to exert control over the region. After a series of conflicts with the Dutch settlers, in the 1850s "the British, now firmly ensconced in the Cape and Natal, accorded a degree of recognition to the two Boer republics of the high veld," an event that further heightened racial tension. A German protectorate was established over South West Africa (Namibia) in 1884. In the late 1880s, Cecil Rhodes used the mineral wealth to "occupy Zimbabwe, Zambia, and Malawi and to give Britain control of Botswana" (Rotberg, 1986, pp. 117-118). In the long run, British efforts to resolve the "Afrikaner problem" failed and Africans have since then remained alienated in their own land. By the time the British left South Africa, they somehow placated the Boers "at the price of the institutionalization of white supremacy" (McCaskie, 1985, p. 18) over millions of South Africans.

The Second World War was a watershed in African history because it weakened most imperial powers. "France, Belgium, and Italy were humiliated; Britain was impoverished; and Portugal and Spain were morally bankrupt as a result of their association with fascism and Nazism" (Mazrui, 1986b, p. 161). As important segments of European opinion and leadership favored decolonization, colonialism was increasingly attacked in Europe and overtly challenged in Africa. Having "witnessed at first hand the fragility" of the European military (McCaskie, 1985, p. 21), Africans became more militant in their demands for self-rule. Imperial Europe was thus forced to respond, albeit with palliative measures. For example, in the 1940s the British passed a series of Development and Welfare Acts that granted more aid to the colonies (McCaskie, 1985). The 1956 French *loi cadre* (enabling law) granted local government for the constituent colonies, but none for the French African Federation. The postwar period (1946-1956) was marked by swift political developments in British and French West Africa, culminating in Ghana's and Guinea's independence in 1957 and 1958. In 1955 only Egypt, Ethiopia, and Liberia were independent, later joined by Libya, Sudan, Morocco, and Tunisia.

The Algerian War of Independence (1954-1962) challenged the French Fourth Republic and led to the Fifth Republic under General Charles de Gaulle, who accelerated France's decolonization in Africa and else-

where. In 1958 de Gaulle introduced a new constitution whose provisions permitted West African colonies to opt either for independence and
"all its consequences" or for the Franco-African Community with restricted autonomy. Sekou Toure's Guinea alone opted for independence
and severely suffered De Gaulle's "consequences." Nevertheless, by
1960 the rest of French West Africa became independent, but with unusual
economic overdependence on France. For instance, the economies of
much of Francophone Africa are tied to the apron strings of the French
economy due to ceding the exchange value of the CFA franc, the currency
of those nations, to the French franc. Thus the fate of their economies
is inescapably tied to that of the French.

Colonial powers were of different strengths, exercised jurisdiction
over unequal territories, and implemented divergent policies and programs. Although the relationship between the colonizers and the colonized varied from place to place, the colonial encounter tended to be a
similar, though negative, experience for Africans everywhere. For instance, Africans were forced to work on European-owned mines and
plantations. In many places they

> were discouraged from living in towns; Africans in Kenya could not
> cultivate coffee in competition with Europeans; Africans in Nyasaland
> [Tanzania] and Zaire were harassed for joining the Watchtower Move-
> ment; Africans in Zambia were not permitted to join white mineworkers
> unions; and Africans in most territories were not permitted to join political
> parties. (Liebenow, 1986, pp. 25-26)

All this applied whether the colonial relationship was established by
conquest or as a result of an innocuous and deceptive "treaty of friendship and commerce," and whether the dependency was ultimately destined
for independence or was "considered an overseas extension" of the imperial state (Liebenow, 1986, p. 25). Consequently, a new generation of
Africans who had never known any other life than that directed by whites
emerged. Africans "adapted easily" to the phenomenal changes; unfortunately this initiated valuation of Western "ways" and encouraged negative attitudes toward things African.

The United States, which had passively watched Europe's balkanization and exploitation of Africa, belatedly questioned colonial intentions. After two wartime visits to the Gambia, President Franklin D.
Roosevelt claimed that "for every dollar that the British . . . have put
into the Gambia, they have taken out ten. It's just plain exploitation of
those people" (Ungar, 1986, p. 44).

Africa's American Connection

Africa's American connection was brought about by an almost four-century-old trade in African sons and daughters across the Atlantic. Today the African presence (for 400 or more years) in the New World is evident from parts of Argentina to Newfoundland in Canada. Slaves arrived in North America in the early 17th century, but their arrival in South America and the Caribbean dates back to the 16th century. The dispersal of African peoples in the Americas and the Caribbean established a triangular link between the legacies of Ancient Africa, Arabia, and Europe and led to an overlapping of African and Middle Eastern studies. The Arabian legacies came to the Americas because some slaves had embraced Islam and imbibed Muslim culture that, like traditional African culture, was never completely extinguished by the "terrible dehumanization and humiliation" (Cummings, 1986, p. 12) of the slave status. Of course, that debasing status did not deter Africans who entered the New World from transmitting to the aborigines of and immigrants to the then emerging colonial societies many African cultural fragments. Some of Africa's cultural survivals are more evident than others, however, and some areas are more affected by them than others. That is, elements of African cultural presence are perceivable throughout the Western Hemisphere, even in the United States where slaves were denied "the opportunity to develop the structures necessary for cultural continuity" (Cummings, 1986, p. 12).

The African presence in the New World has had a tremendous impact on the physical population and cultural systems developed in the Western Hemisphere. In fact, with the presence of millions of African Americans as bona fide citizens the unique experience of the United States is probably the single most critical factor that differentiated American from European civilization. In reality, what distinguishes American political history from African political history, in Cummings's (1986, p. 14) view "is that, whereas, America and Africa were field objects in European expansionism in the Age of Discovery, it was in America that Europe reproduced itself through colonization." This important distinction affected America's images of Africa and people of African ancestry as well as Africa's images of America and Americans. All this notwithstanding, American history is incomplete without the African component. Students of American history will always labor under the shadow of the African-American legacy.

That the slave trade altered the course of American history is undoubted. What is not widely noted is that African Americans have always been active participants in *all* phases of American history, from the American

War of Independence to contemporary American life, although American historians fail to acknowledge outstanding "Black" feats in this history.

Induction of Africa into World Affairs

Although Mediterranean Africa, the Horn of Africa, East Africa, and eventually West Africa had contacts with the non-African world from prehistory, Eurocentrists posit that Africa's effective involvement in world affairs began only with the arrival of Portuguese mariners in West Africa. According to this viewpoint, the induction of Africa into global affairs went through three main phases. First, initial coastal contacts led to extensive European exploration of the African hinterland and culminated in the balkanization of Africa at the Berlin Conference, following Europe's discovery of the richness of the continent. The second phase was the period of formal European colonization of Africa, the high points of which included Westernization of Africa's elites, the capture of the African mind via European versions of Christianity and education, and the effective induction of Africans into the global capitalistic system through their production of export crops for European needs. It must be emphasized that the "Easternization" of Africa by Semitic and Arabian legacies, especially Judeo-Christian, Islamic, and Arabic traditions, far preceded its Westernization. The third phase was the Second World War and the weakening of European imperial powers by the Nazi bid to enter the "scramble" for Africa.

The sowing of the seeds for the externalization of African cultures was acquisition of foreign (luxury) items by Africans through long-distance trade exchanges in North Africa, the Horn of Africa, East Africa, and West Africa (via trans-Saharan trade), first from Arabs, Muslims, and Berbers and much later from Europeans. Long before European voyagers arrived in West Africa, the *camel* gave Muslims and Arabs greater access to and monopoly over the African gold fields. This "heightened the curiosity and jealousy of European traders" whose "sense of deprivation and denial of access" prompted Prince Henry the Navigator to establish the Maritime Academy to study the exploration of the seas (Cummings, 1986, p. 4) in order to gain access to and take over the trade in gold and spices of the Orient. Between the fifteenth and eighteenth centuries, African gold and slaves were the most precious items on the European list of African export commodities. Thus, in recounting Africa's induction into world history, one must point out how the Easternization (Islamization, Arabization) of Africa and trade in African bodies tied directly into its balkanization and colonialism (Westernization, Christianization, monetization).

Africa is now at the heart of a Eurocentric world history. Although not a superpower, Africa's strength or weakness on the geopolitical chessboard derives from its rich natural resources, from its being a flourishing common market for world ideologies and experimentation with such things as new drugs or weapons, and as a source of cheap labor. Before discussing the effects of Africa's cultural hybrid, it is crucial to mention the role of history in understanding present-day Africa.

It is with Africa's rich but traumatic history that any attempt to understand her material base and the psyche of contemporary Africans must begin. It is equally crucial to remember that "the present international economic and legal structure developed gradually out of the interaction between the different nations of Europe, and then the United States and the British Dominions. Their cultures were basically similar, and their knowledge and access to it were primarily similar" (Cummings, 1986, p. 16). It is also essential to note that the underdeveloped world, particularly Africa, despite its starkly different material and economic realities, was not privy to the efforts at Bretton Woods in 1945, or other efforts to draw up rules of the international economic order.

THE CONTEMPORARY ECOCULTURE:
A HYBRID OF A TRIPLE HERITAGE

Africa's encounter with alien cultures wrought irreversible changes in the material, institutional, and value foundations of African cultures (Cummings, 1986; Nsamenang, 1983) and gave rise to a breed of Africans who are more imperfectly than perfectly acculturated to both endogenous and exterior cultures. Some indigenous institutions were used to further colonial purposes: "twisted, distorted, and in the end corrupted African cultures and institutions" (Southall, 1988, p. 5). Thus the successful implantation of foreign institutions and exterior cultural fragments in Africa helped establish alien structures, identities, outlooks, and complexes among Africans and promoted Africans' fresh view of things African. This African attitude, together with imperial policies designed and systematically and coercively applied to eliminate or transform African cultures, saw the gradual atrophy of indigenous institutions and value systems. Fortunately, "nowhere has this led to the total social disintegration of indigenous structures" (Nsamenang, 1987, p. 276). For instance, "African art forms and cultural influences were resilient enough to survive the holocaust of the international slave trade" (Ungar, 1986, p. 14). The political, economic, and food crises throughout Africa today "are visible symptoms of deeper problems in the institutions and structures of many African countries and the world system of which they are part" (Schultheis, 1989b, p. 4).

Although Africa was affected negatively by Europe, it is only fair to acknowledge European contributions to African society and life. Nevertheless, this section focuses almost exclusively on the negative consequences of the external factor. We are stressing negative outcomes with the belief that the defeatist view of Africa as a "lost cause" is unwarranted and should be replaced with an attitude that regards and tackles "problems as challenges which can be overcome with great resourcefulness and sacrifice" (Liebenow, 1986, p. 3). This section looks at the exterior factor in the African environment, political landscape, and the socioeconomic domain.

Environmental Degradation

Sometimes human beings unwittingly exacerbate the impact of the elements on the ecosystem. As mute testimony of the long-standing nature of West Africa's environmental abuse is the reference to the huge waste from the iron extractive industry in the Ghana Empire in the 11th century (Posnansky, 1986). Today the "Africans of the Sahel and elsewhere are dying of starvation because human institutions have failed to stem the tide of desiccation which historians have traced back some five thousand years" (Cummings, 1986, p. 1). The Black Death epidemic of the 14th century is linked to increasing desertification that forced the southward movement of peoples from the desert and Sahel into the wetter coastal areas. The cost of the Sahelian drought has not only been in human lives but in the destruction of the ecosystem and a way of life of millions of people. Some of the

> nomads survived the famine only to face despair, disease, and still uncertain food supply in squalid refugee camps and settlements across six countries. For an already impoverished region, this mass of humanity driven from its economy and culture would be yet another burden, and a potential source of social or political turmoil for generations to come. (Sheet & Morris, 1974, p. 1)

Another growing source of environmental degradation is industrial pollution, "garbage imperialism," and the misuse and misapplication of diverse chemical agents.

Environmental control and reforestation have been attempted in almost
every country, but with only minimal success. Reforestation does not
usually seem to be carried out with the right species of trees. I have
observed that some existing streams and rivers in Cameroon have either
dried up completely or reduced drastically in volume after reforestation
of the watersheds with other than native species. It therefore seems
streams and rivers thrive better in areas whose watersheds are from natural forests than reforested catchments.

Political Organization and Governance

From the history of colonialism in Africa, we learn how "as a direct
result of the African encounters with Europe and, indeed, as a result of
the Africans' reluctance to accept colonial administration, Africa is today
divided into more than fifty states" (Cummings, 1986, p. 13). The emergence of these nations as actors in international politics is startling in
that until the 1950s, Africa "was an area of the globe where outsiders proposed and outsiders disposed of the major interests of the inhabitants
of that world region" (Liebenow, 1986, p. 13). African independence
was precipitated by nationalist challenges of colonialism and Africa's
refusal "to collaborate with a European imperial order under Europe's
terms" (Mazrui, 1986a, p. 269). The transactional encounters between
Africans and imperialists in the field of education, especially missionary education, gave birth to African nationalism.

Missionary bodies were not solely proselytizing agencies; Christian
mission schools were among the major transmitters of secularism in the
total African experience (Mazrui, 1986b). As a result of this development, the basis for African nationalism was laid. In 1948 Hendrick
Verwoerd (later Prime Minister of South Africa) alleged that Christianity had infused Africans with "the wrong expectations" because it evan-
gelized by fostering a new secular order. This was probably the case
since Christian secularism throughout Africa vitalized the struggle for
national independence. For instance, South Africa's outstanding freedom fighters (Mandela, Bishop Tutu, the Reverend Alan Boesak) and
African nationalist leaders like Um Nyobe, Kenyatta, Nkrumah, Kaunda,
Nyerere, and others were/are products of missionary education.

Prior to the Berlin partition of Africa, the nation-state was an alien
concept in Africa. African political frameworks comprised a mosaic of
efficient ethnic polities. Today a system of dual governance exists in
most African communities: the existence of ethnic authority alongside
that of administrators of the nation-state. Because several culture areas

or ethnic groups were indiscriminately split into different colonies, and eventually into nation-states, statehood "still faces a crisis of legitimacy before the tribunal of African pluralism" (Mazrui, 1986b, p. 199). The most critical political problem confronting West Africa today is the process of shaping a sense of national identity and forging a feeling of national community from a multiplicity of constituent ethnic polities. This has been difficult because committed and responsive national leadership that regularly commands the loyalty of the majority of the people, thus far seems to have eluded (West) Africa. The situation is made worse by the fact that the elite group in control seems to be more self-seeking than powerless peasants who are "innocently ignorant" of the significance of nationhood.

Some political regimes lack both the resources and the legitimacy to govern effectively. The political ideologies and forms of government that have been attempted in (West) Africa "have been so various, so often altered and so little correlated with the resolution of the problems of underdevelopment, that one is tempted to question whether they make any difference" (Luckham, 1985, p. 48). To the extent, however, that their common legacy has been the perpetuation of dependent underdevelopment and the fostering of new forms of structured inequality, they do make a significant difference. Despite the divisive effect of truncating ethnic peoples and/or ancestral lands across national borders, "partitioned Africans have nevertheless tended in their normal activities to ignore the boundaries as dividing lines and to carry on social relations across them more or less as in the days before the Partition" (Asiwaju, 1985, p. 3). Of course, this has precipitated numerous boundary disputes between several states, most of which are yet to be resolved.

The political leadership arouses great expectations, which their political and economic programs, always spurious models of imperial versions, have manifestly failed to satisfy. Instead of liberating and harnessing the rich talents of diverse ethnic peoples for greater productivity and vitality of national life, we see the incarceration of talents and unhealthy ethnic rivalry. Instead of the leadership and elites being role models, they alienate citizens and act in their own corporate interest, erecting new ascriptive barriers that limit positive contributions to national life and development. Generations of leaders repeat the cycle of errors of their predecessors, refusing to learn from a conspicuous past. The leadership is more creative in designing and implementing efficient networks to sustain power than to improve economies and standards of living. Due to failed policy programs and the failure of independence to benefit any but a small elite, there emerged a generation of left-wing leaders (Luckham, 1985) and a wave of coups d'état. Since armies themselves are unstable amalgams of interest groups, they have also failed to correct the conditions that tempted them to take over power. This has forced up military budgets and led to political tension, giving rise to a huge population of displaced persons, many of whom face starvation and an uncertain future.

The Religious Impact

The unholy alliance between imperial flags and the Cross was obvious because missionary objections to African religious practices were usually translated into administrative ordinances with legal force (Sanneh, 1986). This alliance fostered the African perception of Europeans as holding the Bible in one hand and a gun in the other. As envoys of a civilization blinded by a superiority complex, the missionaries misconstrued and denigrated African divinity. With the coexistence of Christianity, Islam, and African theodicy the African conscience became a gallery for the display of diverse religious traditions. This gave rise to religious conflicts and/or violence that occasionally flared and still flare in some African communities today.

Eventually, as separatist movements emerged, the imported religions were forced to adapt their practices to the ecology. Today most of them have diverged widely from their original antecedents. Several "independent" churches now exist. As Africans increasingly become aware of the hypocrisy of imported religions, the extent to which they use churches and religious occasions for worship or sociability merits scholarly scrutiny.

Despite continuing denigration of African religious life, the enduring vitality of African theodicy is self-evident (Sanneh, 1986). The coexistence of Islam, Christianity, and their distinctly African sects with indigenous religions has created a profusion of religious practices. Indigenous religious precepts invigorate and inspire both Islam and Christianity (Mazrui, 1986b); the old religion assertively interpenetrates the new, even as they compete for converts, influence, and credibility. The "churches and mosques are crowded, but traditional beliefs are still upheld and the old gods are not forgotten" (Stapleton, 1978, p. 14).

Christian schools played a dual role in that they preached the "good news" as well as taught secular skills and values. On the other hand, Islamic clerics focused all their attention on the Crescent. Although different colonial powers pursued different educational policies, the Westernization of African elites was popularized through missionary schools. However, Western education generally whetted African expectations but prevented their fulfillment through selfish policies. For instance, British colonial education in India, as elsewhere, was to train "at least a class of persons Indian in blood but English in opinion" (Fafunwa, 1967, p. 6). Thus the ulterior goal of colonial education was to crush the indigenous mind and will.

Social Decay and Economic Crisis

"Battered by global economic conditions beyond their control" (A. W. Clausen, quoted in Hubbard, 1985, p. 56), most West African nations have neither achieved the lofty goals set at independence nor even kept pace with the level of economic performance of the 1960s. Poor African nations "bear the burden of policies and institutions imposed and maintained by the powerful and the rich" (Schultheis, 1989b, p. 13), particularly the International Monetary Fund (I.M.F.) and the World Bank whose stringent adjustment policies have forced the contraction of already depressed African economies.

A visible area of decay in West African economies is the infrastructure and public utilities. For example, communication networks are underdeveloped and what exists is in a general state of disrepair. As rural exodus intensifies and the existing transportation and communication structures deteriorate daily, the village is increasingly becoming inaccessible to growing urban populations. The telephone system typifies West Africa's dependency syndrome. There are very few, if any, direct telephone links between African countries. Consequently, most telephone calls between West African nations are relayed via Europe.

The most alarming symptom of economic malaise is the fact that food production lags far behind population growth. Food production is increasingly being abandoned to an aged population as healthy youth flee the countryside, only to face a bleaker future in the shanty towns of crowded cities. "The population shift is caused by the breakdown in the rural areas, rather than being the result of healthy growth in the non-agricultural economic sector" (Schultheis, 1989b, p. 10). Given the fact that about 80% of the population relies on agriculture for a livelihood, the fall in demand and adverse terms of export crops trade literally represents economic genocide against West African peasants.

Instead of per capita income growing, in West Africa it has betrayed a precocity for diminishing returns (Mazrui, 1986b). How can we expect economies to expand when rewards for hard work are the exception rather than the rule? Economic expedience demands that West African governments and entrepreneurs urgently determine the daily man-hours of their employees and the extent to which their work is commensurate with their pay packets. The core of economic crisis in West Africa is threefold: (a) duality of the economic ethos, (b) the local component (unfavorable climatic conditions, bureaucratic ineptitude and corruption, misguided economic policies, human mismanagement, etc.), and (c) trading on "their" (i.e., rich industrialized nations, the I.M.F., and the World Bank) own terms. West African economies do not possess "the objective requirements that are imperative" for Western-type economies (Olurunsola & Muhwezi, 1986, p. 202), unfortunately adopted by all governments, because they are punctuated by a dualistic economic ethos: the idioms of kinship and some rudiments of free market forces.

The scenario is made worse by the fact that "Africa has found no truth in the economic theory that prices are determined by the operations of a free market, that is, by discussion and compromise between sellers and buyers. Rather, they have found that prices of [their] primary products are fixed by purchasers" (Cummings, 1986, p. 17). Both as sellers and buyers, Africans are price-takers, not price-makers. As a result, they sell cheap and buy dear. To be successful, African economic policies and programs must be based on the extremely tenacious indigenous imperatives, which hitherto have been grossly ignored. This is a very complex economic scenario that demands more sophisticated economic planning than in previous failed attempts. African nations should endeavor to live up to the spirit of the *Lagos Plan of Action* (Organization of African Unity, 1981), which, though not flawless, at least advocates self-reliant development.

The overall aim of education is to socialize for a civic role, but one of the most prominent outcomes of African education today is "the dissociation between learning and living" (Basu, 1987, p. 92). Not only is educational infrastructure inadequate or nonexistent, but existing ones are in urgent need of repair. Teachers are generally underpaid; they have become less professional and moonlight in order to ensure a livelihood. Most governments face a dilemma about how best to fund education: whether to provide universal primary education or free higher education. In some countries, students receive monthly stipends but the same governments that pay them often are unable to afford basic educational infrastructure. Curricula "present borrowed versions of western literature, allusions, and examples which virtually have no significance to the life" Africans know (Basu, 1987, p. 93). As a result, the graduates of educational institutions in West Africa are more informed about Western countries than they are about their own. How can such citizens be expected to contribute effectively to building nations and acting as role models in nations about which they are expertly ignorant? When will African scholars focus on their own cultures if they are so obsessed with Western models?

A related topic is the issue of brain drain. While many West African countries continue to hire expatriate personnel, increasing numbers of West African intellectuals are taking jobs in foreign countries because of unfavorable conditions at home (Olorunsola & Muhwezi, 1986). Perhaps they need to be reminded that the "favorable conditions" in their adopted homes were created by the "sacrifices" of the citizens of those nations and that they are helping to improve those conditions at the expense of their ancestral homes. West African governments equally need to learn that, in the long run, it is cheaper and in the best interest of national sovereignty and progress to retain their own citizens than to depend on foreign experts who are unaware of the subtleties of national life. Concerning Canada, Davies (1974, p. 21) perceptively pointed out that "Canadian nationality is an essential condition of insight into Canadian society. . . . Canadian nationality, native or acquired, opens the door for an awareness of Canada's underclass, hinterland status in the American empire." In the same vein, citizenship in African countries permits sensitivity to the harsh realities of the African condition. The situation whereby West African nations entrust certain spheres of national life to expatriates instead of their own nationals tends to mask rather than redress delicate national issues like nepotism and interethnic animosity.

Law enforcement is also in decay. Although the prisons are over-crowded, the law enforcement machinery seems to be crumbling onto itself (Mazrui, 1986b). Public outcry everywhere indicates that people are becoming more confused about the law and less secure in person and property. The crime wave rises but justice is hardly done or ever seen to have been done. Prior to the introduction of Western-type justice systems, there were indigenous mechanisms for keeping the peace and maintaining law and order. In indigenous terms, the protection of the innocent rather than the punishment of the guilty was the main focus of law enforcement (Mazrui, 1986b). The emphasis in litigation has now shifted from shame, a subjective experience with corrective value, to the proof of guilt with calibrated degrees of punishment. In the traditional justice system, legal issues were promptly reconciled by the supportive networks of the disputants in their best interest, but the excessive delay in the due process of law today has itself become injustice inflicted par excellence. Most litigants seem to leave courtrooms more aggrieved than they entered them. Consequently, many people tend to avoid the justice system because its corruption and long delays have made the miscarriage of justice more likely than the administration of justice.

"Europe's greatest service to Africa was not Western civilization, which is under siege, or even Christianity, which is on the defensive. Europe's supreme gift was the gift of African identity, bequeathed without grace and without design, but a reality all the same" (Mazrui, 1986b).

AFRICA'S TRIPLE HERITAGE: PERSONALITY PERSPECTIVE

In Africa today, "the old traditional ways have a continuing relevance, along with the new" (Ellis, 1978, p. 7). The admixture occurs in diverse shades across countries, communities, classes, and individual lives. The current African heritage is thus neither entirely indigenous nor entirely alien, it is a hybrid.

History shapes and sharpens the psyche just as it canalizes orientations and emotions. African history has done this rather perfectly. Hence the pertinence of Hunter's (1962, p. 6) reminder that the sores of slavery, the stigma of bondage and defeat left a "deep sense of inferiority and aggrievement . . . in African minds" that remains a lively force in African behavior today. Liebenow (1986, p. 63) labeled the series of Africa's historical traumas, "the debased Black condition." The intensity of the psychic traumas and the enormity and rapidity of social flux that has taken place in so short a time have left Africans neither the time nor the opportunity to resolve the multiple contradictions inherent in their debased status. When one juxtaposes the rapidity and enormity of change that has occurred in Africa within so brief a period of time with the often contemptuous remark that Africans are resistant to change, it becomes obvious that such assertions are no more than ethnocentric statements.

With centuries of subjugation and assimilation as the mark of their heritage, "Africans had learned to denigrate themselves and all aspects of their traditional culture" (Skinner & Mikell, 1986, p. 219). This is the sine qua non of psychology in Africa. The most assertive psychological attributes of contemporary Africans largely emanate from a reactive response to a debased fate. They are an insidious as well as frank symptomatology of a postsubjugation syndrome. How, really, does it feel to belong to "one group, the focus of this book, whose distinctive culture is little appreciated?" (Ellis, 1978, p. 1). It is the psychology of a people whose cultural tap roots, hence individual and collective identity, have been withering for centuries. It is the parents and caregivers with these kinds of orientations, value systems, and action-tendencies who are bearing and raising children in West Africa today.

The traditional and modern worlds may look so far apart in orientation and content but they are not so far apart in the reality of the contemporary African condition. The twilight zone for the old and new is the psyche and individual lives. At one end of the spectrum is a starkly illiterate villager still wholly submerged in his or her culture and nearly "untouched" by alien influence. At the other end is a partly Westernized graduate, a true citizen of the world, who, having studied, lived, and worked in Europe or North America, endeavors painfully and unsuccessfully to reconcile endogenous values and the acquired Western habits. The uneasy coexistence of endogenous traditions, Eastern legacies, and Western traditions paved the way for the development of three strands of African thought and value system: indigenous African, Arabo-Islamic, and Western-Christian. The outcome is a marginality wherein people are merely "groping desperately for answers to make their existence bearable" (Laosebikan, 1982, p. 1). The extent of this marginality is captured in Obiechina's (1975, p. 37) lucid remark that the West African only has "a thin layer of modern sophistication concealing the deep centre of traditional beliefs and feelings."

Despite the depth of indigenous concepts and modes of life, some people literally strive to eliminate indigenous inheritance from their behavioral repertoires. Others endeavor to belong to both worlds. Both groups of persons wage an endless war to reconcile within their lives and psyches the conflicts engendered in living within the twilight of fiercely competing values and ideologies. Of course, these are no-win battles because it is as difficult to discard centuries of sociocultural inheritance through wishful thinking as it is impossible to function properly within value systems without roots in one's developmental niche or life history. The struggle to reconcile the contradictions and conflicts incidental to marginal existence takes a profound toll on the individual and collective psyche and health. This perhaps explains the restiveness, generalized debility, and general lack of direction in West African societies today.

As purveyors and peddlers of alien goods, ideas, tastes, and cultural fragments, West Africans find that with every concession to externalization, their traditions are compromised and they feel an intensifying sense of alienation and a deepening loss of personal and collective identity (Esen, 1972). Caught in this twilight of value conflicts and moral dilemmas, West Africans find it difficult to preserve their roots and adapt to or benefit from external cultures. In a manner of speaking, they are pawns in a cultural chessboard. African elites have not imbibed the social skills and customary modes of life that confer a sense of confidence in the African world. But they have yet to internalize the modus vivendi that typifies Western life. Such persons can simply be described as mere danglers, living at the fringes of indigenous and alien worlds. Thus at several points in the lives of adults and children, indigenous and exterior modes of life and moral canons coexist uneasily, confront and/or collide with each other (Esen, 1972). As old values and life-styles collide daily with the new, children pick up double-bind cues from parents, peers, teachers, caretakers, friends, and caregiving niches. The anxiety and emotional turmoil this stirs flares up within individual psyches and can be observed in both adults and children. Thus the developmental world in West Africa is one in which several values and life-styles jostle for attention and adoption—in a sense, a "blooming, buzzing, confusion" (William James, 1842-1910). This obviously affects the way children are raised and the orientations and behavioral repertoires they acquire to face our common world.

SUMMARY AND CONCLUSION

Africa's contact with the external world predates recorded history. The three main forces underlying the contemporary West African condition are indigenous inheritance, alien spiritual traditions, and several alien secular influences. As a result, a multiplicity of alien cultural fragments, most of which have not taken root, have been grafted onto Africa's social ecology.

Extensive psychological acculturation means that at various points of life indigenous values coexist or clash with alien counterparts. This can only serve to confuse adults as well as children. Africa's historical traumas gave birth to a debased condition that Africans ought to regard and use as a challenging source of strength. The real challenge is to establish viable economic and political systems capable of meeting the basic needs of African populations and preserving an African identity.

To avoid leaving sociocultural change to chance, West African governments should sensitively design and implement programs to retain African roots and to gain cautiously from the modifying effects of alien influences. The unique wisdom in the West African worldview is unfortunately being abandoned in haste for Western patterns. Researchers in West Africa should think of how best to "assign" 21st century goals to indigenous structures, rather than replace them.

6

HISTORICAL ROOTS
Continuity and Discontinuity in West African Reproductive Ideas and Status Roles

One of the most fundamental issues of human existence is the manner in which procreation is imprinted in the human psyche and located in the life cycle. Every human culture constructs its own pattern of reproduction. Adult members, particularly parents and experts of the culture, dictate or provide the norms by which to make judgments about reproductive life (D'Alessio, 1990). For example, African "elders formulate a pattern of behaviour which they consider fulfils the wishes of their ancestors" (Musoke, 1975, p. 315) to ensure "the supply and maintenance of new members without whom the society would disappear" (Nsamenang, 1987, p. 278). Sexual attraction between a man and woman may lead to sexual intercourse, but in West Africa, "it is the desire for offspring which insists on a social charter for the propagation" of the species (Raum, 1967, p. 70). Although West Africans marry primarily for procreation (Erny, 1972, p. 22), the desire for children cannot be satisfied except in a legitimate marriage. West African cultures therefore sanction procreation and parenthood only within the institution of marriage. Parents are important in the reproductive outcome because they "provide the ideal environment for the child, both physical and psychological" (Musoke, 1975, p. 315).

The focus of this chapter is on continuity and change in West African reproductive ideology and status roles. In it, I have tried to identify some social dimensions of the African child in its sociocultural context: characteristics of the African family in flux, with a profile of the Nso and reproductive ideas in West Africa. In addition, I have attempted to sketch the current state of familial, parental, and status role change and their implications. After a study of an Ivorian community, Dasen et al. (1978, p. 57) concluded that it was a system in total flux, with the contrasts and inconsistencies that engenders.

THE WEST AFRICAN FAMILY: A PROFILE OF THE NSO OF CAMEROON

In order to understand the traditional African family structure, it is important to contextualize it (Dasen et al., 1978, p. 60). The basic nature of the West African family is the extended social network, whose general features were outlined in Chapter 4. Our concern here is briefly to describe trends in and features of a contemporary family as informed by interview data[1] derived from Nso parents. Nso is the largest of several ethnic polities in the Western Grassfields of Cameroon. The bulk of its population of 250,000 inhabitants lives in villages in Nsoland—although some have settled outside the ancestral land, the majority in the town of Bamenda.

The "environments of infancy and early childhood are shaped by cultural values. These values vary widely among populations and become firmly established in the personal preferences and inner regulations of individuals who seek to re-establish them in the next generation" (R. LeVine, 1974, p. 226). Beliefs about children and development form the core of such values. Developmental psychology has overwhelmingly been concerned mainly with the "psychologized" (scientific?) notions of parenting and child care, to the unfortunate neglect of folk precepts that underlie caregiving in the vast majority of human cultures. In order to study the folk belief systems underpinning parental role division and parenting, we interviewed 347 Nso parents (176 fathers, 164 mothers, and 7 parents whose gender was not recorded).

Tape-recorded interviews were conducted using the *Lamnso* (the language of the Nso) version of the Parent Interview Guide—PIG (Nsamenang & Lamb, 1988). The PIG is an open-ended questionnaire with 16 core items about the concept of child, perinatal concerns, and parenting issues. In designated Nso villages and in Bamenda, 7 native Nso fathers conducted home interviews one and a half to two and a half hours long with the 347 parents in a friendly open-ended format at their convenience. The choice of one parent per family reflected rural-urban residence; African, Christian, or Islamic religious affiliation; parents with a child 10 years old and younger or grandparents; and voluntary participation. The interviews were coded by three trained Nso female high school students. The findings reported here pertain only to the characteristics of the sample.

Disregarding homemaking as an occupation because in West African cultures the status of complete housewifery is abhorred, the vast majority of the sample engaged in purely traditional occupations, particularly farming. Of the 347 households in the Nso survey, 46% reported sheltering at least one other-than-biological member at the time of the interview. With such a percentage of *household extendedness* we may begin to question the sense of the ubiquity of the extended household system often conveyed in most discussions of the (West) African family. Whereas 32.6% of rural households were extended, with an average of approximately 2.0 extended persons per household, 60.8% of urban households were extended, with an average of 2.2 extended members per household. That is, the extended household system may be more extensively an urban phenomenon than a rural one. Of course, this "reality" is consistent with current trends in rural exodus and the rapid rate of urbanization discussed in Chapter 3.

The overall average number of children per family was 5.9; 6.2 for the rural area and 5.5 for the urban setting. Although we did not know whether the children reported were actually living in the households of the subjects at the time of the interview, these figures nevertheless suggest the possibility that more persons may be living per unit area in the city than the village, given that the limitations of space and room tend to be more acute in urban than rural neighborhoods, at least in Cameroon. All the respondents who reported 10 or more children were fathers, except one rural, Christian mother who reported 12. The larger number of children reported by fathers might be a function of polygynous fatherhood. This observation is plausible in light of the fact that *only* 11% (excluding the mother just cited) of the 164 mothers (i.e., 18) in the sample mentioned 8 or 9 children. Fourteen of the 18 mothers were rural and 4 were urban. Considering that the projected female life expectancy in Cameroon in 1991 is cited as 57.6 years (Ministry, 1986, p. 5) as well as the high mean age (51.3 years) of the mothers in the sample, it seems safe to intimate that the fecundity rate in Cameroonian women, at least among the Nso, may be less than 8. Of the 11 fathers with 15 or more children, 9 were Muslims (4 urban, 5 rural), while the other 2 were city and village Christians. The observed large number of offspring in Muslim households is not surprising because Islam sanctions polygyny (to 4 wives).

The average number of years of schooling among rural parents was 2.0 years as against 4.7 years for urban parents; for fathers it was 2.9, and 3.0 for mothers. Twenty-seven percent of the fathers versus 31% of the mothers had no schooling. However, although the number of fathers and mothers with 10 or more years of schooling were equal, 13 each, more mothers (6) than fathers (3) had at least 14 or more years of schooling. Twenty-four (92.3%) of the 26 parents with 10 or more years of schooling resided in the city and 2 (7.7%) in the village. The overall lower rate of female education seems to accord with national trends in Cameroon. Half (49.3%) of the enrollees in kindergarten in the 1980-1981 school year were girls, indicating that almost equal numbers of boys and girls start schooling at the same time, although the ratio soon begins to widen as more girls than boys drop out. This perhaps explains why the girl population in the same year was only 45.5% of the total elementary school enrollments (Ministry, 1986).

Although the data do not address causal relationships, they nevertheless depict a picture as well as suggest some trends. Taken together, a Nso child is likely to have other siblings. Rural Nso children are less likely than their urban peers to have schooled parents, or if the parents are schooled, they would, on average, tend to have had fewer years of schooling than their city counterparts. Stated differently, rural Nso parents tend to be less formally educated than urban Nso parents. Nso children in the city are more likely to have extended members in their households than are Nso children in the villages. Because it is more difficult to obtain adequate housing in the city than in the village, Nso children in the city are more likely than their village peers to live in crowded households.

There does not seem to be any apparent reason to doubt that the sketchy profile of the Nso family just painted does not apply to other West African communities, at least in general trends, that may even be more marked in societies with more widespread fosterage than in Nso. The trends in urbanization and household size might even be magnified in such communities as the Yoruba of Nigeria and Benin Republic and the Akan of Ghana who have known urban life for centuries. However, whereas the rural-urban drift and the felt need for schooling might be lower in nomadic and Islamized societies, households in the Islamized societies of the Sahel zone and the pockets of Muslim communities in West African cities and some villages are likely to be larger than the figures reported here, since Islam permits polygyny.

While variations in family structure and characteristics are obvious, their impact lies in the reproductive patterns they foster.

REPRODUCTIVE IDEAS AND PARENTHOOD
IN WEST AFRICAN CULTURES

The way in which fathers and mothers conceive of children and development influences the way their children are raised and, consequently, how their children will turn out (Sameroff & Feil, 1985). In the Nso survey referred to above, more fathers (54.5%) than mothers (37.6%) reported that pregnancy signified an increase in family size and/or strength. This suggests a lurking possibility of differences in the way fathers and mothers view pregnancy. If maternal and paternal ideas or attitudes differ significantly, this certainly carries important implications for reproductive behavior and the task of raising children.

What first strikes an observer of the African social scene is the desire for and high valuation of children. Attitudes about childbearing in Ghana, as elsewhere in Africa, are universally positive (Kaye, 1962). For West Africans, the marriage contract foreshadows the child (Raum, 1967). The main purpose of marriage is childbearing rather than sexuality or the mere satisfaction of a biological need (Kenyatta, 1965). According to Erny (1972, p. 25, author's translation) "the image of Black Africa that readily comes to the European mind is that of free, 'savage,' and unbridled sex. Nothing is further from the truth. What strikes a keen observer is not the excesses but the control to which the African is subjected; it is not the exasperation but the mastery. Not having seen sexuality treated naturally" the Euramerican mind, thus far, has projected no more than erotic obscenity into African reproductive life. High fertility is regarded as a measure of divine or ancestral approval for a couple's marriage and life-style. Using the Nso data, Nso parents perceived pregnancy as primarily signifying family size/strength, divine gifting, proof of manhood/womanhood, proof of fertility, a biological process, and responsibility or maturity, in that order.

Parenthood is a coveted West African goal. The desire is not simply for children; the common feeling is that the more one has the better. Nsamenang's (1989c) report that the mean number of children per family in the Bamenda Grassfields of Cameroon is 4.7, is consistent with the finding that the range of total fertility in West Africa varies "from just over 4.5 in Cameroon to something close to 7.0 in most countries of the region" (Ware, 1983, p. 18). The 5.9 average number of children per interviewee obtained in the Nso survey falls within the Ware (1983) range, but is higher than Nsamenang's (1989c). A possible explanation is that a strong ethnocentric desire for many children probably interplayed with the Catholic pronatalist posture to produce the observed high fertility rate of 5.9 since 68.7% of the sample was Christian, 74.8% of them being Catholic. Sex or gender preferences may also sustain higher levels of fertility than would be the case if the sex of children were a matter of indifference (Cleland, Verrall, & Vaessen, 1983, p. 7). In contrast, the African reproductive practices of "regulating fertility and spacing children" and abstaining from sexual intercourse while nursing is a form of birth control (Hunt, 1983, p. 401).

In the psychological outlook of the West African, "fertility in all its forms represents the primary value" (Erny, 1972, p. 20). Accordingly, the desire for children is so deeply rooted in the hearts of both men and women that they regard procreation as their first and most sacred duty in marriage (Nsamenang, 1987). Parenthood confers a sense of self-fulfillment in West Africans, particularly in women. The expectation that a couple should have children as soon after the wedding ceremony as possible is so strong that parents become anxious if their daughters do not become pregnant within the first year of marriage (Uka, 1966). "A pregnant woman is a happy woman" (Erny, 1968, p. 84). Thus, "confirmation of pregnancy is a time of jubilation even when a woman already has several children" (Ellis, 1978, p. 40). The common thought is that without children a person will leave no heirs to survive him or her. "To die childless is to 'die completely.' By contrast, as a Kongo proverb asserts, 'if you are a father, you are immortalized. A child is the only remedy against death' " (Erny, 1972, p. 21). Consequently, most West Africans prefer to die in poverty and be survived by offspring than to die rich and childless (Nsamenang & Laosebikan, 1981).

Infertility "is felt by both men and women as the greatest of all personal tragedies and humiliations" (Fortes, 1950, p. 262). Thus the slightest indication of infertility precipitates intense anxiety and deep concern about its source (Nsamenang, 1987). As a result, individuals, couples, and families spare neither efforts nor resources to establish, restore, or prove fertility. Couples and individuals usually receive the first blame for being childless until its cause is identified. For instance, "the fact that a couple has no children is interpreted as sufficient proof that they are bad people and their 'badness' is being punished with childlessness by the ancestors" (Nsamenang, 1987, p. 282). Others think that a woman's "unfruitfulness is usually attributed to some fault of her own, on account of which ancestral spirits will not insert a soul in her womb, or be willing to be incarnated in her" (Uka, 1966, p. 37). In this sense, infertility is regarded not as a physiological deficiency, but a cosmo-cultural deficit.

The high valuation of childbearing implies that infertility may precipitate divorce, polygyny, or fosterage. But "divorce is not a necessary and never an instantaneous result of infertility" (Raum, 1967, p. 76). "If divination fails to discover the cause of barrenness, and medical treatment and sacrifices cannot remove it, several schemes are customarily adopted to achieve the birth of a legitimate heir" (Raum, 1967, p. 75). In some cases, the spouse (secretly) arranges for a substitute to raise "seed" for him or her.

In discounting the spiritual component (folk explanations) in human fertility, it is perhaps instructive to reason like the Nso: "Why does it have to be 'this' or 'that' person (with potentially fertilizable eggs or sperm) whose genotype does not shape him or her or 'tune up' for reproduction?"

In West Africa, as in Kenya, "the social position of a married man and woman who have children is of greater importance and dignity than that of a bachelor or spinster" (Kenyatta, 1965, p. 158). After the birth of a first child the couple become the object of greater respect than they were prior to the child's birth (Nsamenang, 1987). In Erny's (1968, p. 84) terms, "the birth of the first child constitutes a more important event than the establishment of conjugal life." The naming of the baby further increases parental status because parents become known and addressed, not in their personal names but, as "this" or "that" child's father or mother. In the case of two or more children, parents are addressed by reference to the parents' or addressor's favorite child—a practice that could have negative psychological repercussions on the child or children not so favored, especially if the favorite is younger. The custom of naming a child after the father is a borrowed one, and has come into use in (West) African traditions very recently (Fox, 1967).

Generally, there is little or no aversion toward having children, even "illegitimate" ones, although illegitimacy does not exist in the Western sense. A child is always the child of "someone." In general, children of unwed or divorced mothers belong to their families of origin. Although wives are usually furious about their husbands' "illegitimate" children, Nsamenang (1987) noted that—in cases where they are not incorporated into the mother's family of origin—the children of the so-called outside wives are generally accepted and integrated into the father's family. Parents may be unhappy about their daughter's unwed motherhood, which seems to be attaining alarming proportions in many communities. Nevertheless, they readily accept and assume responsibility for the care of such children, a practice that now seems to promote teenage parenthood. Parents reason: How can one reject or disclaim a daughter for extending the hearth? Among the Nso of Cameroon, adolescent motherhood is traditionally greeted with a birth song: *"loo wan dzee wan"*—a chant expressing happiness at "the birth of a child by another child." That West African children are born into a basically welcoming atmosphere (Wober, 1975, p. 3) was exemplified by an almost unanimous endorsement (98.1%) of the celebration of childbirth through feasting and singing of birth songs, goodwill visits from friends/community, "showering" of the neonate with gifts, and performance of customary rituals to mark childbirth by parents in the Nso survey referred to earlier.

In Ghana as elsewhere in West Africa, the expectation is that parents should feed and raise their children, "clothe them, send them to school, find jobs for them, and then marry them off" (Kaye, 1962). Consistent with this expectation, more than half of the "yes" responses in the Nso data focused on proper character (59.8%), children's nutrition (58.5%), and education (57.6%). Others centered on children's health (39.6%), clothing (25.1%), filial marital arrangements (24.1%), protection (24.5%), support of the spouse (12.4%), and ensuring filial involvement in community affairs (2.8%).

The relatively low percentages do not necessarily imply that parents were uncommitted to the parenting issues raised; they are relative rather than cumulative because open-ended responses were provided. It seems probable, however, that many parents had difficulty articulating their responses, especially as some of them hinted that the interview was the first time they had ever been asked to verbalize their parenting ideas and strategies. As the contribution by children to the family economy declines and some of the basic necessities of life and family welfare are purchased rather than grown on the family farm, these responsibilities are quite expensive in terms of parental investment and money. In a certain sense, children are seemingly becoming "liabilities" and parental "burdens" rather than the assets they once were. Thus the high cost of raising and educating children appears to be responsible for the sluggish and certain, but as yet unmeasured, decline in the desire for large families. Because children "now have greater freedom to choose their marriage partners and make other personal decisions than in the past" (Nsamenang, 1987, p. 290), parents are increasingly becoming peripheral figures in the lives of their children, particularly in children's marital arrangements.

The pro-life attitudes of West Africans sharply contrast with those of Americans. Research findings published in 1957 by Sears, Maccoby, and Levin (cited in Ellis, 1978, pp. 40-41) indicated that "only 62 percent of the American women interviewed were delighted to be having a first child and they became less delighted at the prospect of subsequent children." A replication of this study today may produce a lower percentage of American women with a similar reaction to motherhood. Ideas about parenthood connote parental goals and parenting orientations.

PARENTING ORIENTATIONS AND GOALS

Cultural scripts, no less than biology and phylogeny, contribute to the ways in which parents perceive the task of raising children. These "ways are rational in that they contain information about environmental contingencies previously [cognized and] experienced by the population and assimilated into its cultural tradition" (R. LeVine, 1974, p. 227). Such orientations are consistent with the collective elaboration of the past and the dynamic reality of the present (D'Alessio, 1990). What are some of the orientations and goals West African men and women bring to parenthood today?

From the Nso data, we learned that half the "yes" responses (51.1%) acknowledged the innateness of some human attributes, while 28.5% favored the view that the human offspring is God's precious gift. More than half (52.6%) of the responses favored differentiable gender socialization. Some of the reasons given to account for gender differences were notions of weaker/stronger sex (36.2%), the protection of girls from exploitation (32.5%), and differences in the rate of biological maturation (0.3%). Although three modes of parental authority were identified —punishment (35.6%), restrictions (26.3%), and intimidation (10.5%)— only 27.6% of the responses sanctioned the use of parental authority. This somehow runs counter to the general feeling that African parents tend to be authoritative. Assuming that assertion of parental authority over children is perceived negatively, one plausible explanation is that parents would consciously tend to dissociate themselves from motivations or tendencies considered to be negative.

What these findings point to is that Nso parents, like all West African parents, are not blank slates regarding the nature of children and that they do not attempt to raise children without intended purposes or expected child outcomes. In this light, parenting among the Nso is meant to instill good character (66.6%), and parents expect filial work (52.7%) and good progress in school (49.8%). Parents also expect filial obedience (35.3%), proper development (25.1%), vocational competence (19.8%), provision of a decent burial for parents (12.1%), and financial support (7.4%).

Child care in West African cultures is not a parental prerogative; it is a collective social enterprise in which parents and kin, as well as siblings and sometimes neighbors and friends, are active participants. Although the parenting literature generally locates the primary responsibility for child care on mothers, in Cameroon as in much of West Africa, children spend much more time and engage in more intensive interactions in the care and guidance of other children and peers than has conventionally been documented (Nsamenang, 1992). Thus 67.2% of girls and 65.2% of boys in the Nso sample participated in child caretaking as well as attended school. The slight difference in the rate of female and male involvement in caregiving is consistent with parental encouragement and expectation that daughters be better careproviders and nurturers than sons (Nsamenang, 1989a). It is difficult to find a West African child who grows to adulthood without having encountered several caring persons and developmental experiences in diverse niches. The prototype of this kind of socialization is the evocation in *The African Child* of Camara Laye's (1977) boyhood and emergence into manhood in rural and urban Guinea and France. The extent to which West African children participate in the care of other children is unmatched in many cultures. Whether positive or negative consequences flow from such a caregiving scenario has yet to be determined by research. In this direction, Weisner and Gallimore (1977, p. 169) remarked that the styles of sibling caretaking are different from parental care and thus "are intriguing in their potential effects on both caretaker and charge."

Parental concern with academic progress, for one example, alludes to the impact of alien values on parental values and attitudes, since formal schooling is not an endogenous West African custom. Because the data presented above involve indigenous as well as borrowed imperatives in the contemporary parenting ecology, this confirms the emphasis in Chapter 5 of the coexistence of both old and new status roles, especially those pertaining to parenthood and family life. The final section of this chapter is devoted to an examination of the enormity of the social flux and role change in West Africa.

THE CHANGING FAMILY STRUCTURE AND ROLES

The data presented above indicate that West Africa's "old traditional ways have continuing relevance, along with the new" (Ellis, 1978, p. 7). The continuities and changes in family structure and status roles exist in varying degrees across rural and urban settings and reflect the ways in which West Africans are coping with the changes in the political, social, economic, religious, and other spheres of contemporary life.

We pointed out in Chapter 3 that the majority of West African families are peasants, producing crops for subsistence with occasional sale of the surplus. We also indicated that men, women, and children contributed to the traditional food production system. In rural communities today this productive system somehow persists, but the urban family has become more a unit of consumption than of production. The urban family has almost become a "pack" of adults and children pursuing disparate goals: paid work, commerce, schooling, wealth and success, leisure and fun, kinship and friendship ties, and so forth. In the exceedingly dynamic and competitive urban centers, there is a "seething scramble to find a niche" (Hunter, 1962, p. 85) by both adults and children. On the other hand, village life is less hectic as the rural family still retains some degree of homogeneity of its primary goals—the production of agricultural crops and crafts and the maintenance of mutual reciprocity.

The West African "culture pattern is changing due to contact with the outside world" (Musoke, 1975, p. 315). The changes are also "profoundly shaped by the existing social structure and culture" (Ouden, 1987, p. 13). Major shifts in the social structure and roles are thought to have begun with long-distance trade exchanges with the Arabian Peninsula and Mediterranean Europe by way of North Africa. With the establishment of monotheistic religions and the advent of enslavement, European cash, taxation, formal education, colonization, and public administration and welfare services, the changes progressively intensified. Visible even to the casual observer of the West African world is the fact that today men, women, and children are taking on roles that were either unavailable or that they previously did not or could not play. Of all role changes perhaps the most dramatic are in work options, especially for women, and children's routines, particularly schooling and children's economic activities.

The most innovative deviation from the custom that adult women should marry, become full-time farmers and homemakers, and as soon as possible, mothers, occurred when taxes and school fees were introduced and crops were cultivated solely for cash. This began to alter family/social relationships, particularly within the food production chain. The total labor time for everyone increased. For example, in 1934 when the Beti of south central Cameroon were faced with high taxes and low cash crop prices (a fate they and other West Africans still face today), women had to work more than 70 hours a week compared to 46 hours in the precolonial period, by far more than men's 25 hours for household heads and 55 hours for the dependent males, which were twice their precolonial averages (Henn, 1978). Export crops are in the sphere of men's responsibility and as men's opportunities increasingly lay outside the ancestral land (Ouden, 1987), women had to intensify their farming tasks to make good the loss of men's labor. While some women had to help with the production of the export crops, others undertook their full-scale cultivation, whereas still others even became plantation laborers (D. B. Koenig, 1977). Today many Cameroonian women, including mothers, are full-time laborers in the Cameroon Development Corporation's varied plantations.

Provisioning in West Africa is somewhat different than in many societies. West African women "are highly prolific mothers of many children and at the same time heavily engaged in productive work both inside and outside the home" (Oppong, 1983, p. 4). Many women now have access to craft and food marketing and play important roles in the labor force and retail trade. Guyer (1984) noted that most West African women have integrated earning an income with housekeeping and child care. Boserup (1970) found that Cameroonian women in Bamenda contributed about 44% of the family income. Some women now have a purchasing power higher than that of their husbands. Most men attempt to control the use of their wives' income in what resembles a deeply ingrained male struggle to retain control over female labor (Henn, 1984). For example, Kaberry (1952) pointed out that Bamenda women can keep small sums of money, but the question of rights to money become crucial when larger sums are at stake. Nsamenang (1987) corroborated this finding with a report that wives' financial independence in the Bamenda Grassfields was the source of husbands' unhappiness and marital discords.

The establishment of schools, plantations, and food processing and mineral extraction industries inaugurated patterns of migration that persist to date. Male migration placed a heavy burden on other family members whose labor increased because they had to produce food as well as take over cash crop cultivation from absent husbands (White, 1984). O'Barr (1984) thinks that the only area in which women's workload did not increase was in the role of wife. With time, single women also migrated into the cities and plantations to provide companionship or sell food and beer to the men who performed tedious jobs for very meager wages (White, 1984). According to O'Barr (1984), recent research on African women has shown that they had played a greater and more influential role in traditional political life than they did during the colonial era and since independence. In traditional dispensations, women's political roles and prerogatives (women's houses), though never on a par with men's, were quite considerable (see Chapter 4). The colonial and the immediate postcolonial governments, however, seemed to have shared the myopic view that women should be kept outside the proper realm of government. The occupations women pursue are as limited as their involvement in government. This may be due to their differential access to education, partially explainable by the gender division of labor (Robertson, 1984).

In the family scene the number of monogamous households and people remaining single and childless throughout their lives, as well as the rates of divorce and absentee spouses seem to be increasing (Nsamenang, 1987). In the struggle between the generations and sexes, the tide is against parents, fathers in particular. As far as the due process of law and political order were concerned in traditional polities, lineage patriarchs and "select" women were responsible for the lineage; were the law and the state. But today, the law is concerned with the rights of individuals: men, women, and children. The net effect of the changes is parental frustration and sense of powerlessness. Parental frustration is typified by the complaint in the Bamenda Grassfields that *"we no know wetih pekin them wan today"* (a Creolized version of "we don't know what today's children want") (Nsamenang, 1988, p. 22). Parents seem bitter that they are becoming merely "other" members of the family instead of the once undoubted mentors. The erosion of parental authority is further facilitated by the fact that nowadays children know more about contemporary life than do their parents. Consequently, most parents are finding it difficult to guide their children in how to behave in a world in which they are the more ignorant citizens. This approximates role reversal: Children, not parents, are the ones who explain how the world functions.

There is also confusion regarding the enforcement of customs for the support of widows, divorced wives, and child custody (Skinner & Mikell, 1986). Wealthy men sometimes find their property so entangled within the traditional inheritance network that they leave virtually nothing for their widows and children to inherit. This state of affairs obtains because wives are more loosely anchored in the extended family networks than previously. This and many similar trends in West African life have yet to be investigated.

As mothers are combining motherhood and career roles, an increasing number of young husbands are slowly though hesitantly beginning to take on some caregiving and domestic roles that they could not previously play (Nsamenang, 1987). It remains to be studied how these changes are affecting children, families, and the society. The starting point for such studies may be the fact that motherhood has become more difficult as mothers are assuming full-time roles outside the farm and the marketplace. Even more difficult for children of working parents is the task of figuring out and comprehending the working life of parents and the nature of their work. Sometimes the exigencies of work or formal education separate spouses or they may be separated from their children and kin for extended periods of time. Such separation of network members has obvious implications for the experience of childhood. Urban children are increasingly being placed in the care of baby-sitters; often relatives, but sometimes nonrelatives hired solely for this purpose. The impact of the baby-sitting arrangement on African children has rarely been studied. Even casual observation, however, may reveal that in stressful situations like illness and hospitalization, some baby-sat children prefer being handled more by their sitters than by their mothers.

The potential impact of role change on children is magnified by the school system. Increasing numbers of children are entering the school system and spending longer periods of their waking time in educational environments. This obviously limits the impact of their home environments and reduces their role as careproviders as well as contributions to family subsistence. Unlike in the past, when knowledge was limited to the ethnic history and folklore, the school system greatly expands children's horizons and experiences. This, in turn, influences their orientations and patterns of behavior. Most of the skills needed for gainful employment and modern life-styles are acquired through formal education, not by imitating mentors or by being assigned lifework and being trained at it. Strictly speaking, this statement is misleading because school attendance does not necessarily preclude children from subsistence chores, particularly in rural communities. Rather, some reorganization of time rather than a real reduction in the tasks to be accomplished is the usual solution (Bekombo, 1981). Endogenous education, the sacred duty of the family, kept children in contact with their social context and activities of daily life. But today, "traditional education, disrupted by the numerous changes taking place, has to some extent lost its regulatory role" (Federal Republic of Nigeria, 1983, p. 8) because the break between the past and present has occurred fairly quickly. In juxtaposing the claims of the ethnic polity as opposed to those of the nation-state, Sharp (1970, p. 20) warned "against destroying too abruptly the traditional background of the African," which is still "the best guarantee of the child's welfare and education."

To conclude, contemporary West African "families seem to be in trouble not so much because of the problems of poverty, ignorance, and disease but because the inherited conception of the family is rather tenacious and inadequate for coping with the requirements for living in a society in a critical stage of transition" (Nsamenang, 1987, p. 291). Daily, the traditional and modern directives of family life and parenthood conflict. The clash between traditionalism and modernity produces dilemmas and incompatible role demands that serve to confuse both parents and children. As a result, parents are literally waging endless struggles to reconcile the multiple contradictions. The outcome is parental confusion and inadequately parented children. This has given rise to parental bitterness as well as "an increasing incidence of psychological disturbances in children" consequential to faulty parenting (Nsamenang, 1983, pp. 6-7). Thus the challenge facing West African parents and communities "is to forge new conceptions of the family and of family life" (Nsamenang, 1987, p. 291). This may be facilitated, not impaired, by the recognition of the complexity of the issues and a revision of the gender division of family roles to reflect the stark realities of West Africa's triple heritage (see Chapter 5).

NOTE

1. The work reported here was a collaborative research effort between Cameroon's Institute of Human Sciences, Bamenda, and the Laboratory of Comparative Ethology—NICHD, Bethesda, MD, and carried out by Nsamenang and Lamb between October 1988 and April 1989. It was funded by the National Institute of Child Health and Human Development (NICHD).

7

CHILDHOOD AND HUMAN DEVELOPMENT IN WEST AFRICAN CULTURES

In Chapter 6 we discussed the reproductive ideas and parenting orientations of West Africans. In the present chapter we shift focus to the notion that every culture constructs childhood and socializes children in its own terms (Erny, 1968). The focus of attention here, then, is on the West African conception of the child as this determines the nature of developmental and caregiving environments West Africans prepare, the kinds of resources and experiences they provide, how they raise children, and the conditions under which they endeavor to meet children's needs. An attempt is also made to outline the way West Africans partition the human life cycle, a partition based more on social ontogeny than on biological maturation.

CONCEPT OF THE CHILD

Folk ideas about children are integral components of the cosmology or frame of reference of a society. A West African concept of the child is theocentric in nature—children serve a spiritual function. The link between human beings and God is through filiation; God can give or deny fertility. Personal comportment and spiritual and moral probity are critical determinants of God's decision to "give" or "not give" fecundity. Whereas pregnancy is seen as signifying divine blessing, the child is regarded as God's precious gift, "given" through the mediative approval of ancestral spirits. That is, pregnancy denotes God's approval of the ancestors' wish to send "a representative through the couple into the community" (Nsamenang, 1987, p. 282). This viewpoint acknowledges the role of biology in procreation by positing God's use of couples to propagate the species.

While some children are God's free gift, others are ordinary children or reincarnations of dead ancestors. Of course, reincarnation is impossible without divine approval. Although all children have a divine origin, societies like the Nso of Cameroon attach special socio-religious significance to a class of offspring referred to as *woon-ah nyuy* (children of God). In Nso thought, ordinary and reincarnated children are bona fide Nso citizens, whereas *woon-ah nyuy* are special emissaries (strangers) God sends to "tempt" human goodwill, hence the reverence accorded such children and their parents.

Children are not thought to belong to this world until they have been incorporated into the community of the living through naming. Prior to the conferment of a name—usually when the umbilical stump falls off or about the seventh postnatal day—the neonate is generally believed to belong more to the spirit than to the material world and could be "taken away" (i.e., die) at any moment. "Just as the ancestors are thought to have gone from the land of the living, though not far, the newborn are regarded as not fully and securely with the living and are thought to have special links with the spirit world" (Ellis, 1978, p. 42). Children who are stillborn or those who die during birth or prior to their naming ceremony are usually suspected of being "spirit" children. In some societies, they "are buried without ceremony and are not mourned" (Ellis, 1978, p. 42). The naming of a child therefore marks the dawn of personhood in West African ontogeny. This is an occasion for thanksgiving and rejoicing; the point at which the child might "remain with the living," that is, survive. Hence its initiation via naming into the community of "other" humans.

Pregnancy and birth are only two positive indicators of the process of divine gifting. Because infant mortality is high, one week in a baby's life is a critical period for assessing God's willingness and final decision regarding the parents' worth for his precious gift. Thus "the named baby is felt by all to have had its existence confirmed and strengthened" (Maclean, 1971, p. 56). As a result, there is a tendency in some communities not to count children who die before they are named as having lived. On the other hand, all children who die just after naming will always be remembered (Ellis, 1978). This is a crucial point worthy of note in demography and obstetric history. Thus West Africans use beliefs and practices to rationalize the excessive waste of infant life, a practice that functions to soften the pain of such losses (Wober, 1975).

Virtually nothing is published about the essential nature of the child in West African thought. Extrapolation from the socialization literature and observation of the manner in which children are treated, however, justifies the statement that the West African mind sees the child as an empty vessel to be filled. The quantity and quality of "material" with which the filling is undertaken determine how the child turns out. The presumed innocence or emptiness of the newborn is true only from the standpoint of socialization. There is a widespread belief in the innateness of certain attributes such as the gift to heal, some forms of wickedness, and other traits. In the Nso survey (see Chapter 6), half (51.1%) of the sample reported that some human traits are inborn.

In the sociological realm, the child is considered a "plant" growing up in a field—the kin group (Nsamenang, 1987). The metaphor of the plant connotes tending and development to maturity and fruit-bearing, that is, children, whom the Bambara regard as the *"grain du monde"* (Erny, 1968, p. 21). The functional dimension of this conception is that from early in life, children are introduced to their kinfolk who have responsibility toward and rights over them. This viewpoint is consistent with the belief that only unborn babies belong to their parents. From birth on, children belong to those who make up their agnatic kernel. Such extended networks readily share in child care, although wicked or envious kin may not want the child to thrive.

Although children are conceived of in lofty spiritual terms, mundanely they are regarded in utilitarian terms and the way they enhance the status of their parents. Thus children are a source of family strength and parental prestige. They "improve" the social standing of the parents and are their "walking sticks"—a parental social security system, especially in old age. An Ewe wit succinctly captures this mode of thinking:

> A mother's son is a buttress:
> if you have none
> down falls the house.
> A mother's daughter is your
> everyday apparel:
> if you have none
> you're cold, exposed
> (Ellis, 1978: p. 39).

This poem clearly portrays the differential valuation of male and female children. The view of children as a parental support system means that parents, the father for example, can literally "call on his children for assistance at any time and can even intervene, without being considered as intruding, in the affairs of a married child, particularly his son" (Nsamenang, 1987, p. 286). Expectations in terms of social development and competence and fruit-bearing are core concepts underlying the developmental path in West Africa. An overview of developmental milestones in the West African worldview is the focus of the next section.

DEVELOPMENTAL STAGES
IN WEST AFRICAN ONTOGENY

In discussing the concept of precocity of development in African children, Wober (1975, p. 3) remarked that "the notion of precocity assumes that there may be a 'natural' schedule of development for newborn babies and infants, which will be followed at least until cultural differences make their effects felt in the pace and directions of growth." The inference here is quite clear: Cultures infuse their own agendas onto a natural, biological program. Stated differently, various cultures may recognize, define, and assign different developmental tasks to the same biological agenda. In other words, although there may be a "natural" developmental path, every culture superimposes its own imprints on it. In this sense, the developmental tasks contained in most English language developmental texts may be no more than the cultural agendas for the development of Western middle-class children. Thus the experience of childhood in West Africa, for instance, may not necessarily accord nor exactly correspond with the definition and experience of childhood as portrayed in the current developmental literature. My task here is to attempt a sketch of the social construction of the life cycle within the West African ontogeny.

For West Africans, the infant is a "project-in-progress." In West African thought, the human neonate—in lay, mundane terms—is a human frame that shelters a spiritual self-hood onto which a social self-hood begins ontogenetic development on the assignment of a name, that is, from the moment of incorporation into a community of the living. Thus naming is an ontogenetic event of primal importance because it marks the dawn of human, in a more restricted sense social, development. Since West African ontogeny visualizes the cyclical nature of the human person, infancy, like old age, is an intermediate, transitory stage. Whereas the infant is entering the world of the living, the old person is preparing to leave it (Erny, 1987). In this light, West African ontogeny recognizes three basic dimensions of personhood. First, there is a spiritual self-hood beginning at conception and ending with naming. Second, the social self-hood extends from naming until death (in old age). Third, the ancestral self-hood follows biological death (and extends, perhaps, to the ritual initiation of the ancestral spirit into a higher spiritual realm [see Chapter 4]).

Social ontogeny does not deny biology. In fact, except for the ancestral self-hood, social self-hood and part of the spiritual self-hood are contained in a biotic structure, the human body, that itself possesses a "natural" ontogenetic path. Biogenetic development, as explained in Chapter 2, nevertheless requires ecocultural primers. The human body, then, is a temporary, mundane habitat for the manifestation of human presence, personhood. In the natural order of things, the human body per se is less important than what (the human presence) it contains. Regardless of the shape, size, color, and other attributes of the anatomical framework, the importance of what it houses is the critical factor. Our primary concern here is with social self-hood, the purely earthly dimension of personhood.

In West Africa, developmental phases are premised, not on chronological age, but predominantly on "socially recognizeable stages by reference to physical events like smiling, starting to walk, cutting teeth and beginning to talk" (Nsamenang, 1988, p. 16). Different behaviors are thus expected from children at various life stations during ontogeny. Whereas the behaviors expected during the early years of life tend to be biological in nature—smiling, sitting, teething, walking—the phases from when children can walk about are marked by reference to socialized behaviors such as running errands, "good" conduct, generosity, helpfulness, and so forth. The emphasis is on social maturity rather than biological maturity because of the lurking possibility that some persons who are mature by virtue of chronological or biological age, may fail in social maturity. The presumption of biological maturation, however, is evident in the statement that "the child is more reasonable (responsible) than his or her age."

The first stage in social ontogeny is the period of the newborn, marked by happiness for the "gift" and safety of birth, with the simultaneous projection of the kind of socialized being the neonate should become. In some cases, the name given to the child may epitomize the expectation or reassert gratitude to and resolute trust in the Supreme One. Thus West African names are neither arbitrary nor innocuous "tags." The "passive" habit of naming the child after the father is a borrowed one that came into West African custom very recently (Fox, 1967). Generally, West African names, determined primarily on the basis of historical and circumstantial factors (Erny, 1987), address an inherent force that transcends human biology and consciousness. Perhaps the inherent vitality and "soulfulness" of African life, especially music and dance, emanate from an acute awareness of the pervasive presence of this "vital force."

Representing the expectations of significant others, West African names carry potentially critical implications for personality development. For example, among the Akan of Ghana, as in much of West Africa, "a powerful element of uniformity is introduced by the existence of socially determined beliefs about certain defined categories of children" (Jahoda, 1982, p. 116) who may be named after the day on which they were born or their names may be derived from a profile of culturally defined situational factors. The *woon-ah nyuy* in Nso cosmology represent such culturally defined classes of children. Social expectations not only foreshadow social destiny but also "what type of character may emerge" in persons so defined (Jahoda, 1982, p. 116).

The second stage of social self-hood, which approximates the period of infancy, is the presocial phase, identifiable by such biological behaviors as, for example, smiling, crying, teething, and sitting up. Implicitly, the biological markers are regarded as the precursors of social functioning. The major developmental task of this stage is success in social priming; failure usually provokes anxiety, with efforts to remedy it.

The third developmental stage, which may roughly be equated to childhood, begins with walking and extends to the throes of adulthood. This is the period of the social novice (social apprentice) during which children are gradually and systematically initiated into various social roles. The principal developmental task is to recognize, cognize, and rehearse social roles, to be an active agent in the endeavor to become a socialized novice. Social roles pertain to three hierarchical spheres of life: household, network, and public. At various levels of social maturity, the novices, each according to ability, are expected to learn and to attempt to enact roles within each sphere.

The fourth and fifth stages, the transitional phases from social novice to the socialized neophyte, heralded by the appearance of secondary sex characteristics, may be designated social entrée. Societies that still practice initiation ceremonies mark this phase with the so-called puberty rite, others mark it with accentuated efforts to allocate more responsibilities and to co-opt the neophytes into adult social groups and roles. This marks the beginning of social probation or internship; a period of intense social induction, the definitive preparation and training for adulthood. The developmental task of social induction is to become a socialized intern—an emerging adult.

The sixth stage is adulthood, with implications for marriage and responsible parenthood. Individuals acquire only proto-adult status on marriage, however, increasing their seniority with the birth of each child.

That is, a person is not considered "man" or "woman" enough if he or she is unable to reproduce. Full adulthood (personhood) is thus synonymous with "married with children." Ordinarily, unwed childless "adults" are viewed with contempt, but the definition of "full" adulthood seems to be changing in face of social change, at least to a certain extent. For example, some unwed, childless persons who have attained a high level of formal education are generally not assessed with as much contempt as unwed, childless illiterates.

The seventh stage of social self-hood is old age. Old people are expected to be grandparents, who, though frail, are usually regarded as the epitome of social competence. The confidence level with which old people face death depends on the number of competent offspring who live with their "blood." Thus biological readiness, inclusive fitness, and social competence are implicit concepts in the West African social ontogeny.

In sum and in terms still in need of refined phraseology, the West African social ontogeny posits nine cycles of human life, namely: spiritual self-hood, period of the newborn, social priming, social apprenticing, social entrée, social internment, adulthood, old age, and ancestral self-hood. There is urgent need to undertake research in order to demarcate and describe each of these stages as well as their core developmental tasks. Some children are more precocious in social development than others, hence the notion of "the child being more mature than his or her age." Without other humans, a human offspring cannot attain social self-hood (personhood). Social ontogeny does not discount biology because without biological maturity, developing persons cannot attain social maturity. For instance, the substantive induction of social novices into the adult world does not begin in earnest until the secondary sex characteristics start to unfold. Accordingly, social ontogeny assumes—rather than gives primacy to—a "natural" agenda. Furthermore, socio-ontogeny is not an entirely ethnocentric perspective. Every culture designs and implements a unique cultural program to "transform" their offspring from biotic imperatives to socialized humans. Whereas some cultures emphasize academic and cognitive modes of social integration, others stress subsistent and socio-affective socialization. Social agendas cannot succeed without biogenetic maturation. Because human offspring everywhere undergo long periods of social priming and social internship under diverse cultural programs, the developmental path of any culture may be fitted into the present social ontogenetic framework.

Table 7.1 presents the stages of the life cycle in social ontogeny, which may be approximated to the conventional developmental stages as follows: "A newborn child is not yet a social being. It becomes one

Table 7.1 Ontogeny: West African View of Life Stages

Socio-Ontogenetic Stages	Conventional Developmental Stages
Spiritual self-hood	Prenatal stage
Period of the newborn	Neonatal period
Social priming	Infancy
Social apprenticing	Childhood
Social entrée	Puberty
Social induction/internment	Adolescence
Adulthood	Adulthood
Old age/death	Senescence/death
Ancestral self-hood	—?—

through socialization—being taught all the things he or she needs to know to function as a member of a specific society" (Peil, 1977, p. 47).

THE SOCIALIZATION AND CARE
OF CHILDREN IN WEST AFRICA

Socialization and parenting in West African societies are predicated on two basic maxims: Personhood is acquired during functional maturation; "the child is passive and simply has to learn to adapt to the requirements of society" (Ellis, 1978, p. 39). The overriding aim is to prepare children for adulthood, with expectations of moral probity and competent parenthood. Training is pragmatic, apprenticelike in nature, and systematically "graduates" children from one role position to another, until the assumption of adult roles (Nsamenang, 1988). However alien it may appear to readers whose worldview emphasizes individualism and freedom of choice, understanding the significance of respect for seniority and obedience to elders and superiors is one of the keys to decoding West African behavior. Western observers are often amazed at the bonds and deference in the West African peer culture and the caring roles of older siblings. Such cultural patterns are the product of a socialization with emphasis on the notions of locus of authority, seniority, and filial service.

Socialization literally begins at birth. It is therefore erroneous to hold the view, promoted by Ellis (1978), that West Africans do not talk to babies because of the belief that babies do not understand "baby talk." This viewpoint stands in sharp contrast to a widespread practice wherein everyone who handles the neonate freely verbalizes about whom the baby resembles, what his or her name should be, what it signifies, and expectations about what he or she will turn out like as an adult (Nsamenang, 1988). In this direction, Jahoda (1982) alluded to the plausibility of considering how the expectations of others may affect personality development.

Babies are also cuddled and teased to smile along with adults from the earliest months of life. From about the first year of life, parents and other caregivers offer infants food items and playthings, and lure them both verbally and through nonverbal communication to return the "gifts." This is an example of social priming, a preliminary step to more extensive training in gifting, sharing, and generosity that is continued until marriage. As infants and social novices grow, they increasingly come under the influence of what Jahoda (1982, p. 131) called "the sharing and exchange norms" that bind siblings and the entire social system together. Thus as children mature through socially recognized life stations they are assigned gender-appropriate roles and tasks. Initially, a Baoulé boy of 6-7 years of age, for example, goes on errands in the village, fields, or a neighboring village (Dasen et al., 1978). Elsewhere, village boys of this age may tether goats, while girls tend chickens and city girls hawk a variety of wares.

During the induction stage, including definitive preparation for marriage, "children learn vocational, marital and citizenship roles under the tutelage of their parents or fostering kin who must ensure that they are properly socialized into those attitudes, values, skills, expectations, and aspirations necessary for effective group membership" (Nsamenang, 1988, p. 17). Fosterage, wherein "natural" parents delegate the care of their child to foster parents without losing parental rights, is commonplace. The preferred placement is the home of a more affluent kin or friend (Laosebikan & Filani, 1981). Fostering is an African way of rearing children within the extended social network (Ware, 1975). It cements kinship or friendship bonds and sometimes provides companionship or household help to a childless person or an "empty nest."

Ellis (1978) alleged that appropriate child-training in West Africa "is axiomatic" and that parents do not question the basis of their actions. This viewpoint contradicts his acknowledgement in the same paper that "punishment and close surveillance" occur "within an accepted framework" (Ellis, 1978, p. 39). Perhaps what Ellis meant was that African parents were unaware of child-rearing concepts and principles as elaborated in the Western literature. This indeed may be true, as we revealed in Chapter 6 that Nso parents were guided by "their own" notions of development, desirable child states, and caregiving. For instance, parents apply some unwritten, as yet unexplored, criteria to assess the extent to which children are thriving. They readily take action to remedy the perceived deviation from the expected developmental trajectory. These are discernible by anyone who is sufficiently motivated and genuinely interested in studying them.

Whereas Westerners revert to what they legally define as child abuse, West Africans depend on an unwritten cultural code for gauging when punishment exceeds culturally permissible levels. The enforcers of such codes are "plenty of people around to see what is happening and to prevent punishment going too far" (Ellis, 1978, p. 49). These "punishments . . . are unlikely to get out of hand and go beyond what is culturally acceptable" and West African parents "are unlikely to reach the level of exasperation of parents in Britain" (Ellis, (1978, p. 49). Abusive parents are usually advised to refrain from child mistreatment. There are few parental stigmas comparable to the shame of being labeled a harsh or wicked parent. Most parents avoid such stigmas, perhaps because of the cultural belief that cruelty to children is itself punishable by ancestral spirits. There are compelling folk expectations about the safety and welfare of children, some of which are not at variance with the precepts of scientific psychology. For example, aversive techniques are strategies for behavioral control in both scientific and folk psychology and may be applied positively, negatively, or to the scale of abuse.

Parenting strategies in West Africa, as in every society, range from extreme permissiveness through loving tenderness to neglect and extreme abuse. And on this continuum, what might be considered parental neglect or abuse in West Africa could be the opposite in other cultures. However, West African parents are very concerned that their children acquire the correct affective and behavioral posture with respect to appropriate gender roles and social competence, especially in communicating with elders and traditionalists (Nsamenang, 1988).

The bulk of knowledge and skills is acquired by simply observing and imitating what adults, elder siblings, and mentors do, with little or no instruction. Children are expected to observe roles or the performance of tasks and to rehearse them during play within the peer culture. Consequently, it is commonplace to see toddlers playing mother or father, more under the corrective surveillance of elder siblings or peer mentors than of parents or other adults. Many lessons, however, are taught in proverbs and folktales that contain moral themes and virtuous acts for children to emulate, or in tales that are suffused with myth to give a sense of the strange and fearful to deter children from wrong-doing. There is a strong belief that praise can induce pride in children. But the remark that parents do not reward children (Leis, 1972) stems from a probable misunderstanding of what "reward" is, since we know that parents occasionally entice children to perform tasks or services with food, favors, other objects, and sometimes with Western toys.

Failures in learning are verbally admonished—usually with a terse proverb or verbal abuse—and sometimes punished by the withdrawal of privileges—usually food—and by spanking. The children are expected to, and in fact do, take punishment without rancor and to accept a parental "right to deal with them" as they think fit (Jahoda, 1982, p. 110). Parents rationalize the strictness of their upbringing by recourse to such folk maxims as: "If a person is trained strictly then that person becomes a good person" (Ellis, 1968, p. 156); "to beat a child is not to hate it" (Jahoda, 1982, p. 111). Children accept parental punishment because "my father punishes me to correct my behavior; my mother rebukes me because I am wrong" (Ellis, 1968).

Parental authority does not cease when children are adults but continues to be asserted when the offspring is trying to make his or her own way in life (Jahoda, 1982). As long as one's parents are alive, "a child is always a child" and must come under "some" sphere of parental authority, even vicariously (Nsamenang, 1988). The objective of parental authority is neither to suppress children nor to indulge in personal whims, but to promote the best interest of the children and the family (Nsamenang, 1983). From parental authority over children is derived that of older siblings over the younger. With such authority, older siblings are usually charged with the care of younger brothers and sisters whom they can reprimand and correct. Younger siblings obey their older peers because "a mechanism of self-regulation exists in the fraternal group, due to the power inherent in the word of the adult, whose direct intervention is no longer needed" (Zempleni-Rabain, 1973, p. 233). Caregiving, then, is a collaborative enterprise in which siblings participate.

Although fathers are not involved in routine caretaking, it is wrong to equate child care to maternal care. The bulk of the day care of children who have been weaned is provided by someone other than mother (Nsamenang, 1989a), usually the peer group. Among the Wolof of Senegal, for example, "some of the fundamental social norms of the culture begin to be systematically and, in the main, painlessly instilled into the children almost immediately after weaning . . . the powerful role of the sibling group in this process is" quite remarkable (Jahoda, 1982, p. 131).

Peer caregiving is more widespread in villages than in towns because parents consider most city neighborhoods too unsafe to leave children by themselves. Sibling or peer caretaking is usually practiced in groups since most children are members of age, gender, or neighboring teams. In a typical scenario, multiage, dual-sex teams of children ranging in age from 20 months to 6 or 7 years of age are often found together in the neighborhood under the guidance and mentorship of one or two elder siblings, often but not exclusively girls of 8 to 10 years of age. The team spirit fosters collective role performance, responsibility, and peer mentoring. The "free" atmosphere within the peer culture breeds conflicts as well as compromises, thereby enabling children to learn the "ways of the world" from each other. In previous times, such social clubs were used as a training ground for leadership roles and, when members became old, as part of the instruments of government and law enforcement (Ohuche & Otaala, 1981, p. 20). Today they participate in building such community projects as markets, health centers, or schools. In addition, school children belong to competitive dancing, debating, and sporting associations.

Ohuche and Otaala (1982, p. 18) summarized the current difficulty in securing safe and quality care for children while parents are at work in the following terms:

> With the disintegration of family ties, caring for the young children becomes a problem. Those in the pre-school years now must be looked after by house maids, who may or may not be relations. Older children go to school and if there is no substitute help, they stay at school, while mother goes to the farm, the market or to work. The educated working wives usually make a more durable arrangement with their hired help.

The magnitude of the problem varies within and across countries according to the rate of participation of the extended-network members in caretaking and the incidence of school enrollment in the child population. I have seen how some "busy" parents in the Bamenda Grassfields of Cameroon sometimes encouraged their toddlers to "sneak" into classrooms or follow elder siblings to school in order to be under the watchful eyes of teachers and the peer group. The school system, especially the urban day-care facility, has almost become a caring agency as many parents tend to perceive the role of kindergarten teachers not as educators, but as caretakers.

PROFILES OF CHILDREN'S LIFE-STYLES IN DIVERSE ECOLOGIES

West African children live and grow in a variety of physical settings that provide diverse ecological opportunities and experiences that may exert differential developmental demands. The following are some profiles of such existential experiences.

The Grassfield Farms

A typical day in the life of a 3-year-old boy in the open savanna begins around 7 a.m. or 8 a.m. when his mother cleans, dresses, and feeds him with a maize couscous and huckleberry or pounded cocoyams and meat soup. Some portion of food for the day is stored in a place where the boy or his peer caretaker can reach it easily. On leaving for the farmfields, the mother places her son under the care of an older sibling or hands him to an elder peer (to whom he is more closely attached) in the compound or neighborhood. She may simply ask the boy to meet his peers in a mate's or neighbor's house. As stated earlier, a multiage, dual-sex team of children move about together under the supervision of older peers. As they play make-believe, group-circle, and other games in the neighborhood, they are expected to fetch water and carry firewood as well as complete any chore they were assigned. When they are hungry, they return to the house to eat the food their mothers left for them; older children feed younger ones. Adults, especially grandparents and sometimes fathers, are usually within shouting or running distance to intervene or help when disasters such as a serious fight, injury, or snake bite arise.

The City Slums

Lola is an 11-year-old elementary school girl in a West African city slum. Her mother cooks and sells food in a makeshift kiosk in the city center. Her father is a laborer in a beer factory in the city suburb. He leaves home at 5 a.m. and rarely returns earlier than 7 p.m. Lola's mother takes her 2-year-old daughter with her to the marketplace. After school, at 2 p.m., Lola and her 8-year-old brother join her at the kiosk and eat their lunch. After the meal, Lola is given peanuts or any other available item to peddle on the streets until about 5:30 p.m., when she returns to the kiosk for their 25-minute walk home. At home, the 2-year-old girl and her 8-year-old brother play together while Lola and her mother prepare dinner and the food for the next day's sale. It is usually after the chores have been completed and they have had dinner at about 8 p.m. that Lola and her brother can study or do their school assignments. The two children are interested in school and judging from their annual school reports, they do not seem to be underachievers.

The Fishing Village

Kiwo is the only son of Lon, a plantation supervisor and Bih, an office clerk in a firm. They live in a fishing village along the river Loum. Being in the terminal year of the primary school, Kiwo is expected to sit for the highly competitive qualifying examination into secondary school. His parents work very hard to provide his school needs and prepare for his college education. Unfortunately, instead of attending school Kiwo often goes fishing with "village" children during school hours. There is a ready market for the fish because the village is located on a major highway to and from the hinterland. At the end of the first semester, Kiwo's parents were embarrassed about their son's high rate of school absenteeism and poor academic record. They soon learned that Kiwo spent more time fishing than attending school. Earlier, perhaps because of their self-perception as "competent" parents, Kiwo's parents did not take kindly to sneers in the village about their son's truancy and poor behavior.

Nomadic Pastoralism

Ali is a 15-year-old son of a Muslim livestock breeder who attends a "mobile" elementary school in one of the countries in the West African Sahel zone. At the onset of the dry season in late December, Ali and his dog accompany his father's three hired herders for a southward march with the cattle in search of water and pasture. This "search" often takes them across national borders. Ali only considers resuming schooling after their return to the homestead at the onset of rains in mid-March.

It is evident from the foregoing discussion that the mode of socializing children in West Africa not only differs from one ecological region to another, but that a West African child presumably experiences a different kind of social reality from that of a Western peer. An inquisitive child, for example, would likely be approved in Britain, but in West Africa such a child is likely to be rebuffed (Ellis, 1978). Further, in Ghana, as throughout West Africa, a good child is one who does not interrupt adult conversation until he or she is asked to speak (Kaye, 1962). One reality that clearly stands out, nonetheless, is that there are culturally competent parents and children in West Africa as elsewhere. A noteworthy fact in this regard is that West Africans who were raised under the patterns of care and socialization described above, considered inimical to proper personality development in the contemporary psychological literature, have adapted remarkably well and have excelled in character and learning, to earn recognition outside West Africa. For example, the

Nigerian literary luminary and professor of comparative literature, Wole Soyinka, won the Nobel Prize for literature in 1986. The Cameroonian electrical engineer, Khan Tasinga, has been a city engineer in Los Angeles and an adjunct professor of electrical engineering at the University of California, Los Angeles, for several years.

From these profiles, one feature that seems to distinguish socialization practices in West Africa from those in Western cultures is the role children are required to learn and play, namely, filial service or child work.

CHILD WORK

In this section we overview child labor, a ubiquitous parental expectation in West African cultures, evaluating whether child work is an evil to be eliminated or an essential component of socialization worth promoting.

West African children work, or at least perform certain services. A great deal of child labor consists of parental services, domestic chores, subsistence tasks, and caregiving to younger siblings. Children are thus expected to run errands, keep the living environment clean, care for younger peers, and obtain supplies of water and firewood, as well as engage in activities in family support and production as part of domestic, agricultural, vocational, and parenthood training (Nsamenang, 1988). Filial service begins with errands around the house from when children merely start to walk; the spheres of activity increase with age and perceived competence. In Ghana, for instance, children "may have simple household duties allotted to them from the age of three or even two" (Kaye, 1962, p. 194). In eastern Nigeria, "children take an active and important part in the work of the compound and village" (Uchendu, 1965, p. 2). Thus "children in West Africa contribute in many ways to the life of the group and are able to recognize themselves as useful members of it" (Ellis, 1978, p. 50). As a general rule, all male and female infants and toddlers come under maternal care. Boys and girls of 4-6 years increasingly come under the companionship and tutelage of the same-sex parent and multiage, dual-sex peer groups.

Although children in West Africa are generally seen and not heard, as are children in Western cultures, their integration into economic life parallels their participation in adult social life. Children may literally be taken everywhere—the farm, the marketplace, the family or lineage meeting, funerals and feasts, as well as religious ceremonies. In this way, they are part of the adult world and are generally not regarded as being "in the way" in a way that children in many cultures are not. In juxtaposing the roles of British versus West African children, Ellis (1978, p. 50) mused "whether in Britain too little is expected of children, their activities being restricted almost entirely to play." While discussing the valuation of children in the United States, Boocock (quoted in Zelizer, 1981, p. 208) expressed the view that: "Although one would not wish to return to an era of exploitative child labor, . . . one still has the feeling that children in societies like ours are underemployed."

Child work is an indigenous mechanism for social integration and the core process by which children learn roles and skills. It also has a high economic significance. The minimal extra income some children bring home often makes the crucial difference between family starvation and sufficiency (McHale & McHale, 1979). Schildkrout (1981, p. 93) believes that "children who perform errands for their mothers, care for younger siblings or assist in domestic chores, are contributing to the maintenance of their households as well as reducing the opportunity cost of women's work." Child work thus constitutes an essential adjunct to the family economy as children's caring responsibilities reduce parental work load and free parents, especially mothers, for other duties vital to family existence and welfare.

A legitimate concern regarding child work is the extent to which schooling and urbanization have affected it. According to Bekombo (1981, p. 119), "school attendance does not release children from their duties in rural family communities. A reorganisation of time rather than a reduction in the tasks to be accomplished is the usual solution." Obviously school attendance reduces the amount of child labor because children are no longer full-time family labor-suppliers. Thus nonacademic work for the majority of West African children has become parttime because they must share their time between services or domestic chores and academic work. In urban centers some children are also parttime hawkers of food and other wares as well as aides in the house. The extent to which some children maintain a delicate balance between academic demands and the performance of domestic chores and services and are still high achievers in school is rather surprising. This needs more focused research attention.

Thus far, schools seem to have failed to provide education to foster understanding of West African existential realities (Ohuche & Otaala, 1981). To the extent that education and farming have erroneously been made to appear to be incompatible and employment openings are scarce, children should be required to learn at least the basic agricultural skills for survival in agrarian economies. To the extent that children are not exploited or as long as their performance of services and chores permit their enjoyment rather than mere endurance of childhood, child labor should be encouraged rather than eliminated. Child labor is an indigenous educational strategy that keeps children in contact with existential realities and the activities of daily life. It represents the participatory component of social integration; it is a necessary preparation for economic participation in societies where the school system has failed to provide the basic skills for dealing with subsistence problems. Child labor eases children's passage from play to productive activities and appears to render relatively painless the transition from play to productive life (Bekombo, 1981). For example, because it is not a West African tradition to provide children with toys, they are usually encouraged to create their own, making miniature replicas of common objects (Nsamenang, 1988). What children "create" is immediately recognized as a "product." Such recognition undoubtedly enhances their self-image. The genesis of the rich tradition of African sculpture, woodcuts, embroidery, leather-work, and pottery is rooted in this form of socialization. The artistic productions of the founding fathers of this tradition adorn many a museum worldwide.

CHILDREN'S NEEDS

Children are affected more adversely by social and other problems than are adults. "It is for this reason that most societies make special provisions—traditional, legal, administrative, etc.—for the care and protection of children" (Lukutati, 1983, p. 46). Unfortunately, "the needs of all families and children are not fully or adequately met in any country. Personnel and physical resources are often insufficient and . . . existing resources are not always fully utilized" (Sicault, 1963, p. 134).

This assessment was as pertinent three decades ago as it is today. Despite the harsh realities of life today, the vast majority of African children are not willfully neglected or deprived. Poverty, hunger, ignorance, disease, and the exploitation of humans by each other are the five major problems that constrain the ability of West African countries to create the conditions and supportive climate conducive for meeting children's needs.

This section focuses on the conditions under which West African countries endeavor to meet children's needs. It is organized around the following themes: child-care niches, health, nutrition, shelter, education, employment, social security services, and child-centered legislation and policies.

Child-Care Niches

The welfare of children depends on the niches in which they live. The main features of child-care niches include the family, child-care arrangements, caretaking resources, the residential neighborhood, the social ethos and its inherent dynamics, and the imperatives of the overall ecosystem. All forms of social change affect child-care niches. For instance, changes in the socioeconomic and demographic profiles of a society imply critical shifts in human needs. High birthrates in West Africa, for example, pose immediate needs for care and food. In addition, a growing child population requires expanded housing, schools, health care facilities, social services, and jobs. As the population balance shifts, institutions that satisfied the needs of the present generation may be inadequate to meet those of future generations. Development planning must take full cognizance of such trends.

Poverty or affluence gives rise to differential standards of living and access to health care and education. It equally shapes life purposes and aspirations. The quality of nutrition and dwelling affects the quality of growth and resistance to infection. The quality of residential milieus and the family are key ecological forces in development because values, aspirations, and living standards filter onto children through the family. The effects of environmental hazards are usually more adversely felt by poor communities and families than affluent ones. The networks of services or social support available for children and families in such circumstances determine matters of death or life and its quality. Where children are not injured or killed in such disasters, they are often orphaned, left homeless, or emotionally traumatized. In this sense, one hidden cost of the refugee problem is that "refugee children have limited access to formal or informal educational opportunities. This deprivation affects them for the remainder of their lives" (Schultheis, 1989a, p. 1).

West African communities are high in mutual supportiveness but low in agency-based social services. Reciprocity of the support system obviously promotes some, but certainly stifles other, aspects of development. For instance, there may be loss of individuality or personal freedom with obvious gains in the security that comes from being a member of a supportive social network in which roles are interchangeable in ways they are not in many cultures (Nsamenang, 1989c).

The Need for Wholesome Health

Health is an expensive commodity (McHale & McHale, 1979). The affluent tend to be healthier and live longer than the poor because they can purchase health services and basic amenities. The mean child mortality rates (150 to 200 per 1,000) and high morbidity rates bear witness to the extreme vulnerability of African children to communicable diseases (most of them preventable), particularly tuberculosis, measles, poliomyelitis, whooping cough, tetanus, and typhoid, without counting the diarrheal infections. "The health facilities that exist are far from providing a solution to the problem in most countries. They are inadequate to meet population demand and, because of the failure to adapt them, they are unable to provide the preventive primary care that children need" (Mostefaoui, 1983, p. 8).

To overcome the shortages of facilities and health personnel, especially in rural areas, the concept of primary health care (PHC), which encourages community participation in health intervention, was introduced. According to Colgate, Carrièere, Jato, and Mounlom (1984), the success of this program in Cameroon is shown by the fact that some communities now participate in the prevention and treatment of endemic diseases. A more certain strategy is to infuse health education into the school curriculum in order to increase the health awareness of the population, especially students.

The Need for Adequate Nutrition

Malnutrition caused by a combination of poverty, ignorance, unbalanced diets, and poor food hygiene is one of the key determinants of nutrition status in West Africa. Deficiencies in food and nutrition create a breeding-ground for diseases, especially in the vulnerable group: pregnant women and children. Hunger and ill-health stunt not only physical and mental development but lower the capacity for food procurement. "More than one child in four does not have enough food in Africa" (Mostefaoui, 1983, p. 7). Even more alarming is the fact that food production is, with few exceptions, lagging far behind population growth in African countries.

Breast-feeding offers the baby a head start in life because it provides wholesome nutrition. The decline in breast-feeding among poor, ignorant populations who cannot afford the high cost of formulas, or often over-dilute and contaminate them, is a major health hazard in West Africa today. It has increased infant mortality rates and the incidence of infections and diarrheal conditions, with consequent lowering of growth rates in children. Intestinal parasites are a common cause of malnutrition in West Africa, even where the child has a relatively good diet. Malnutrition is often exacerbated or induced by the practice whereby cattle, poultry, dairy products, and vegetables are not consumed but are sold to raise cash for commodities with little or no nutritional value.

The Need for Shelter

Although children everywhere need decent, clean dwellings that provide personal and family privacy and security, the degree of protection required against the elements varies by climatic conditions. But how well and how securely children live is very much determined by the quality of the residential milieu and its sanitation and supporting supplies of water and other utilities. Many children in poor rural and urban communities do not have a home worthy of the name. In addition, hectic socio-vocational agendas and overcrowded living conditions often leave parents too exhausted to give close and meaningful attention to children.

As a whole, all West African countries require programs to modify existing dwellings, curtail current housing shortages, and plan the construction of culture-relevant and climate-appropriate houses and residential neighborhoods to meet the needs of the rapidly growing population, especially the urban poor.

The Need for Education

"The family is the first educational environment a child encounters. The foundation of all aspects of development of the child is laid in the family even before the child is born" (Durojaiye, 1983, p. 39). That is, the seeds of education and learning are sown in the family long before a child ever starts formal education. Hence the dire need to strengthen families and to raise their educational awareness. Paradoxically, it is the years when much learning is taking place that are the least provided for in formal education. This suggests that allocations of educational attention and resources should be revised toward more emphasis on the preschool period, which, because of the child's dependency, are also its most vulnerable years (McHale & McHale, 1979). Unfortunately, preschool education, an essential link in the development of children, is confined to the towns and to the privileged population strata.

A critical challenge in education is basic literacy, not necessarily higher education. Although education is not insurance for a trouble-free life, illiterate children increasingly find themselves disenfranchised from full and active participation in modern political economies. The literacy of children and families is often the key to improving health, nutrition, and standards of living as a whole. For example, the constraining effects of illiteracy are evident regarding spreading information about sanitation, family planning, and agricultural extension. Self-help programs are much harder to undertake in illiterate than in literate communities. The literacy status of girls is worse than that of boys because all over West Africa, female school enrollment is lower than that of male enrollment. This reinforces the cycle of female illiteracy; when illiterate girls become mothers they are less motivated and are unlikely to help their children become literate. In addition, difficulties in attending school are compounded by the high rate of teenage pregnancy.

A major constraint in the education of both boys and girls is the apparent irrelevance of the school curricula to cultural realities, especially the immediate needs of children and their families. "The consensus of opinion in many African countries is that the curriculum of schools is inadequate for the purpose envisaged for education in Africa.... Schools, it is desired, should make pupils more of job makers and less of job seekers" (Durojaiye, 1983, p. 42). Together with large-scale unemployment, perhaps these are responsible for the high rate of school dropout and the low parental motivation to support education. There is therefore a crying need for creative reforms to make education relevant to the cultural environment and to integrate children into their societies. An important component of the economic chaos in contemporary West Africa is the school system that is at variance with local and national realities. For instance, what logic supports the preeminence of white-collar education over technical and vocational education in largely agrarian societies?

The Need for Full and Gainful Employment

By ILO regulations, children 15 years of age or younger are legally excluded from the labor force. If *labor force* is defined in terms of participation in subsistence life, then enforcing a minimum working age is almost impossible in societies in which child labor is integral to the process of social integration. As long as such communities are unable to guarantee all children a place in the school system or are unable to prevent school dropout, children will continue to perform traditional work roles, engage in paid work, or to be used as "exploited" domestic aides and/or apprentices.

In *The African Child and His Environment*, Ohuche and Otaala (1981, p. 17) noted that "the children of farmers have either to absent themselves from school temporarily in order to farm, to avoid attending school altogether, or to attend school, often against family wishes and with a firm resolve to escape completely from the land." They further indicated that the work African children perform provides additional income with which to pay fees or purchase essential commodities. Children who work for pay face increasing competition from older peers and will face unemployment as they themselves grow older (McHale & McHale, 1979). Unemployment, particularly of school-leavers and graduates, has already attained critical dimensions in some countries. The prospects for employment throughout Africa as children rapidly attain adolescence and adulthood are becoming even bleaker.

Social Welfare Services

Although the amount, quality, and distribution of child-related resources and benefits vary considerably across the globe and national territories, concern about children's welfare has recently entered the public realm and has taken various forms in almost all countries. The situation of the child in Africa constitutes a double dilemma: The child is wanted, but the basic services coverage of children is appalling despite the fact that all African states promote positive ideologies and political commitment in favor of children (Lukutati, 1983).

The basic intent of the welfare programs is to reach the most deprived population groups, particularly women and children in both rural and poor urban communities. The aim is to expand opportunities that enable children who otherwise would not have had them to get a head start in life in order to optimize their potentialities. The programs are also meant to minimize the health risks all families run in terms of parental surveillance during pregnancy, birth, and nursing, and in nutrition and health, especially during the first five years of the child's life.

Some of the programs are concerned with the regulation of parental employment, others give family allowances based on economic circumstance, and many graduate benefits to the number of children, either as direct cash payments or as income tax rebates. Unfortunately, however, the principal beneficiaries of most programs are usually families of working parents. This excludes the large majority of the most needy segment, peasant families. Even for families for which such schemes are directed, the extent to which the allowances or services are used on behalf of the target population—neonates, infants, and their mothers— seems questionable. For instance, in Cameroon some fathers who take paternity leave when their wives give birth do not use it for the benefit of their parturient wives and newborn babies. Most fathers use it for socializing with friends, ostensibly for celebrating the child's birth.

Changes in the status and roles of West African women have occurred and certainly have critical consequences for the welfare of families and children (see Chapter 6). Paid employment, the marketplace, and school enrollment have made child care, especially maternal care, more difficult. As urban life becomes more difficult and it is more stressful to support self and children, the urban parent or émigré is "forced" to abdicate parenting roles to paid baby-sitters or nursery schools, neglect children, or leave them to their own devices. As milieus in which psycho-emotional insecurity is the dominant motif, slums seem to be more detrimental to children than village communities. It is more difficult for slum children to combine fending for themselves with school work than for rural children. Rural children are more firmly anchored in their supportive niches and have more ready protectors than slum children do. In consequence, slum children seem more likely than rural children to become truants, delinquents, vagrants, or school dropouts (Sicault, 1963). The lure of urban settings and the push of the village have resulted in the massive rural-urban flight of both male and female adolescents. There appears to be a practice in many West African cities today wherein female teenagers prostitute themselves, ostensibly to raise the cash for school fees and the necessities of "modern" life. This requires urgent research attention and appraisal. "In all African countries, legal and administrative provisions exist prohibiting prostitution and carnal knowledge of female minors" (Lukutati, 1983, p. 49).

CHILD-FOCUSED LEGISLATION AND POLICIES

According to McHale and McHale (1979, p. 9), the obligations for the care and welfare of children are "being less left to traditional precept and custom and increasingly placed under larger moral and legal scrutiny and social legislation." This is evident in the ways in which nations, including West African countries, have adopted or established social policies and regulations for child care and welfare.

International recognition of the rights of children began when the League of Nations adopted the "Geneva Declaration of the Rights of the Child" in 1924 (Ethiopia and Liberia were the only "free" Africa states at that time). In 1948, the United Nations General Assembly approved "A Universal Declaration of Human Rights," within which the rights of children were implicit (only three nations in Africa were then independent). The special needs of children were incorporated into this Declaration as the United Nations "Declaration of the Rights of the Child" in 1959 (only three West African countries were independent). Since then, West African nations, the majority of which gained self-rule in the early 1960s, have devised social policies for children and have adopted or created legislation to govern child labor, safeguard against child exploitation, and foster the education of children and the special problems of the retarded and handicapped as well as adoption, custody, and the welfare of children under dispute.

Considering the short span of public concern for children in West Africa, however, appreciable progress has already been made. Despite these positive strides, the prescriptions for child care and welfare in much of West Africa are still on trial in the supreme court of traditional precepts. Many policies and legislation disregard or contradict emotive endogenous precepts and practices. The child-centered policies and legislation in most West African countries are best described as frag-mentary, ambiguous, and insensitive to the cultural realities of the people they are meant to serve. Even where explicit policies or legisla-tion exist, they are neither clearly understood nor properly implemented or enforced.

Statistics show that investments in children have not reached the majority of children in Africa, particularly the underprivileged classes (Mostefaoui, 1983). Nevertheless, the primary constraints on public efforts to improve the care and welfare of children in African nations remain due to the irrelevance of some policies and/or programs, the scarcity of material and manpower resources, and the limited scope of most programs, rather than because of incoherent policies and legisla-tion per se. "Most African countries have planning instruments but national development policies do not yet contribute efficiently to the protection of children and young people, to their training and assimila-tion into society" (Mostefaoui, 1983, p. 11). The needs of children cannot be fully provided for without a reorientation of national devel-opment policies and programs. In order to do this, African governments must be ready to adopt culture-relevant approaches and be more willing to listen to their populations.

The Ecocultural Framework

The human person is not a decontextualized organism floating in a universal sea of civilization. Human beings live in diverse environments that are culturally perceived and reacted to.

Part IV concentrates on the need to bring environmental inputs into developmental research. The main thrust of an ecocultural conceptualization is "to expand both the methods and vision of psychology beyond the individual as an exclusive focus of analysis" (C. M. Super & Harkness, 1986).

Many theories spawned in Western industrial society (North America and Europe, including the Soviet Union and Japan) not only are ethnocentric but tend "to be disseminated to the Third World as gospel truth" (Dasen & Jahoda, 1986, p. 413). Poincaré (1908) cogently pointed out that "science is built up of facts, as a house is built of stones; but an accumulation of facts is no more a science than a heap of stones is a house." Developmental facts therefore need a theory to give them form and meaning. But to what extent do developmental facts in Third World cultures fit extant theories? The nonexistence of a theoretical paradigm articulated to be specifically sensitive to developmental facts in the Third World justifies our efforts in this book, especially in the four chapters of this section, to address this theoretical gap by sketching how this may be attempted. The ecocultural mode of conceptualizing research is suggested as an heuristic device that can permit and facilitate appropriate developmental research in different ecocultures, particularly in other-than-Western contexts or the Third World.

8

CONCEPTUALIZING DEVELOPMENTAL RESEARCH IN ECOCULTURAL CONTEXT

Human development occurs in diverse ecocultures. "For every child the processes of development, socialization and acculturation proceed hand-in-hand within the child's own social and physical environments" (Hinde & Stevenson-Hinde, 1990, p. 63). But psychology's primary concern in its early history was with psychic processes, how we perceive and learn, for example. There was minimal, if any, effort to make the " 'person-acting-in-setting' the unit of analysis" (Jahoda, 1986, p. 429). Thus insufficient or no attention was given to the context in which development occurs (Grossen & Perret-Clermont, 1984).

The purpose of this chapter is to highlight the need for and process of contextualizing developmental research, especially in the Third World. We begin with a brief historical perspective on contextual thinking in psychology, then proceed to outline the main features of contextual theorizing and the criteria for environmental assessment. Next, we discuss the analytical coordinates for mapping the effective context of developmental phenomena and the guidelines for building contextual theories in developmental psychology.

CONTEXTUAL THINKING IN PSYCHOLOGY: A BRIEF HISTORICAL PERSPECTIVE

The first contextual study in psychology was perhaps Schwabe and Bartholomai's 1870 Berlin investigation (Bronfenbrenner & Crouter, 1983) of how children from different "social addresses" were "differentially affected by the contexts in which they were raised" (Pellegrini,

1987, p. 11). Although there was evidence of ecological concern in the works of Koffka (1935), Lewin (1936), Murray (1938), and Tolman and Brunswik (1935), contextualism virtually disappeared from the psychological research scene until the unprecedented social turmoil and extensive environmental damage of the 1960s forced an awareness of the deficiency of decontextualized research (Stokols, 1987). Scientific efforts to understand and redress the problems eventually culminated in the emergence of environmental psychology—a subdiscipline concerned with the systematic exploration of psychological phenomena in context (J. Russell & Snodgrass, 1987).

Berry's (e.g., 1966, 1971, 1975, 1976, 1986) long-standing advocacy of ecological research, Bronfenbrenner's (1979) *The Ecology of Human Development,* and Stokols and Altman's edited *Handbook of Environmental Psychology* greatly boosted ecological thinking in psychological research. Recent books by teams of cross-cultural psychologists (e.g., Berry, Irvine, & Hunt, 1988; Berry, Poortinga, Segall, & Dasen, in press; Pence, 1988; Segall et al., 1990) stress a central thesis of the ecocultural approach: "that the conditions under which human beings live have a powerful effect on how they develop" (Bronfenbrenner, 1988, p. x). John Berry, one of the foremost cross-cultural psychologists, has taken non-Western ecologies seriously and, besides having conducted "appropriate" research in other ecologies, he has carried out an intensive study of neighboring Pygmy and Bantu populations in the Central African Republic (e.g., Berry, 1986). C. M. Super and Harkness (1986) have narrowed down Bronfenbrenner's (1979) general notion of the ecology to the metaphor of the "developmental niche," which has "enabled them to explore cognitive, and to some extent affective development in novel and fruitful ways," particularly among the Kipsigis of Kenya (Jahoda & Lewis, 1988, p. 14). R. L. Munroe and Munroe's (1977) "series of ecological studies in Kenya" (Jahoda & Lewis, 1988, p. 14) further attest to the relevance of the ecocultural framework for Third World ecologies.

The seminal concept of contextualism is embeddedness or nicheness. Every developmental phenomenon is embedded in a nested network of ecocultural components (see Chapters 1 and 2). This implies that development cannot be appropriately studied out of its ecocultural context; it must involve a clear understanding of the "niche" (C. M. Super & Harkness, 1986) in which the development occurs. Current views of the ecocultural model "share a common awareness of behavior and development as interactive elements in a fluid and changing interplay among" socioecologically nested systems (Pence, 1988, p. xxiii). However, the interactions between humans and their ecocultures generate probabilistic rather than deterministic characteristic patterns of internal and external adaptations (Berry, 1979). The two main sources of development within the ecocultural framework (see Figure 2.1) are ecology and acculturation, with humankind's biologic and cultural adaptive systems as intermediary processes (Berry, 1981, p. 482). Due to differences in human habitats and cultures, societies establish different learning situations for their members. In other words, learning opportunities for socioaffective, cognitive, and performance skills vary across cultures and developmental niches.

The ecocultural model, narrowed down to the metaphor of the developmental niche, "has the advantage of allowing the analyst freedom to range from personal schema, script or mental structure to the social contexts and the macro forces shaping them" (Jahoda, 1986, p. 429). The thrust of the ecocultural framework "is far more conceptual than methodological, more a call to thoughtful, systematic awareness than an operationalized, methodological guide" (Pence, 1988, p. xxii). It is an heuristic device whose value lies "in the questions it generates, in the framework for answering these questions that it supplies, and in the kinds of answers it renders appropriate" (Sternberg, 1984, pp. 319-320). It is a way of opening up (Goodnow, Wilkins, & Dawes, 1986) to new sources of developmental data, especially in the so-called exotic cultures. Because the ecocultural framework emphasizes "different pathways of development" (Berry, 1981, p. 482), there may be no single developmental trajectory for the diverse peoples of the Third World (Witkin & Berry, 1975). It is therefore essential to assess development as a culturally adaptive phenomenon (Berry, 1981) whose path varies across cultures, rather than to judge it in terms of some nonexistent, absolute, or universal criteria.

If the ecocultural framework inspires appropriate research, what then are the main features of contextual research and the importance of adopting a systematic approach to conceptualizing and executing developmental research in context?

FEATURES OF CONTEXTUAL
AND NONCONTEXTUAL RESEARCH

Developmental research may be noncontextual or contextual. Noncontextual research focuses entirely on the relationships between independent and dependent variables and excludes intervening variables as much as possible. A noncontextual approach to the study of a sexually transmitted disease (STD), for example, would simply focus on the identification and elimination of its causative organism. In contrast, contextual research incorporates all the intervening variables assumed to be related to the incidence of the disease. A contextual approach to the study of an STD would endeavor to identify and eliminate the causative agent in both the patient and contacts. In addition, an exhaustive history of the patient's sociosexual behavior and the impact of the infection on his or her life and social network would be undertaken.

Given a particular research problem, the delimitation of contextual variables can proceed either in an exploratory, atheoretical manner or on the basis of theoretically grounded assumptions about the target phenomenon. The nonexistence of systematized indigenous conceptual systems handicaps researchers in the Third World. By employing the exploratory approach they may begin with a tentative hunch about one or more situational mediators of the target phenomenon. Research on high academic achievement in Cameroon, for example, may begin with the clue that the majority of people who have earned doctorates are not from economically privileged classes. Exploratory "analyses can play a useful role in the early stages of theory development by revealing situational factors that significantly influence the target variables and by excluding from further consideration those that do not" (Stokols, 1987, p. 45). A more robust form of contextual analysis occurs when the research design and the empirical assessment of situational outcomes and target variables are explicitly guided by an extant theoretical metaphor, for instance, the developmental niche (C. M. Super & Harkness, 1986). Researchers ought to cast their research problems in some theoretical context, and measurement strategies should flow from methods congenial with the theory (Guthrie & Lonner, 1986).

A contextual theory attempts to explain why the hypothesized cross-situational variations in the target phenomenon occur. For example, as lower class West African children realize their disadvantaged social position, they probably develop higher achievement motives than their upper class peers who may already be contented with their current status. Contextual theories thus attempt to specify situational factors that qualify the relationships among independent and dependent variables. In contrast, noncontextual approaches do not predict nor attempt to explain the cross-situational variation in the relationships among target and outcome variables. They simply explore and explicate the variables.

Contextual theories elaborate and account for the situational specificity of the environment-behavior nexus. The discovery of environment-behavior contingencies in developmental research often occurs inductively rather than deductively. In other words, contextual relationships are often discovered in a nonprogrammatic, happenstance manner in the process of comparing findings from separate, independently conducted studies, rather than through programmatic strategies. In citing the Whitings' (Whiting & Whiting, 1975) six-culture study as an example of post hoc theorizing, Jahoda (1982) nevertheless qualified it as "the most extensive and ambitious study" of aspects of socialization ever undertaken in non-Western cultures. Of the many lessons it provides for further work in this sphere, "the single outstanding one is that one needs a more systematic scrutiny of the 'learning environments,' which the Whitings brought in only *ex post* in order to substantiate the model" (Jahoda, 1982, p. 128). Knowledge of the ecoculture is thus essential for building contextual theories. Without an adequate understanding of the contexts in which development occurs, it is impossible plausibly to hypothesize the relationships between outcome phenomena and ecocultural variables.

"By making the explicit consideration of contextual factors a routine part of the research process, important aspects of the target phenomenon might be revealed that otherwise would have been neglected" (Stokols, 1987, p. 46). This is not to suggest, however, that all target phenomena are equally amenable to contextual analysis. For instance, when the threshold level of noise, an ecological stressor, is exceeded, habituation operates and its impact becomes relatively uniform across individuals and milieus and it consequently ceases to be an ecological variant in the true sense of the term. In other words, there might be a point at which larger doses of certain contextual variables may cease to exert varying (additional) effects.

In practical terms, whether or not a contextual research design is actually operationalized may depend on the researcher's ecological awareness, the availability of baseline data bases, and guiding concepts as well as logistical support.

Environmental assessment is integral to contextual research.

CRITERIA FOR ENVIRONMENTAL ASSESSMENT

Four basic assumptions about phenotypic dimensions of behavioral development (Stokols, 1987) underlie ecocultural conceptualization.

First, psychological phenomena should be viewed in terms of the spatial, temporal, and sociocultural milieus in which they occur.

Second, in the short run a focus on individual responses to discrete stimuli or events should be supplemented by long-term molar analyses of daily activities and settings.

Third, the search for lawful, generalizable relationships between behavior and
   environments should be balanced by a sensitivity to, and analysis of,
   the situational specificity of developmental patterns.
Finally, the criteria for ecological and external validity should be explicitly
   considered along with the internal validity of the research when designing
   developmental research, as well as when judging the applicability of
   research findings to policy issues and intervention programs.

Four key questions are related to contextual assessment (Stokols, 1987).

First, what features differentiate a contextual analysis from a noncontextual
   one?
Second, for which developmental phenomena is a contextual analysis war-
   ranted and for which is it not?
Third, what considerations should guide decisions about how narrowly or
   broadly to delineate the contextual boundaries of phenomena?
Finally, which appropriate concepts and methods should be applied in the
   analysis of the relationships between the target phenomenon and the
   specific contexts in which it is observed?

Environmental assessment is "a general conceptual and methodological framework for describing and predicting how attributes of places
relate to a wide range of cognitive, affective, and behavioral responses"
(Craik & Feimer, 1987, p. 891). It provides a systematic means of
viewing the relationship between environmental parameters and behavior or developmental outcomes. The approach is based on the recognition that the manner in which people perceive, use, and evaluate their
milieus can yield important developmental data. Since human behavior
is influenced not only by the terrestrial environment, but also by enculturation and acculturation, environmental assessment is an extension of
psychological assessment to the ecocultural sphere. Acculturation is an
important dimension, because "unless the researcher can gauge" its
"influence, and its impact on the individual, inappropriate conclusions
could be drawn about the sources of cross-cultural variation in behavior" (Berry, Trimble, & Olmedo, 1986, p. 291). Berry, Trimble, and
Olmedo (p. 320) further highlighted the potential impact of acculturation by revealing that "performance on cognitive tests becomes 'better'
as the test taker becomes more acculturated to" the culture within which
the test was originally developed.
   Environmental assessment entails a "population" of environmental
parameters that can be identified and indexed on the basis of some
criteria. The clarification of the meaning of *environmental quality* is an

extremely crucial preliminary step (Craik & Zube, 1976). Stokols and Altman's (1987) edited volume reviews a wide array of components that subsume the construct environmental quality. For instance, Carp and Carp's (1982) 147 attributes of the residential environment yielded 15 factors. Environmental quality is but one of several components of the ecoculture, a representative sample of which must be considered in any assessment process. We need to give serious consideration to the "individuality" (Barker, 1987) of settings when assessing ecocultures. In Oskaloosa, Barker and his collaborators (Barker, 1987, p. 1418) "identified 884 places in the public areas of the town with distinctive patterns of behavior." The notion of place-specificity of behavior is highly appropriate for endogenous sectors of West African life where cultural scripts unambiguously prescribe definite, identifiable patterns of behavior and modes of action for specific places, events, or social encounters. Several advantages can accrue from environmental assessment. For West Africa, it can identify and describe the hitherto assumed elements of West African developmental niches. This can furnish the missing baseline data on the image of humanity in West African cultures not only to the scientific community but also to parents, educators, and policymakers.

Environmental assessment involves valuation, an important component of the general construct of environmental quality; hence the significance of guarding against "using the sentiments and ideas that we have within us as other human beings" (Redfield, 1959, p. 4) in our characterization and evaluation of others. That elements of the ecoculture exist is obvious, but the crucial problem is how best to study, assess, and understand them, particularly as "assessment in and across cultures other than one's own is fraught with conceptual, epistemological, and methodological difficulties" (Guthrie & Lonner, 1986, p. 235). The difficulty is exacerbated by the human tendency of "looking out" at phenomena from their "own position" (Redfield, 1959) rather than from that of owners of the culture. As agents of social service organizations or representatives of civilizations or social classes engaged in planning, in implementation, and in evaluating other humans (Segall, 1986), researchers must acknowledge and seriously consider the felt needs, wishes, viewpoints, and other relevant dispositions of their target communities or subjects. Perhaps psychologists need alerting that they hold no monopoly on evaluations. An urgent scientific "challenge is to understand judgments by both" psychologists "and others on both formal and informal occasions of evaluations" (Goodnow, 1984, p. 392). This implies, for instance, that "for each class of environmental entities, surveys of representative samples of lay-persons and experts can assist in clarifying the salient constituent elements of the construct" (Craik & Feimer, 1987, p. 894). Because most psychologists have had little "opportunity to learn very much about the local ecologies and cultures" (Jahoda & Lewis, 1988, p. 13) and seem to have arrogated the role of sole evaluators of psychological functioning, the long-term goal of conceptualizing and assessing locally sensitive psychological phenomena continues to confront and elude (cross-cultural) researchers (Berry, 1984). No research project can be better than the quality of the assessments it attains. Assessment is a means to an end and not an end in itself. The purposes and methods of measurement must be congenial with the research questions or theory being used or tested (Guthrie & Lonner, 1986). The "choice of measurement technique would be among the last decisions to be made in planning" a research project (Guthrie & Lonner, 1986, p. 238).

Craik and Feimer (1987) identified five steps in the process of environmental assessment. First, delineate aspect(s) of the ecocultural setting to be assessed. Second, establish assessment criteria. Third, outline the sampled context. This entails the identification and description of an array of environmental properties. Fourth, relate descriptive attributes (age, sex, social class, residential neighborhood, etc.) to some stated variable such as academic achievement, high blood pressure, self-concept, and so on. The relationships thus obtained provide a preliminary indication of potential predictors of the criterion measures. The fifth step requires cross-contextual validation of the predictive relations on a new sample of places in order to validate the model.

The indexing of environmental parameters may be evaluative, descriptive, or predictive (Craik & Feimer, 1987). Evaluative assessments appraise the extent to which settings meet explicitly stated criteria. Descriptive and predictive assessments identify specific attributes of the ecoculture that relate to known criterion measures. Evaluative measures can be obtained by gauging the extent to which the goals of the initiators, consumers, or managers of a project have been realized (Cooper, 1975; Friedmann, Zimring, & Zube, 1978). Descriptive environmental assessments may be technical or observational. Technical assessments are based on an explicit technical system of measurement like standard metrics of weight or distance, apparatus for monitoring physiological functioning (e.g., blood pressure, sugar level), instruments for determining water or air quality, or the seismogram, to mention only some. Observational analyses are based on self-reports or the consensual views of panels about the places being assessed. Predictive environmental assessments involve predictions based on empirical data or simulations. Data derived from descriptive and evaluative assessments constitute the basis for empirical generalizations. Claims for empirical generalizations require the confirmation of the replications of observations in diverse settings; multivariate statistical analyses are very useful in this direction. Predictions based on such data hold only for general trends and not necessarily for specific cases. They can, however, guide the formulation of focused environment-behavior hypotheses.

A crucial point in assessment is not which test items or tasks constitute the content of testing, but how best to present them to the subjects in ways that are meaningful to them (Berry et al., 1986). The task of how best to describe or represent developmental environments also is not an easy one. The difficulty stems from two basic reasons. First, ecocultural units are complexly multifaceted. Second, most ecocultural properties, especially in Third World contexts, have not yet been explored, much less explicated. There is thus a scarcity of ecocultural concepts and taxonomies. Accordingly, environmental assessment should be an open-ended, multivariate endeavor (Craik & Feimer, 1987). We should avoid adopting specific sets of standard procedures and techniques as the panacea for assessment. Rather, the conceptual or taxonomic door should be left open so that assessment is graduated as an ongoing process that is refined at each level of research and with every new insight. This approach is plausible in light of Craik and Feimer's (1987, p. 895) assertion that "the future vitality of environmental assessment depends not on a devotion to its scientific aims but on drawing upon a larger appreciation of places and a fascination with the subtle variations among them."

Once the researcher opts for an ecocultural approach, a crucial question arises: Which criteria afford the greatest analytic leverage for understanding the embeddedness of the target phenomenon?

CRITERIA FOR EVALUATING CONTEXTUAL THEORIES

Stokols (1987) proposed four organizing themes around which to delineate target phenomena in contextual research. These are effective context, contextual validity, relative power and efficiency of theories, and "generativity" of contextual theories.

The Effective Context

Because developmental settings are multidimensional, their analyses necessarily involve a variety of variables. Thus a "key challenge in developing contextual theories is to identify from among the myriad of potentially relevant situational factors those that are most crucial to the understanding of the form and occurrence of the target phenomenon" (Stokols, 1987, p. 46). A subset of these factors has been designated the "effective context of the target phenomenon" (Stokols, 1987, p. 46). It may be difficult, even impossible, to specify completely the effective context of a given phenomenon because the full range of factors impinging on a phenomenon is potentially infinite, often covert and unmeasurable. This implies that the determinants of development can only be estimated, rather than specified unequivocally (Manicas & Secord, 1983). Nevertheless, the notion of effective context reminds developmentalists not to lose sight of the possible range of contextual forces that may impinge on development. At our current state of knowledge and technology only some of such forces are measurable. The concept of effective context raises three fundamental questions about the adequacy of contextual theories (Stokols, 1987). First, how accurately does a theory specify the relationships between the target phenomenon and contextual variables? Second, how completely does the theory represent the full range of both overt and covert moderators of the target phenomenon? On this issue, Irvine (1986, p. 206) holds that conventions and rules on human assessment "increase with the degree of theoretical uncertainty." Third, what is the generative potential of the theory?

Contextual Validity

The degree to which a phenomenon is niched in an ecoculture represents its contextual validity (Berry, 1981). A contextual theory therefore refers to the accuracy with which the theory specifies the full range of relationships between a target phenomenon and all its contextual determinants (Stokols, 1987). For instance, if a theory predicts that juvenile delinquency is related to family size and poverty, with evidence from several lines of research in diverse ecocultures confirming the pattern, then such a theory is assumed to possess contextual validity. Although definitions of contextual validity vary, they all stress the extent to which a target phenomenon is similar to one in another context (Bronfenbrenner, 1979; Brunswick, 1956; Winkel, 1987; Wohlwill, 1978). Thus contextual validity implies an appraisal of the extent to which theories apply across settings or situations. That is, transcontextual validity is ascertained when a theory accurately predicts the same phenomenonal outcome across a number of ecocultures.

The contextual validity of a theory is low to the extent that it incorporates ecocultural factors that have only minimal or no influence on the target phenomenon, or factors that affect the target variables in a manner that contradicts or confuses the predicted pattern (Stokols, 1987). Construct validity generally refers to the extent to which research methods match conceptual constructs. Whereas construct validity implies the elimination of all confounding variables, the goal of contextual validity is to incorporate all identifiable sources of variance into more integrative and ecologically contingent theoretical explanations of target phenomena. The sources of variance in contextual validity are important not as a means of achieving uncontaminated representation of phenomena, but as a basis for their inclusion into theoretically broader pictures of phenomena in context.

Because ecocultures contain both overt and covert forces, we do not have to lose sight of subtle mental or transactional dimensions of environments that impinge powerfully on development (Stokols, 1987). A more balanced analysis of context should consider transactional as well as subjective and objective criteria of environmental assessment, because all three sources of data are relevant to psychological functioning. This is an important point because the impact of the environment, as stated in Chapter 2, depends on an individualized perception and experience of environmental conditions.

Contextual theories may be evaluated in terms of their relative power or efficiency in predicting the observed phenomena.

Relative Power and Efficiency of Contextual Theories

A contextual theory may correctly identify some of the conditions that influence developmental processes but may exclude several others. For example, a theory may accurately account for the impact of self-concept and job dissatisfaction on the relationship between anxiety and psychosomatic symptoms. If other contextual variables such as marital schism and role conflict are also significantly implicated, the theory that focuses only on self-concept and job dissatisfaction would be less powerful than one that includes the influence of marital schism and role conflict. The relative power of a contextual theory may be assessed by gauging the extent to which it encompasses the full range of situational factors that qualify a target phenomenon (Stokols, 1987).

On the contrary, if a contextual theory incorporates factors that exert only trivial, marginal, or no impact on the target phenomenon, another evaluative criterion, namely the efficiency of a theory, may be applied.

"A contextual analysis is efficient to the extent that it includes those and only those situational factors that exert a significant influence on the target variables" (Stokols, 1987, p. 49). If empirical evidence demonstrates that self-concept and job dissatisfaction, not marital schism and role conflict, qualify the relationship between anxiety and psychosomatic symptomatology, then the theory that focuses on job dissatisfaction and self-concept would be more efficient than one that incorporates marital schism and role conflict. The former theory is more parsimonious than the latter because it excludes marginal or trivial variables from its framework.

The relative power and efficiency of theories address the questions raised earlier about the phenomena that are amenable to contextual analysis and delineation of the effective context. These concerns are central research issues "because the range of influential factors varies across psychological phenomena (with some being impervious to situational influence and others being highly dependent on the context in which they occur)" (Stokols, 1987, pp. 49-50). It is therefore important for researchers to give careful consideration to the effective contexts of the phenomena they study in order to determine which variables should be incorporated into research conceptualization and measurement.

Generativity of Contextual Theories

The generativity of a contextual theory is its "capacity to provoke new insights about important contextual moderators of a target phenomenon that were not explicitly stated in the initial version of the theory or in earlier theoretical and empirical work" (Stokols, 1987, p. 50). Some theories that are low on contextual validity and relative power and efficiency may instigate research beyond their overt propositions. It is even possible for a theory to propose wrong causal or explanatory relationships but in so doing excite scientific interest or curiosity that has the "conceptual advantage of opening up new questions" (Goodnow, 1984, pp. 391-392) and discovery of alternative explanations or relationships. Freud's psychosexual theory, for one example, did this perfectly.

It is difficult to evaluate the generative potency of a theory in the short run, but over the long haul we can judge the impact of a theory on the conceptualization and generation of empirical data about other developmental processes. The generativity criterion thus underscores the provocative power of theories and their potential contribution to the evolution of more powerful and valid explanations of the relationships between ecocultural factors and developmental change. Progress in developmental psychology in the Third World depends ultimately on the generative power of the ecocultural or other relevant theoretical approaches. The value of a contextual theory also lies in the extent to which it facilitates problem solving, that is, its applied utility.

Applied Utility of Contextual Theories

Because the Third World cannot yet afford the luxury of strictly basic research, applied research should constitute the main thrust of research efforts in Third World countries, at least initially. The litmus test for contextual theories in the Third World should therefore be the extent to which they contribute to the understanding of endogenous phenomena or provide policy guidelines for effective services and intervention programs. After all, every research project is said to be a form of social intervention (Warwick, 1980). As such, research in the Third World should play a "role in aiding the understanding and solutions of problems of development" (Hefner & DeLamater, 1968, p. 2).

All this implies that part of the contextual variables a theory specifies should be sociopolitical in nature (see Chapter 9). The effectiveness of public policies or programs derived from decision-driven research depends largely on the adequacy of the theoretical guidelines on which the research was based. Theories that do not specify the full range of contextual qualifiers of a problem may appeal to policymakers by virtue of simplicity rather than their relevance to problem resolution (Stokols, 1987). The low contextual validity of theories thus jeopardizes the effectiveness of policies or intervention programs derived from them. The duality of Third World societies makes theorizing in them less straightforward and more laborious than hitherto undertaken. Consequently, Third World ecocultures call for more "sophisticated" theorizing than the hitherto simplistic approaches to problems of these "simple" societies. In relation to developmental science, this conceptual difficulty is compounded by the scarcity of data on Third World childhood, hence an overwhelming Third World reliance on Western data bases and sources of developmental norms.

Having examined the features of contextual theories and the criteria for evaluating them, it is necessary to shift focus to the coordinates for mapping out effective research contexts.

COORDINATES FOR MAPPING
THE EFFECTIVE CONTEXT

According to Stokols (1987) the four coordinates that can guide the mapping of the boundaries of effective contexts include contextual scope, objective and subjective representation of variables, individual and aggregate levels of analysis, and partitive and composite representation of people and settings.

The contextual scope of environmental analysis involves the range of spatial, temporal, and sociocultural forces that interplay to determine a phenomenon. The context of research tasks can be described in terms of scale of complexity, ranging from specific to complex and involving situations and settings, life domains, or the entire span of life. *Situations* are sequences of individual or group activities that occur at a particular time and place (Forgas, 1979; Pervin, 1978). *Settings* are terrestrial locations in which various personal or interpersonal situations recur on a regular basis (Barker, 1987; Stokols & Shumaker, 1981; Wicker, 1987). *Life domains* are different spheres of personal life such as family, education, religion, recreation, employment, and commuting (A. Campbell, 1981; Stokols & Novaco, 1981). An even broader unit of contextual analysis is the individual's overall life span (Magnusson, 1981), a composite of all life domains. Consequently, the contextual scope of research refers to the scale of the ecocultural entities included in the analysis of the target phenomenon. A developmental process can thus be examined in terms of narrower versus broader and proximate versus remote segments of the life history.

The analysis of environments and developmental processes can be undertaken at the spatial, temporal, or sociocultural levels. Spatial analysis involves places, events, and processes occurring within a narrow or broad space in the individual's geographic location, for example, the house, compound, workplace, place of worship, village, and so forth. The temporal scope of analysis involves situations, events, and processes experienced within a brief or extended time frame, such as a calendar of events for one year or for two weeks. The sociocultural scope of analysis incorporates relevant dimensions of the sociocultural milieu, for example, social structure, belief systems, family patterns, day care, kinship, ethnic stereotype, and national character. So far, most developmental research has not seriously considered the metaphysical and sociocultural conditions whose influence on development transcends research settings and time frames. For instance, the impact of refugee status goes beyond the migrants to future generations of their offspring.

An important research issue concerns the researcher's decision about how narrowly or broadly to conceptualize the problem and measurement of parameters that exert a significant rather than trivial impact on the phenomenon. The broader the contextual scope of analysis, the greater the potential range of overt and covert factors that can impinge on development. For any problem, the researcher must determine at what point increasing or decreasing the scope of the contextual variables brings diminishing returns in terms of the explanatory power of the theory (Stokols, 1987).

When a researcher has access to valid data about the contextual variability of a phenomenon, decisions regarding the appropriate scope of analysis become relatively easy and straightforward. But when one lacks such information, as in most cases in the Third World, it is useful to adopt broader conceptual frameworks during the early phases of investigations. Such an approach expands "ecological sensitivity" (Pence, 1988, p. xxi), eschews a premature narrowing of contextual scope, and permits the gradual sharpening of a theoretical base through the progressive deletion of irrelevant contextual variables as additional insights and data about the phenomenon accrete. Because longitudinal developmental research is inchoate or virtually nonexistent in many Third World nations, the adoption of too narrow a contextual framework at the outset may unduly limit the possibilities of uncovering effective contexts of developmental phenomena. This highlights the appropriateness of an exploratory "map" possessing sufficient range and flexibility. The exploratory mapping process does not, however, imply the inclusion of all contextual mediators of the phenomenon. By being systematic in approach and broad in scope, it enhances the possibility of including relevant mediators that might otherwise be excluded in haphazard, unsystematic approaches.

Ecocultural variables may be represented in objective or subjective terms. For example, anxiety level can be measured objectively using physiological monitors such as pulse rate, blood pressure, and biological assays of urinary adrenaline, or in terms of self-reports. Whereas many research programs rely exclusively on either objectivist or subjectivist sources of data, the ecocultural framework underscores the value of using both objective and subjective representations of target phenomena or variables (Stokols, 1987). The combination of objective and subjective measures may offset the limitations of single-measurement approaches. It can also help to assess the degree of convergence or divergence of the various measures employed (A. Campbell & Fiske, 1959; Cohen, Evans, Krantz, & Stokols, 1980).

Contextual analysis may focus on the individual or on an aggregate of individuals. For example, crowding and noise at work may be viewed as external conditions of an individual's occupational life. But when the focal unit of analysis is the organizational framework of the workplace, crowding and noise become integral parts of the work environment. The relationship between individual behavior and ambient work conditions such as competitors' strategies, monetary policy, and political climate may be modulated by membership in various social groups and other conditions of the macrosystem (Bronfenbrenner, 1979). A researcher's decision to represent an individual or an aggregate perspective of the environment depends on issues at hand. The adoption of an integrative, cross-level approach to the conceptualization and measurement of phenomena can offset the limitations inherent in purely individual or purely aggregate frameworks.

Developmental niches may also be represented in terms of their partitive or composite properties as they reflect the interdependence among people and their milieus. Partitive analyses view places and their occupants as independent entities and emphasize the interactive effect of person-environment relationships on developmental change. For example, we can assess the effects of rural versus urban school environments on achievement motivation and academic performance. The central concern of composite analysis, on the other hand, "is the mutuality of an animal and its surroundings" (Gibson, 1984, p. 243). That is, humans and their habitats are mutually bounded systems. A major goal of composite analysis is to develop taxonomic concepts for representing the interdependence between humans and their niches, for example, behavior setting (Barker, 1968), social climate, home atmosphere, community spirit, person-environment fit, or place identity (Caplan, 1983; Kaplan, 1983; Stokols & Shumaker, 1981). The primary units of assessment in composite analyses are patterned situations or settings that provide the theoretical concepts for describing and classifying environments. Composite analyses also attempt to explain how the relationships among specific environmental and developmental variables (e.g., achievement motive, academic performance) are qualified by the contextual conditions in which they are observed (e.g., social class, rural vs. urban residence, extended vs. nuclear family).

The distinction between partitive and composite theories is crucial because it indicates that the boundaries of psychological phenomena do not always reside in the overt features of settings or in the demographic characteristics of the occupants. The effective context of certain phenomena is better represented in terms of covert, abstract dimensions of the relationships between people and their surroundings (Stokols, 1987).

Consider, for instance, the subtle but potent influence of the sharing and exchange norms that sustain peer bonds in West African cultures (Jahoda, 1982). A partitive analysis also differentiates environmental settings into several elements like history of the place, social groups, buildings, activities, and so forth. A composite analysis might identify contextual elements in terms of the degree to which each constitutes a traditional or nontraditional setting. According to Jacobi and Stokols (quoted in Stokols, 1987, p. 56), "a traditional behavioral setting is an environment where the activities of its occupants directly reinforce the historical continuity of the place and the perceived ties between past, present, and future generations of occupants." In other words, the composite construct portrays the interdependent parts of settings and then "chunks" them into a new summary concept—the traditional versus nontraditional behavior setting (Stokols, 1987).

The distinction between traditional and nontraditional behavior settings provides a valuable conceptual tool for comparing the dualism of Third World ecologies in terms of the degree of traditionalism versus modernism—that is, the degree to which they retain endogenous identity versus the extent to which their outlooks, especially Third World views of childhood, have been externalized by acculturation. Since places accord symbolic significance to the occupants, a sense of security may be felt by individual members of a place by virtue of mere presence in the milieu. Analyses of the effect of support systems on social competence tend to ignore the role of the physical environment in fostering these kinds of noninteractional support. One advantage of composite analysis is its ability to reveal previously neglected contextual processes that moderate target phenomena. Stokols (1987) advised the representation of person-environment relationships in terms of the statistical interactions among multiple predictor variables, typified by multivariate analyses of trait-by-situation contingencies (Endler & Magnusson, 1976).

In some settings, phenomena may be masked by contextual factors; for instance, the incidence of noise in urban transit stations or marketplaces and its relative absence in funerals or libraries. This implies that contextual factors may alter the meaning or impact of target variables. The utility of partitive versus composite approaches depends largely on the level of interdependence that exists among subjects and their milieus. Interdependence, in this sense, is not a constant, but a variable that truly varies; or, one that exhibits "both stability and susceptibility to change" (Bronfenbrenner, 1988, p. xi). As a result, the interpersonal encounters that occur in transit stations, for instance, are less stable than those that occur within homes or school settings.

One question that persists in spite of the foregoing discussion is how
to proceed with the process of building contextual theories?

DEVELOPING CONTEXTUAL THEORIES

Having identified the core properties of contextual theories and the
main criteria for evaluating them, it seems expedient to outline the
phases of contextual theorizing and to specify the guidelines for developing contextual theories.

Phases of Contextual Theorizing

According to Stokols (1987) contextual theorizing is a two-tier enterprise. First there is a contextual mapping phase in which ecological
and behavioral or developmental target variables are examined. This is
most expediently done within the broadest possible scope of analysis,
and its major goal is to include all potentially salient contextual markers
of target phenomena. Second, there is a contextual specification phase
in which efforts focus on demarcating and defining all relevant contextual variables most pertinent in understanding target phenomena. The
goal of the second phase is to identify and specify the effective scope
of the target phenomenon. In contextualizing academic achievement in
Cameroonian students, for example, the mapping phase is likely to
involve consideration of, among other things, personal attributes, social
addresses, home climate, and life histories. For the demarcation phase
we may identify pertinent variables such as age, sex, ordinal position,
IQ, self-concept, emotional adjustment, achievement motive, performance
tasks, time and conditions of evaluation, mode of instruction, institutional
membership, socioeconomic status (SES), family size, residential neighborhood, and ethnic background, among many others.

In developmental research, the exploratory mapping phase of contextual theorizing is often ignored. In the haste to maximize construct
validity and explicit operationalization of variables, investigators often
narrow the contextual scope of analyses prematurely and move too quickly
to specify predictor variables and outcome criteria. Heuristically, it is
crucial to note that contextual validity, power, efficiency, and generativity of contextual theories depend on the completeness of the mapping
process—that is, the extent to which a given phenomenon is charted in
terms of the largest possible range of contextual variables that define
or modulate the phenomenon (Stokols, 1987).

Guidelines for Theory Building in Contextual Research

The seven maxims Stokols (1987, p. 61) outlined as guidelines for theory development in ecological research are listed and discussed below. They derive from the fact that "behavior is more a function of the situation than of inner dispositions" (Guthrie & Lonner, 1986, p. 237). They are also rooted in the fact that "there is no sharp division between people's physical and social universes"; the two "intermesh, since apprehension of the physical world does not merely arise from individuals' actions, but is also socially mediated" (Jahoda, 1986, p. 427).

(a) The specification of contextual moderator variables should become an inherent part of psychological theorizing. As a general guideline, the relationship between independent and dependent variables should be hypothesized prior to data gathering instead of in a post hoc manner. If the contextual mapping and definition stage of theorizing is coupled with cross-setting empirical research it can provide broader conceptual frameworks for developmental theories and research than can inductive assessments of external validity alone.

(b) A shift of conceptual and empirical focus of research interest from an exclusive emphasis on people's reactions to discrete cause-effect relations to the ways in which behavior or developmental processes are qualified by the ecological settings, life domains, and overall life situations in which they occur is essential. Such broad contextual models permit examination of both genotypic and phenotypic sources of developmental change.

(c) Ordinarily, psychological phenomena should routinely be examined in their temporal context. However, every effort should be made to conceive and study the temporal dimensions of phenomena as embedded within spatial and sociocultural contexts. In other words, the demarcation and definition of the temporal context should involve consideration of how sociohistorical circumstances and anticipation of the future qualify experience and responses to temporal conditions. For instance, how a brief paternal absence in early childhood affects an adolescent's self-concept and academic achievement and life purpose.

(d) The tendency toward psychological reductionism (Sampson, 1981) that characterizes many behavioral theories should be avoided and systematic consideration accorded the sociocultural dimensions of individual and collective behavior. In this regard, Jahoda (1982, p. 115) pointed out that "showing the ideas about personality and character held in various cultures may be of potential value when assessing personality development, and should not be neglected." In other words, indigenous ideas about the determinants of personality should be incorporated into theoretical

models because "they may influence modes of handling children and
thereby be self-validating" (Jahoda, 1982, p. 115).

(e) It is useful to examine the effective context of the target phenomenon
from the perspectives of both individuals and groups. The representation
of contexts from both individual and aggregate perspectives can loosen
"the traditional 'mooring lines' " in favor of novel approaches (Pence,
1988, p. xxi) to developmental research.

(f) The combined use of objective and subjective representations of contextual parameters or target phenomena can reduce some sources of bias in
developmental research: For example, the tendency to depend only on
either subjective or objective measures of developmental outcomes and
the failure to consider the transactional and psychically mediated effects
of environmental forces on behavior. A systematic representation of
objective and subjective features of phenomena can contribute to the
development of comprehensive theories that are sensitive to two main
types of contextual effects: those that are mediated by cognitive, affective, volitional, or interpretative processes, and those that are not.

(g) It is important that the representation of contextual factors either in
partitive or composite terms be congenial with the degree and quality of
the interdependence that exists among humans, their niches, and their
activities. For example, how does the parent, family size, density of
social network, and the subsistent economy affect the types of social
behavior manifested by preschool children in West African societies?
The selective and expedient use of partitive and composite constructs
can enhance the systematics of theory development-in-context.

The agenda for conceptualizing and conducting developmental research
in context is quite formidable. The world expects Third World psychologists to take up the scientific challenge of exploring and presenting
the image of humanity in their own part of our planet. However, an
important, as yet unanswered, question remains: the extent to which the
conceptualization of research in context as discussed in this chapter is
tenable in Third World ecologies.

CONTEXTUALIZING DEVELOPMENTAL RESEARCH
IN THIRD WORLD SOCIETIES

This chapter has explored the theme of ecological thinking with the
hope of stimulating sensitivity, especially in Third World contexts, to "the
environment in which the organism must live and to which it must accommodate itself" (Gibson, 1984, p. 243). This implies that research concep-

tualization in West Africa, for example, must transcend the individual to incorporate the hunch that "the developmental processes taking place in the immediate settings in which human beings live, such as family, school, peer group, and workplace, are profoundly affected by conditions and events in the broader contexts in which these settings are embedded" (Bronfenbrenner, 1988, p. x). It is thus important to clearly identify and describe not only features of children's familiar environments and daily routines but also the macro forces shaping them as an essential precondition for ecologically sensitive research. Unfortunately, research reports in West Africa too frequently contain such "packaged" concepts as the extended family and socioeconomic status as proxy variables, but the degree of family extendedness, for instance, has yet to be explicitly specified (see Chapter 6).

Appropriate ecocultural research therefore requires a mapping out of features of the developmental niche that impinge on development. As explained earlier, the mapping of environmental features is best achieved through the systematics of environmental assessment. For instance, to determine the impact of the family on academic aspiration, we need to know the size and conditions of rural and urban families as well as those of settled and nomadic peoples. In addition, it is critical to assess the value systems and occupations of different families. These and other factors should not be assumed; they ought to be known and explicitly stated, and where possible the researcher should at least gauge if not "allocate relative contributions to development and behavioral variation" of various sources of influence (Berry et al., 1986, p. 323). The assessment of the environmental contingencies of development should be an integral part of every research effort.

The ecocultural framework seeks to understand what phenomena are actually in place locally (in our present consideration, the Third World) and their contextual embeddedness (Berry, 1984). Research within the framework is characterized by analyses of developmental phenomena as they occur in local ecologies and cultures. The core research issue in efforts to understand West African behavior or developmental pathways, for instance, is to take into account an understanding of what West Africans think they are doing. The value of the ecocultural framework thus depends on the extent to which it promotes the understanding of biobehavioral development in the Third World in indigenous terms. The long-term utility of this conceptual framework will also depend on the extent to which it provokes fresh theorizing and offers novel insights into the development of the human being as a global species. Finally, contextual research should foster an understanding and solution of problems of underdevelopment in the Third World.

In conclusion, to make our conceptualizations of human

development fit the new facts from non-Western societies, existing conceptualizations will have to be divested of their Western value assumptions and either revised or replaced to accommodate a broader way of
human variations. When this is done, developmental psychology would
have changed, not just at its outer edges but in its central theoretical core.
(R. A. LeVine, 1977)

9

CROSS-CULTURAL
DEVELOPMENTAL PSYCHOLOGY

By its nature, cross-cultural developmental psychology is not simply comparative, but essentially "an outlook that takes culture seriously," especially as "human development always occurs in a specific cultural context" (Dasen & Jahoda, 1986, p. 413). The history of cross-cultural developmental psychology dates back only about 20 years, and the discipline may be said to have come of age around the turn of the 1970s with the appearance of a number of textbooks (Dasen & Jahoda, 1986), including Serpell's (1976), Segall's (1979), Warren's (1980), and Adler's (1982), all focused on human development. The books by E. Werner (1979), C. Super and Harkness (1980), Wagner and Stevenson (1982), and Volume 4 of the *Handbook of Cross-Cultural Psychology* edited by Triandis and Heron (1981), as well as the landmark *Handbook of Cross-Cultural Human Development* by R. H. Munroe, Munroe, and Whiting (1981), are devoted to developmental research. Some recent works have either dealt with methodological concerns and advances in cross-cultural research (Lonner & Berry, 1986) or with introductory issues, as in *Human Behavior in Global Perspective* (Segall et al., 1990), in order to point to the character of variations in behavior across cultures and ecologies. An earlier volume edited by Marsella, Tharp, and Ciborowski (1979) focused on general issues in cross-cultural psychology.

The purpose of this chapter is to examine the present state of knowledge about the global human condition and psychological research in the Third World, as well as some polemical issues in the cross-cultural research enterprise, especially cross-cultural developmental research.

THE STATE OF KNOWLEDGE ABOUT
THE GLOBAL HUMAN CONDITION

Much of what is known in the scientific world about the "real" conditions of human life in the Third World is derived from myths, stereotypes, media reports of crises, reports of itinerant researchers, and (often derisive) documentaries. In spite of the high level of academia in the West, only a small minority of Westerners have made the Third World the primary focus of their scholarship. The gap in knowledge between the few "Third World specialists" and the Western public is enormous. The enormity of the ignorance in the United States, for example, is captured in Ungar's (1986, p. 14) remark that an African visitor to the United States today "would still find it difficult to meet an American who knows his country well or has even the vaguest acquaintance with general African affairs." Even "in the government bureaucracy and on Capitol Hill, Africa has low priority until it is the scene of a crisis relevant to American interest" (Ungar, 1986, p. 20). The Third World as a whole and Africa in particular "never had a chance to be taken seriously" by the West. From the earliest references in both scholarly and popular literatures, Africa "suffered from a vision of 'darkest' " continent (Ungar, 1986, p. 21). An African diplomat in Washington, D.C. remarked how Africans learn "so much in school [and from the mass media] about Western cultures," but make "the naive assumption" that with all their resources and technology Westerners were learning about Africa, too (Ungar, 1986, p. 25). Although the Third World shelters the bulk of humanity, it is the most unknown part of the planet in terms of developmental knowledge. Wagner (1986, p. 298) mused over the poor state of developmental research in the Third World and wondered why there is no "application of child development research in an international and cross-cultural perspective."

In light of the above, the scope and extent of developmental knowledge and the impact of resources and child support programs are lopsided in geographical reference in favor of the Western world where, paradoxically, children are a declining population.

STATE OF PSYCHOLOGICAL RESEARCH
IN THE THIRD WORLD: AN APPRAISAL

The majority of academic persons in the Third World whose work involves human behavior and/or development are not always concerned with psychology, per se, but are chiefly interested in the advancement of other disciplines like education, health, and human services. That is, a fair picture of the current state of psychological research, especially with regard to Africa, is that it is an inchoate science.

Third World researchers "encounter a variety of practical problems such as lack of resources, writing in a foreign language, inadequate information flow and others" (Dasen & Jahoda, 1986, p. 415). Such conditions greatly reduce their capacity to generate psychological knowledge and produce developmental literature. In Latin America, as elsewhere in the Third World, "one reason for the difficulties is that work that is done in the field [of environmental psychology] is often not published" (Sanchez, Wiesenfeld, & Cronick, 1987, p. 1337). A review of the literature in sub-Saharan Africa revealed that an overwhelming amount of "printed psychological research has been offered by non-Africans, and must embody the different perspectives which such expatriates bring to Africa" (Wober, 1975, p. ix). Serpell (1984, p. 113) corroborated this alien factor in the psychological literature in Africa by noting how "a systematic survey of trends in the research being undertaken on the continent is easier to conduct from outside Africa than from inside." This is not only because the major sources of psychological literature on Africa are foreign authors, but more so because its bulk is more readily available from foreign than African archival sources. Andor's (1983) nonjudgmental, annotated bibliography (1960-1975) of 3,122 entries on psychological and sociological studies in Africa south of the Sahara indicates that a great deal of the literature cannot successfully withstand the acid test of scientific rigor.

Three main trends emerge from Andor's (1983) bibliography. First, the growing amount of the literature from African authors. Second, a general departure from the study of specific abilities or personality traits to the study of people living within the twilight of two value-systems: indigenous and alien (see Chapter 5). "The extensive dualism of developing nations serves as a reminder to psychologists from developed nations of the subtleties of dualism that operate even within their own society" (Moghaddam & Taylor, 1985, p. 1145). Third, a change in the topics studied from cross-cultural differences to an emphasis on the characteristics of the subjects (gender, age grades, rural-urban, literate-illiterate, continuity-change, etc.). The high point of Andor's bibliography is African attempts to adapt to the world as evolved by Western civilization.

Wober's (1975, pp. ix-x) prediction that the 1970s would be a time when "psychology in Africa turns a corner, in that it will be increasingly in the hands of new people, its own people, with their own outlooks, needs, and directions of enquiry" came true to some extent, but research orientations are still entirely Western in outlook. The research focus has almost exclusively been on issues that are more pertinent to Western social reality than to the harsh realities of life in African communities. By adopting the theoretical models of the developed world for their nations, Third World researchers unwittingly ignore the realities that daily stare them in the face, and instead advance Western concepts, methods, and perspectives in their ancestral homes. In this light, Durojaiye (1984) reported how psychological testing in the educational systems in Africa often use tests that do not have references to data bases in Africa. In fact, there exists in the modern sector of Africa, as elsewhere in the Third World, a rapidly growing system for propagating the view of humanity offered by imported psychology. Hence, Moghaddam and Taylor's (1985, p. 1145) claim that "the social sciences probably entail the most important, systematized set of values and ideas that have been imported to assist the modern sector of developing societies in achieving conceptual systems compatible with those of the developed world."

Concerns about imported psychology and limited success in the search for universally applicable psychological laws and principles bring to the fore contentious issues in cross-cultural research. Polemics in cross-cultural research oblige the contemplation of the strengths and limitations that may inhere in psychological laws and principles, as well as critical appraisal of scientific rigor and the soundness of the methodology by which they may be uncovered.

SOME ISSUES IN CROSS-CULTURAL RESEARCH

Psychology is a representational science. The choice of which features of behavior to represent at the expense of others is determined by "the subject whose behaviour is to be explained, the author who proposes the explanation, and the audience to whom the explanation is addressed" (Serpell, 1990, p. 100). As such, polemics in cross-cultural research hinge on values, familiarity with the research setting or task, research methodology, validity of context and measures, interpretation and target audience for dissemination of findings, research sponsorship, and the politics and ethics of research.

Values in Scientific Research

Scientists are not insentient, uncommitted, neutral fact-finders. Scientific choices and target "facts" tend to be consistent with the value and motivational systems of researchers and their sponsors. As researchers, "we look from our position . . . using the sentiments and ideas that we have within us as other human beings" (Redfield, 1959, p. 4). Hence, Wober's (1975, p. x) provocative but germane contention that "psychology in Africa done by outsiders may be different from psychology as it will come to be done in Africa" by Africans, perhaps because psychology draws the person-in-the-scientist and his or her sociohistorical background (Cole, 1988) into the orbit of the questions under study. This produces and admits the difficulty that presuppositions are as much in the mind of the audience as of the author (Wober, 1975).

The best coping strategy for dealing with this state of affairs is "a combination of vigilant perception and emotional relaxation" (Wober, 1975, p. xi); an assumption that "there exists some consistent reality of environmental and behavioral events" that empirical psychology can construct (Poortinga & Malpass, 1986, p. 37). Such rationalization is needed in face of the admission that the phenomena psychologists study "are capricious and unstable across time and setting, influenced by the free will of the subjects, colored by the values of the investigator who studies them, affected by the public's assimilation of prior information . . . and so overdetermined that complete experimental control is impossible" (Weisz, 1978, p. 2). In other terms, all researchers bring "disguised beliefs and culture-bound assumptions" to their research (Badri, 1979, p. 14). This teaches us that short-term contextual validity may be the best any researcher may hope to attain and that "value-free" research, even by members of the research context, is wishful thinking.

The Goals of Cross-Cultural Research

"With few exceptions," little cross-cultural "research has been undertaken with the explicit goal of being applicable to Third World settings from which the data were gathered" (Wagner, 1986, p. 298). The overriding goal in cross-cultural research has often been to "confirm or disconfirm Western theories" (Wagner, 1986, p. 298); to find out "the range of generalizability of Western theories" (Serpell, 1984, p. 113) to the neglect of two anterior goals: discovering endogenous covariation between cultural and behavioral variables, and bringing into focus the total range of variability in human behavior. The discovery of cultural universals per se is undoubtedly significant (Adler, 1977).

Although comparative cross-cultural paradigms are expected to employ broad conceptual lenses in order to capture the potential range of target variables, so far they have offered limited insight into the understanding of human development in non-Western contexts. With "limited data, only partial structures may be discovered" (Berry, 1980, p. 5). The generation of cross-cultural developmental data can reveal a wider range of diversity in human behavior (Berry, 1980), leading to a depiction of a more global picture of the nature of humanity than can data from traditional comparative approaches. If there are any universals in human behavior (Lonner, 1980), they can emerge only when all variability is available for analysis, hence the dire need to uncover cross-cultural variation in behavioral development.

Three main factors (Serpell, 1990) constrain the integration of non-Western behavioral profiles into mainstream psychological literature, namely: a culturally biased subject data base in favor of Euramerican middle-classes, a Eurocentric enculturation of authors of psychological literature, and the production of literature for a predominantly Euramerican audience. The Euramerican slant in scientific psychology even extends to the realm of cross-cultural research, where it might have been anticipated that psychologists who are attuned to the cultures of Third World societies would be supported to explore and document the developmental patterns in those communities. As a result, there have been few systematic, longitudinal cross-cultural efforts devoted to the cumulation of developmental data in the Third World as a prerequisite step for juxtaposing, in the long run, the data bases so obtained against developmental norms and knowledge in ecologies for which such data already exist. In spite of these constraints, considerable progress has been made to fit the conceptualizations of human development to the "new" facts from non-Western societies (R. A. LeVine, 1977). Unfortunately, however, despite efforts to study human development in global perspective, today "developmental psychology as a whole remains unduly parochial" and the domain of only a small circle of scientists (Jahoda, 1986, p. 417). Gardner's (1974, p. 271) assertion that "in truth, the developmental psychology of today is the story of the development of Western children," is basically as true today as it was then.

The results of the first wave of cross-cultural studies surprised Western authors because non-Western responses to "the same nominal stimuli" differed remarkably from Western profiles. A second wave of research was undertaken to explain the "errant" behavioral patterns of Third World people from those of Western subjects. "Satisfactory" explanations were typically phrased in terms of Western norms rather than in light of indigenous terms and epistemologic systems. Fortunately, an important early insight of researchers using the cross-cultural paradigm was that some of their descriptions tend to miss the point of what they seek to interpret, because they fail to connect appropriately with the ways in which the people whose behaviour is described think about that behaviour themselves. (Serpell, 1990, p. 109)

It is difficult to understand what people are doing "without trying to understand what they think they are doing" (Beattie, n.d., p. 1). The inference is that no investigation of a people is complete that does not "embrace a study of their psychology" (Jahoda, 1982, p. 19).

The Emic-Etic Debate

The essence of the emic-etic analogy is "how to describe behavior in terms which are meaningful to members of a particular culture (the emic approach) while at the same time to compare validly behaviour in that culture with behaviour in another or all other cultures (the etic aim)" (Berry, 1984, p. 338). Being monocultural in focus, the emic approach is not strictly a cross-cultural method. The etic approach characteristically compares phenomena in at least two cultures. The best approach in cross-cultural research (Adler, 1982) is collaboration among (a) members of the home turf who can obtain the data and decode them from an insider's viewpoint, and (b) "outsiders" who can observe and interpret the data from the position of an outsider "looking in." In this way the entire research process, especially data interpretation, will be enriched rather than colored by uncontrolled ethnocentrism. But the best raw data are likely to be obtained by well-trained natives (Dasen, 1984; Nyiti, 1982). Because most Third World communities are virtual virgin terrains in developmental knowledge, an emphasis on emic approaches is essential, at least initially, to establish needed data bases for educated etic research.

Although cross-cultural research data eventually become "established" as psychological knowledge, it is important to note that such forms of knowledge are "scientific" knowledge, not the naked truth as it occurs out there in the natural world. Neither "psychology nor any other science deals with a complete real world. The content of science is an abstraction" (Poortinga & Malpass, 1986, p. 20). "Psychologists only reflect and translate the dominant cultural values in a particular historical context" (Dasen, 1984, p. 409). Because psychologists "are engaged from the beginning in an enterprise of translation" and selection, they, like social anthropologists, should "be constantly aware of the difficulties and dangers of extrapolating the terms and concepts of their 'own' cultures into their representations of other cultures" (Beattie, n.d., pp. 8-9). In this sense, to what extent does computerized "cleaning up" of data and video-tapes recorded in exotic cultures and mailed to industrialized nations for analysis, interpretation, and publication reflect the realities of the human condition in the real world (Nsamenang, in press)?

Conceptualizing the Research Context

In stressing the need vastly to increase our power to describe environments for behaving, the Laboratory of Comparative Human Cognition cautioned against the tendency to regard psychology laboratories as culture-free and to use culture as a surrogate for ecological variance (Laboratory of Comparative Human Cognition [LCHC], 1979). If cross-cultural research has offered any challenging lesson to psychology, it is the forced recognition that no research context, even the "carefully" constructed laboratory, is culturally neutral. It is thus noteworthy that laboratory tasks—like walks in the jungle, marks in mud, works of art, or paper-and-pencil tests—are examples of culturally embedded phenomena. Research settings are components of the macro forces shaping them. In addition, research subjects possess some "special knowledge" by virtue of membership in a particular society, behavior setting, or group that organizes the research task (LCHC, 1979).

Whether the research setting is a laboratory or a jungle, participants in every research setting conventionally rely on their sociohistorical tradition (Cole, 1988) and current state to make sense of the task and organize the response in line with their cultural modus operandi. Psychology was sterile in its early history because "it operated with the theory of the existence of an absolute mind, not subject to the environmental setting in which it lives" (Boas, 1911, p. 133). The assumption that behavior in laboratories is culture-free thus has no scientific merit in face of the submission that "the existence of a mind absolutely independent of conditions of life is unthinkable" (Boas, 1911, p. 133). The "content of thought [reflects], in its concreteness, environmental factors" (Weisz, 1978, p. 1).

The foregoing discussion by no means renders the laboratory a worthless tool for cross-cultural research; rather, it hints of the potential problems the laboratory may pose. Because the properties of laboratories are culture-laden, their potential impact must be studied and understood as part of the research enterprise, in much the same way as understanding the "field" context is an essential precondition for field work in cross-cultural research.

Contextual Validity

Contextual validity addresses issues of veridicality of norms and laws across situations and contexts (Weisz, 1978). To the extent that a developmental norm or principle can be shown to hold good across ecocultures, time frames, and subject cohorts, it can be said to possess transcontextual validity (see Chapter 8).

Psychological Tests and Research Tasks: Assessing Development

Psychologists administer diverse devices and contrivances to assess different aspects of behavioral development. Regardless of the extent to which we subscribe to the philosophy that well-normed or standardized tests or tasks provide the most valid means of assessment, we must recognize that if developmental environments are themselves culturally constructed, it is virtually impossible to develop culture-free tests or tasks. Researchers ought to be sensitive to the cultural embeddedness of all research measures. Furthermore, because research subjects come from different social addresses it is important to consider this in test/ task selection and in the interpretation of findings. Goodenough (1936, p. 5) argued strongly that the concepts and items in a test or task should be "representative and valid samples of the ability in question, as it is displayed within a particular culture." "Given cultural differences in patterns of child rearing, are the methods of assessment used" in attachment research, for example, "equally suitable in every case?" (Hinde & Stevenson-Hinde, 1990, p. 67).

The essential task of cross-cultural assessment should be to find out how well subjects perform their own skills, rather than "how well they perform our [Western] tricks" (Serpell, 1990, p. 101). That some cross-cultural studies using known instruments yield "errant" results (Serpell, 1984) raises doubts about the cross-cultural "validity of tests and measures that constitute the hard data of the cross-cultural effort" (LCHC, 1979, p. 827). Serpell (1984, p. 113) revealed that differences in test or task performance were often presented as "developmental lag." But Dasen, Berry, and Witkin (1979, pp. 78-79) "jointly" rejected "the automatic ascription of any 'deficiency' . . . to populations on the basis of variation in task performance." Their position is plausible in the sense that subtle and not-so-subtle differences may set apart subjects, even with the same cultural background (Sattler, 1988).

In responding to research cues, differences among subjects may be magnified by the lurking possibility that the instructions may have been poorly understood, the procedure not followed, "the stimuli meaningless, the subjects bored or frightened. In short, rather than indicating crucial differences in psychological makeup . . . research may do little more than rediscover problems in the conduct of developmental research" (LCHC, 1979, p. 828). In reality, "response to interviews, standardized or open-ended, and to written schedules or scales are subject to as much distortion in foreign settings as they are in our own" (Guthrie, 1979, p. 358), that is, Western, society. Rarely do researcher and informant interact as equal partners. It is therefore "important for the researcher to understand just what kinds of decisions informants are making when they agree to being interviewed. For many Africans . . . whether or not to impart information to an outsider is a volatile existential concern relating to issues of autonomy and control" (Lance, 1990, p. 338). This means that researchers must be sensitive to the difficulties Africans confront when the researcher, especially if a stranger, presents a research task.

There is also a likelihood that "subjects from one group may not understand the materials, motives, or procedures demanded by the experimental setting in the same way as subjects from the comparison group. Second, the tasks which are appropriate to one group may fail to tap abilities that are actually present in the other group" (LCHC, 1979, p. 828). Such possibilities point to the importance of considering ecocultural inputs and the construction of research tasks that sensitively tease out and measure "native" ability and phenomena. For instance, concrete operational reasoning characterizes Western thought as well as that of Inuit and Baoulé children, "albeit with differences in the rate of development depending on which conceptual areas are valued by each culture" (Dasen, 1984, p. 411). That is, Piagetian tasks are "prone to contextual modifications" (Dasen, 1984, p. 408; Okonji, 1971; Tapé, 1977). In other words, what is considered "culture-appropriate" in one society may not be so appropriate in another (Adler, 1982). Perhaps "different things are being measured in different cultures and to an unknown degree" (Segall, 1979, p. 53). This accords with Ogbu's (1988, p. 15) report that "anthropologists and scholars studying minority groups in the United States have shown that the competencies minority children acquire in the community are often different from the competencies the children are required to demonstrate at school." Because responses to research cues reflect "ethnically acquired modes of responding" (Adler, 1982, p. 86), it is futile to decontextualize developmental phenomena.

Some scientists, among them Frijida and Jahoda (1966, p. 118), have warned that "the notion of 'fairness' looks suspiciously as though there were an underlying feeling that, given appropriate measures, cultural differences ought to disappear." Of course they cannot, but will continue to enter task performance in research. One plausible solution is to integrate ecocultural considerations into every phase of the research process. In the heat of such dialectics, Ohuche and Otaala (1981, p. 55), taking the lead from Scribner and Cole (1973), claimed "that basic intellectual mechanisms are universal, but that environment determines the situations in which they are applied." In other words, "abilities develop differently in adaptation to" differing ecocultural contexts (Berry, 1984, p. 342). Thus "it does not make sense to impose one culture's test upon another culture, no matter how fair the test may be for that first culture, unless the adaptive requirements of the two cultures are essentially the same. This sameness is probably a rare event" (Sternberg, 1984, p. 418).

Proxy Variables

Culture and literacy/illiteracy are among the proxy variables commonly used in psychological research—literates being the subjects frequently used. Research has persistently demonstrated that schooling enhances cognitive performance on some tasks. It even "seems that cognitive-developmental research in the United States has been measuring years of schooling using age as its proxy variable" (LCHC, 1979, p. 830). If school-based tasks are the sine qua non of cognitive ability, as the literature unwittingly intimates, the forced conclusion is that cognition occurs only in a small percentage of the world's population, given the current global literacy rate. If literacy is not the only means through which cognitive competence can be expressed, then psychology has a more herculean challenge than hitherto recognized, namely, to develop tests or tasks for "unpackaging" and measuring cognitive abilities among literate as well as illiterate or unschooled populations. It "can hardly be too strongly emphasized that neither intelligence tests nor the so-called tests of personality and character are measuring devices, properly speaking. They are sampling devices" (Goodenough, 1936, p. 163). This statement further highlights the gulf between the contemporary measuring devices and units of psychological phenomena. "Any definition of intelligence and any attempt to measure it," for example, "will amount to a sampling of skills (or concepts, or processes) that is influenced by cultural values" (Dasen, 1984, p. 408). In addition, "cultural values may have a profound effect on the relationship between the child and his or her caregiver. Furthermore, they are labile, differing not only between cultures but also with time in any one culture" (Hinde & Stevenson-Hinde, 1990, p. 64).

Because most psychological tests and research instruments are no more than deliberate samples of the tasks that assess mainly the outcome of schooling and the degree of Westernization, they are likely to be inappropriate as samples of the "native" abilities in unschooled, imperfectly Westernized societies. What is the explicit significance of tests satisfactorily unpacking the independent variables and demonstrating the anticipated variance in the cognitive functioning of literate and illiterate populations? Are we to conclude from the differentiable scores of schooled and unschooled subjects that intellectual abilities do not exist among illiterates because they cannot perform "our" tests? How can we objectify the comparison of cognitive competence in subjects whose socialization emphasizes cognitive development with that which stresses socio-affective development? With only minor differences, studies in Niger, Nigeria, Uganda, and Zambia (Dasen, 1984) allude to cognitive and social aspects of intelligence as well as to the general feeling that individual abilities are useless unless they are applied in service of the commonweal. Thus the distinction between social intelligence and school intelligence is crucial because the Baoulé of the Ivory Coast, for instance, believe that "one may know how to read and write, but be quite dumb"; "You may know much of Baoulé intelligence without knowing much on paper" (Dasen, 1984, p. 427). There is therefore "no single notion of intelligence that is appropriate for members of all cultures" (Sternberg, 1984, p. 310; see also Berry, 1971; Boas, 1911).

Cross-Cultural Comparisons

Scientific comparisons are expected to be based on common parameters (Berry, 1979). Sufficient baseline data are needed for informed cross-cultural comparisons. But the extent to which cross-cultural researchers "have indiscriminately gone after finding differences among various sub-cultural groups without bothering to work out a proper rationale for making comparisons" exemplifies "empiricism running riot" (Sinha, 1983, pp. 4-5). Cross-cultural data are often "interpreted out of a cultural context" (Ogbu, 1988, p. 12). Because the "environment shapes what constitutes intelligent behaviour," intelligence has no meaning outside "the context in which it occurs" (Sternberg, 1984, pp. 308-311). Differences in intelligence or task performance need no longer carry value judgments like "deficiency" or "superiority." Dasen, Berry, and Witkin (1979, pp. 78-79) suggested that the ecocultural orientation (see Chapter 2) "provides a value free context for the interpretation of differences as unique adaptation(s), rather than as differential developments." Thus the ecocultural perspective is perhaps an ideal framework for comparing subjects across cultures and ecologies.

People with differing cultures and ecologies tend to develop and maintain different repertoires of skills (Berry, 1966). The content of the human memory, for instance, varies by ecological input and worldview; performance by the cultural relevance of the task presented and the skills it demands. As pointed out in Chapter 2, we also possess differential genotypic thresholds for incorporating experience and ecological inputs into biogenetic agendas. All this implies that ecocultural imperatives may afford children of one culture greater or lesser acuity for processing some, but not other, forms of information than those of another culture. To compare children from diverse cultures with tests assessing memory content without explicit consideration of ecocultural influences therefore is to engage in scientific unfairness. For instance, how can we "objectively" compare middle-class North American children—who essentially undergo academic socialization—on the same paper-and-pencil tests with their West African peers—whose primary form of socialization is socio-affective—without reference to the seemingly dramatic differences in the content and patterns of socialization? Even when we use culture-fair tests or tasks, we must be deeply aware that individuals experience them in personalized ways. Personal experience appears to be one of the most ubiquitous sources of variance in life and psychological functioning.

Given sufficient data for informed juxtapositioning at this stage of the cross-cultural endeavor, process or thematic comparisons on such things as, for example, reproductive ideology, household composition, use of free time, daily routines, socialization values, and parental expectations, may offer the best leverage and give a global picture of the phenomena. Outcome comparisons are best undertaken after the basic nature of the phenomenon in the target cultures has been explored and adequately understood. Consequently, it is only after the essential nature of the patterning of behavioral development in Third World contexts, for instance, are known that "educated" and scientifically sound cross-cultural comparisons of developmental outcomes are advised.

Interpretation of Research Findings

The "authentic" meaning of a test or research task depends on the subject's motivation and "genuine" cooperation in completing it. Current thinking in cross-cultural testing "begins with the axiom that no true-score variance is measurable until the stimulus is represented in operational form within the subject" (Irvine, 1986, p. 229). Test or task performance are profoundly affected by transient states such as anxiety, ill-health, and testing procedures and conditions. For this reason, conclusions should never focus exclusively on one test score or source of data. As samples of behavior, tests "do not directly reveal traits or capacities, but may allow inferences to be made about the examinee" (Sattler, 1988, p. 5). Test results should therefore be interpreted in light of the child's ecocultural background and facilitating or handicapping conditions in relation to other sources of data (Sattler, 1988). In other words, test scores or research data should never be interpreted in isolation, but in biographical perspective. To the extent that tests and other assessment techniques are powerful tools, their efficacy will nevertheless depend on researchers' knowledge and expertise in using them ethically and efficiently. When properly constructed, and wisely and cautiously used, assessment procedures can assist researchers in obtaining reliable and valid developmental data.

Research data are usually used as guides for action and policy decisions. As such, research carries considerable potential for fostering relief or causing grief, because research "results do have an impact on many people, directly affecting the lives of children and their parents" (Sattler, 1988, p. 5). When misused, research tasks can mislead the consumers of research. Consequently, researchers must be careful about the language of cross-cultural research, the dissemination of research, and communication with children, families, colleagues, and the public. Although labels are integral to the research process, researchers should ensure that their classificatory labels do not become stigmas. However, labels should not excessively regiment or impede scientific progress.

WHAT CROSS-CULTURAL RESEARCH ENTAILS

Cross-cultural research inexorably leads researchers away from familiar into unfamiliar terrain. The more genuinely we undertake to understand research settings other than our own, the more sharply we are made aware of ecocultural differences. For instance, a visit to the Torres

Straits or any other part of the Third World today would reveal that childhood there stands in sharp contrast to its picture portrayed in the developmental literature. When we come across "new people" in alien cultures, we encounter "absurd" behaviors and modes of life.

"When professional social researchers set out to investigate the human situation, a way of thinking about and describing their work travels with them" (Agar, 1986, p. 11). Not only do they realize that most of the concepts, taxonomic labels, and conceptual systems they are familiar with become inapplicable, they equally find it difficult, even impossible, to employ the technology they know so well to make sense of phenomena in exotic ecologies. This is consistent with Brislin's (1986, p. 137) remark that "many researchers find that their well-laid research plans must be modified after arrival in another culture." This sort of scientific "decompensation" instigates a series of critical questions. First, are a majority of the world's peoples to be treated as a residual scientific category simply because we have no accepted or available techniques to study the ways they organize life in their own terms in the contexts that have a profound impact on them (LCHC, 1979)? Second, why do cross-cultural researchers search for universals when their data bases exclude the great majority of humankind in the Third World (Triandis, 1980)? Third, why are unschooled peoples incompetent at performing psychological tests or research tasks but so competent in other spheres of life? Finally, why do apparently competent house-servants and nannies become incompetent citizens or potential labor force participants?

In apparent attempts to address these kinds of questions, a new line of research that promises a deeper understanding of illiterate populations is emerging. An initial attempt in this direction is represented by the study of "everyday activities of people within their own indigenous culture" (Jahoda & Lewis, 1988, p. 12) by Gay and Cole (1967), who explored how Liberian peasants used mathematical knowledge. They found that although the subjects were unaware of mathematics as a systematic body of knowledge, they were experts in the use of endogenous calculational and measurement systems (LCHC, 1979). The most obvious area of such expertise in West Africa is cooking. Indigenous West African women do not normally use standard recipes, cookbooks, or standard measurements when cooking. They rely on a (high?) sense of estimation to prepare delicious dishes. There is no reason to doubt that "unschooled" people employ discernible folk principles and methods in other domains of life. Honig (1978, p. 25) substantiates this by remarking that in her travels to Japan and China, she "did not encounter a child-care person who, when I inquired, was familiar with Erikson or Piaget's work. Yet everywhere I saw the evidence of a superb 'equilibration' process by which the ideas of both theoreticians were applied in ingenious and creative ways to the rearing of children." Berry's (1971, 1975, 1976, 1986) ecocultural model (see Chapter 2) inspires and facilitates "research on local ecologies and cultures" (Jahoda & Lewis, 1988, p. 13).

The discovery of "striking differences" in the global experience of childhood is expected to increase the range of independent variables (LCHC, 1979) and to extend correspondingly the scope of conceptualization in developmental research. The expectation, reinforced by the fact that psychology's legitimate subject matter is human behavior regardless of context, is that cross-cultural research should yield universally enduring developmental norms and principles. Unfortunately, most current psychological laws are anything but universal.

Psychology's failure to yield universally enduring norms stems from the fact that its theories were "built on a limited set of paradigms" (Wagner, 1986, p. 301) derived mainly from the social reality that characterizes Western middle classes (Jahoda, 1980). Researchers have tended to present their unrepresentative data as addressing the global human condition. Despite the obvious fact that psychological functioning is a universal human condition, not the perquisite of one segment of humanity, all but a handful of psychologists "still labor under the misapprehension that one can learn universal truths about human nature by studying one's fellow citizens" (Jahoda & Lewis, 1988, p. 13). The "little contact among the specialists involved" in developmental research (Wagner, 1986, p. 289) exacerbates the failure to evolve a global image of humankind. In order to expand the frontiers of psychology, cross-cultural research should endeavor to include societies other than Western industrialized communities and to incorporate data from them into the corpus of mainstream psychological knowledge.

Will mainstream psychologists sustain and foster the present limited models and methods or will they, despite difficulties, respond to the lead of their cross-cultural peers in opening up to new questions and creative approaches in order to capture the rich diversity in human behavior worldwide? The answer to this question will influence the scientific agenda enormously and determine the future direction of developmental psychology.

There is need for researchers to adopt a learning posture in order to avoid the scientific decompensation that accompanies research in alien terrains. When cross-cultural researchers assume a learning posture, "hypotheses, measurement, samples, and instruments [become] the wrong guidelines" (Agar, 1986, p. 12). In such situations, rather than hold compulsively to preexisting modes of thought and action, there should be "an openness to new ideas and ways of investigation" in order "to go beyond the Western paradigms typically used in cross-cultural research" (Wagner, 1986, p. 301). That is, "the researcher's most valuable commodity" is "careful thought, not methodological rigor" (Brislin, 1986, p. 137). There is therefore need to follow Agar's (1986, p. 12) suggestion that transcontextual research "requires an intensive personal involvement, an abandonment of traditional scientific control, an improvisational style to meet situations not of the researcher's making, and an ability to learn from a long series of mistakes."

The sociopolitical matrix of research settings affects what can and cannot be studied in a particular context (Zuniga, 1975). Because political and ethical considerations are integral to the research process, these topics are the focus of the next section.

THE POLITICS AND ETHICS
OF CROSS-CULTURAL RESEARCH

Whereas *politics* connotes jurisdiction and sphere of influence, *ethics* refers to code of conduct. In this sense, it is difficult to imagine any kind of social science research bereft of political and/or ethical implications.

The Politics of Research

Cross-cultural research is political to the extent that it reflects or affects the ability of the researcher to have access to and enjoy legitimacy in carrying out research in a particular context. Every research project "is as much a political exercise as it is an intellectual one" (Lance, 1990, p. 338). What is studied, how it is studied, and how the results are handled, reported, or used are all susceptible to intellectual and sociopolitical influences and considerations (Warwick, 1980). Through research personnel, auspices, contents, processes, or products,

> a cross-cultural study may impinge on, or be perceived as impinging on, the characteristics and relationships of parties ranging from the principal investigator to one or more national governments. Sometimes the impact of the intervention is so trivial as to deserve little attention, while in other cases it may take on the proportions of an international scandal. (Warwick (1980, p. 320)

"As in politics, in order to gain a constituency the fieldworker must be willing to negotiate and compromise" (Lance, 1990, p. 338). This implies that no research project can be entirely apolitical. For example, "the question of population differences in behavior is so deeply politicized that one can scarcely approach it without some armor of ideology, and the question of sex differences is gaining the same distinction" (Konner, 1981, p. 3). Attempts to make a research project look politically innocuous by choosing topics, methods, and sponsorship that arouse minimal political controversy, itself reflects the anticipatory influence of or aversion for politics. Such considerations should, however, not deter research effort. Rather, they should alert and challenge critical awareness of the cultural and political assumptions built into the concepts and methods researchers use.

The Ethics of Research

Cross-cultural research raises a host of ethical questions. These pertain to access to the research setting, the researcher's obligations to subjects and/or the community, the adoption of a scientific posture, and adherence to the rules of professional conduct. Ethics should be primarily an inherent, internalized part of a scientist's professional arsenal, rather than a bundle of imposed external constraints. The core moral canons expected from researchers are that they enforce the principle of "informed consent," avoid inflicting mental or physical torture, guarantee that benefits outweigh inherent risks, protect research subjects from procedural incompetence, and accept that initial consent becomes void when side effects are potentially or overtly harmful (Ajayi, 1980).

Strictly speaking, research ethics must be derived from the sociocultural conditions of the research context vis-à-vis sound scientific methodology. The operationalization of ethical ideals, however, continues to elude researchers as they are often frustrated by ecocultural exigencies under which they work. For instance, *to inform* requires an efficient system of communication and *to consent* implies understanding. How can high research morality be upheld in societies like those of Africa with a low level of research awareness and a high degree of communication breakdown due to linguistic diversity and an absence of common communication codes? This difficulty is exacerbated by the duality of African sociocultural ethos, wherein researchers have a hard time figuring out how to resolve the ethical dilemmas engendered in the existence of endogenous moral imperatives at variance with scientific ideals.

Despite these constraints, researchers must recognize that the fundamental human and moral rights of every research subject must be upheld. Under no circumstance should ethical thinking fail to enter the research agenda because they are considered irrelevant for a particular subject or context. Concern for the best interest of the subject and community must always prevail over the interests of science.

Political and Ethical Interface

While analytically distinguishable, politics and ethics in research are tightly intertwined in practice. For instance, insensitivity to the political implications of a research project is a grievous breach of professional ethics. Similarly, a developmentalist who undertakes a cross-cultural study without advance knowledge of the target community is also guilty of professional misconduct. A disregard of research ethics could precipitate local, national, or international political contretemps (Warwick, 1980).

Every research situation raises or presents both ethical and political questions. In reality, there is no standard situation in cross-cultural research. Every project possesses a unique profile of political and ethical issues. This implies the handling of every cross-cultural project with cautious expertise. The fact that the sociopolitical milieus for research in Third World nations differ markedly from those of the West increases the incidence of ethical, political, theoretical, and procedural conflicts and dilemmas in cross-cultural research. The nascent state of psychology in the Third World worsens this scenario.

Any discussion of the politics of cross-national research is incomplete without the mention of Project Camelot, which Warwick (1980, p. 324) characterized as "the single most devastating event in the history of this enterprise." In the 1950s and early 1960s, the usual practice was for studies to be designed in the funding nations of Europe and North America, with negligible, if any, input from researchers in the target nations. The proposals were then "farmed out to" the non-Western world for fieldwork (Warwick, 1980). The data were "parceled out" to the funding nations and the participating Third World countries were usually never given any feedback regarding the outcome of the research. This had the semblance of colonialism. Of course, this eventually stirred up bitter reactions in Third World countries. It is thus essential that all phases of cross-cultural research, especially the interpretation and publication of findings, should involve the active participation of researchers from both the funding and recipient nations.

Camelot may be dead, but its legacy is quite alive. "Even today, its ghost rises up, like a genie from a bottle, in cloudy international research incidents" (Warwick, 1980, p. 326).

SUMMARY AND CONCLUSION

Psychology in the Third World is constrained by lack of resources, the adoption of alien models that are inadequate for studying indigenous phenomena, and a nearly exclusive focus on the modern sectors to the neglect of the traditional sectors, true laboratories for indigenous behavioral development. The comparative paradigm typically employed in cross-cultural research generally is inadequate because, meant to confirm, disconfirm, or expand Western theories, it gives little or no room for the generation of psychological knowledge in target cultures. Emic approaches allow for wider research contexts and generation of indigenous data bases necessary for etic research. To engage in cross-cultural comparisons without explicit consideration of the common grounds for comparison is to engage in scientific unfairness. By deriving its literature mainly from Western data sources, scientific psychology unwittingly excludes the bulk of humanity from the discipline. Cross-cultural collaboration and exchange of developmental data among child development experts is necessary to give a more universalistic image of humankind. Every cross-cultural research project carries political and ethical implications that must be given serious thought in the design and execution of research. It is essential to involve members of the target culture in *all* phases of the cross-cultural research endeavor than has hitherto been the case. "Generally cross-cultural psychology has devoted comparatively little effort to the study of emotional development, a challenging area beset with special difficulties" (Jahoda, 1986, p. 432). In conclusion, psychologists need to examine critically whose interests psychological research represents and to reflect on the fact that they may encounter different contents in different ecocultures.

10

THOUGHTS ON DEVELOPMENTAL RESEARCH IN THE THIRD WORLD

Efforts to understand human development have a long past but a short scientific history because humankind's attempts to explain the nature of the species predates the emergence of developmental science. Views about development have evolved from folk notions and philosophical speculations about human nature to "a theoretically grounded empirical science . . . the primary battleground for contests among sets or families of theories concerned with explaining development" (Bornstein & Lamb, 1988, p. 1).

The purpose of this chapter is, first, briefly to appraise developmental theories; second, to argue for the appropriateness of the ecocultural perspective for the Third World; and finally, to suggest broad research directions and priorities for Third World contexts.

DEVELOPMENTAL THEORIES:
A BRIEF STATEMENT

> Give us theories, theories, always theories. Let every man who has a theory pronounce his theory.
>
> —James Mark Baldwin

> Never trust an experimental result until it has been confirmed by theory.
>
> —Sir Arthur Eddington

Theory development is integral to the scientific process. Developmental theories are frameworks for scrutinizing developmental processes and research data. They give meaning and coherence to a "select" set of the "facts" of human development. As scientific tools, they guide and organize research and help psychologists keep their faith that development is an orderly process and a legitimate area of study. They have saved developmental psychology from drowning in the sea of data on children (Miller, 1989). In view of the complexity and multidimensionality of development, the emergence of a wide variety of theoretical models is not surprising. A multifaceted phenomenon like development cannot be understood from only one theoretical position (Weiten, 1989). Diversity in theories of development is not a sign of weakness; rather, it indicates scientific rigor. Divergence in theoretical viewpoints breeds scholarly discourse and enlightening empiricism, alerting researchers against oversimplified explanations of complex phenomena. The history of science reveals that the eventual convergence on common grounds from several clashing theoretical perspectives often yields more profound understanding of the contentious issue than would be possible from only one position. In this sense, it is "most effective to think of the various theoretical orientations as complementary viewpoints, each with its own advantages and limitations" (Weiten, 1989, p. 21).

Although theories of development "differ in their content, methods of investigation, and formal nature, they are similar in that they are forced to take a position on certain core issues of development" (Miller, 1989, p. 20). The major theoretical "wars" are about human nature, the role of nature versus nurture, whether development is qualitative or quantitative, what actually develops, the sequence of development, and whether development is continuous or discontinuous. Over time, major shifts have occurred in both the definitions of development and the manner in which key theoretical issues are handled within each family of theories. Recent theoretical trends are converging on the idea of the bioecology of human development—that is, that the genetic code is as central to development as the developmental ecology (see Chapter 2).

Theoretical wisdom assumes that psychological phenomena can best be understood by "reducing" them to their constituent elements or descriptive units. This undermines the concepts of wholeness and embeddedness—the fact that the human person is a biotic entity submerged in a dynamic network of overt and covert forces. The elementarist approach is perhaps due to the fact that our language can only permit a priori breaking down of phenomena for descriptive purposes, with subsequent attempts to integrate the disparate components into a coherent picture.

A theorist's view of development is closely tied to his or her view of human nature, a view intimately tied to his or her conception of how the universe works. This suggests the futility of discounting "the problems of epistemology and motive in the social sciences" and "the relations among science, social structure and ideology" (MacGaffey, 1981, p. 228) in research. This means that researchers are usually inspired by theories or concepts that organize their thoughts, guide data collection, and give meaning to the data obtained. Developmental theories "vary in their distance from observable behavior" (Miller, 1989, p. 3). Researchers pose questions to fit their place and time and get answers to fit their theoretical niches (Scarr, 1985). In this way, societal, scientific, and biographical considerations complexly interplay to sensitize and orient researchers to some but not other phenomena. To view something in one way is a way of not viewing it in another. Thus, by its nature, there is an element of partiality in the scientific enquiry. In light of this logic it is not at all whimsical to demand to know the extent to which current research is "tuned" to the realities of the Third World. "If the research of cross-cultural psychologists has had little impact on personality theory or other aspects of psychology, it is because research done in second cultures is not rooted, and only slightly related to, current theories" (Guthrie, 1979, p. 352).

THEORETICAL ORIENTATIONS FOR THIRD WORLD CONTEXTS

Third World researchers ought to derive their research hunches from indigenous maxims and precepts. The high point of the critique of theories typically developed in Western cultures and imported into the Third World, is that the sociophysical realities of Western societies in which the theories were developed differ markedly from those of Third World societies. Nevertheless, to varying degrees some Western theories are applicable to some aspects of developmental phenomena in non-Western contexts. The core of their irrelevance stems from the fact that the research findings obtained from Africans, for instance, are often seen by Eurocentric scholars "as they themselves would wish the former [the Africans] to be seen; thus they have cast their subjects entirely in their own mould" (Ojiaku, 1974, p. 210).

The ecocultural framework is rooted in the fact that "genes are never expressed directly in behavior. There is a long chain of events involving genes, physiological processes, and the environment" (Miller, 1989, p. 24). As explained in Chapter 2, the way the genetic code is expressed depends on the nature of ecological press in which the expression occurs. That is, a given genetic program may have different behavioral effects in different environments. The ecological paradigm thus fosters sensitivity to both ecocultural forces and biogenetic imperatives that undergird development. It therefore seems to be a useful heuristic device that can guide research in culture, particularly subsistent cultures. The model "is far more conceptual than methodological, more a call to thoughtful, systematic awareness than an operationalized, methodological guide" (Pence, 1988, p. xxii). Within it, "a range of methodological approaches are possible in undertaking ecologically sensitive research" (Pence, 1988, p. xxii). As a heuristic stratagem it permits opening up to new lines of investigation (Moore, 1987, p. 1371). This openness is not an ideological threat, but a scientific challenge.

Considering the short history of the discipline in Third World societies, what is important at the moment is not the conceptualization and execution of grand research designs but the acceptance of the ecological model. The appreciation of the significance and usefulness of the paradigm per se already represents progress. In scientific traditions, researchers usually first accept a theoretical model prior to designing and carrying out the research it inspires in order to cumulate the data bases required for sharpening and refining it.

The ecocultural framework seeks to draw and focus research on the environment-behavior nexus, thereby discouraging exclusive dependence on either biology or environment as the primary source of developmental data. Research in context demands the explicit specification of relevant ecocultural variables (see Chapter 8). Where the developmental data base does not yet exist or is scanty, environmental specification becomes difficult and requires time to be cumulated. It is best undertaken in a piecemeal, systematic manner. Long-term research programs, approached in a manner that permits and promotes the gradual, cumulative emergence of unifying concepts, norms, and principles, are more appropriate than the itinerant, unsystematized nature of current research in much of Africa. This kind of strategy is likely to follow orthogenetic principles of development (H. Werner, 1978). That is, the initial, usually difficult and confusing exploratory phase is likely to be followed by a period of intense research activity to evolve systematic but cohesive explanations of developmental phenomena in context. This phase eventually culminates in the emergence of unifying developmental concepts and themes derived from Third World ontogenies. Eventually, the nature of human personality can be discerned from the cumulated body of knowledge.

In Chapter 8 we explained how sociohistorical forces inspired the emergence of environmental psychology in Europe. Which ecocultural imperatives instigate contextual research in the Third World? Intense dualism of social systems, harmony with nature and land reverence, or the territorial imperative seem to be the three major forces that compel an ecological awareness in Third World nations. Bringing ecocultural considerations into the conceptualization of developmental research would mean, for example, that there is far more to a pupil's score on a standardized temperament test than the score per se. The test may predict a child's potential behavior in school or in social encounters, thereby revealing a critical personality trait. The test score does not, however, reveal the conditions of test performance nor the children's sociohistory and biography that reflect on the scores. Given the biogenetic dispositions of two children from two ecologies, one of poverty and the other of affluence, each is likely to experience differential patterns of socialization and may bring different perspectives and action-patterns, over and above the biological variance, to the performance of either a test or a task. These and other ecocultural sources of variance are integral to every human research question and require concerned consideration in every research design.

If the ecological approach is pertinent for developmental research in Third World nations, what research directions and priorities does it inspire?

RESEARCH DIRECTIONS
AND PRIORITIES: A PROPOSAL

It is best to situate the answer to the above question within the context of the current marginal and poor condition of the Third World, which can hardly optimize development. Battered by a devastating economic crisis, the capacity of the Third World to provide decent living conditions or fund developmental research has been drastically reduced. Marginal existence and rapid erosion of cultural traditions have given rise to a scenario wherein parents are literally waging an endless struggle to reconcile the contradictions the situation engenders. "The outcome is parental confusion and inadequately parented children" (Nsamenang, 1987, p. 291). Genuine psychological understanding of the African must consider not only his or her historic totality but also his or her geographic, ethnic, and cultural globality (Ojiaku, 1974). As such, an important research focus is to determine "what aspects of culture can be maintained, and what aspects must be changed" (Triandis, 1979, p. 395). That is, what cultural elements can be meshed with the domesticated alien fragments and what elements are completely incompatible with them? In other words, there is need to determine through research ways by which indigenous precepts and maxims can contribute to progress, harmony, and feelings of satisfaction in face of inescapable, intrusive ideologies.

Since the root of the human sciences is the developmental niche (C. M. Super & Harkness, 1986), every research setting requires a detailed, comprehensive descriptive analysis of its constituent elements. Developmental research should thus begin with an understanding of the ecology in which children live and develop. For some nations, literature on some aspects of the ecoculture already exists and can be discerned from a variety of sources. Many components of the African ecology, however, need explication. For example, although the African family is typically described as extended, its exact composition, degree of extendedness, and potential lines of social influence have yet to be specified.

The remark that the knowledge of children in African cultures is sketchy and incomplete (Ohuche & Otaala, 1981) is true and poignantly reinforces the desire for relevant research. Psychologists in Africa have a social responsibility to begin the stagelike process of systematically building up the scientific knowledge required for making informed decisions about African children. In light of the foregoing, the Third World in general and Africa in particular cannot yet enjoy the luxury of basic research. In other words, research in Third World communities should initially be policy-driven, exploring and documenting endogenous developmental precepts and pathways. It should also focus on resolving developmental problems and providing services to promote the enjoyment—rather than the endurance—of childhood. Research should further endeavor to understand the roots of underdevelopment.

The ecocultural framework affords the opportunity to depart from the current view of development, which trivializes the ecology. Within this framework, research may be undertaken at four levels. First, to describe contextual variables and their potential mode and extent of influence. Examples of themes in this phase are caregiving niches and children's routines. Second, to clarify the interconnections among ecocultural parameters, children, and developmental outcomes, examples of which include social networks, lines of social influence, and specific behaviors. Third, to describe the psychological processes that ecocultural factors evoke. This phase should include a focus on psychopathology and indigenous psychotherapy and psychiatry. The fourth phase could rely on the cumulative data bases of the first three phases to formulate definitive developmental hypotheses for higher order research. Over the long haul, attempts could be made to pool together, cohere, and integrate data from the different levels and sources to yield developmental norms, clarify previous theoretical assumptions, sharpen existing theories, and provide the leverage for formulating *informed* conclusions about the development of African children.

This research path is suggested in my own order of preference, with the understanding that in some countries research has already been conducted or that data already exist in some domains. The sequence is no more than a guideline. The design and execution of research should be determined by the work already done and the realities and priorities of each research terrain.

In sum, researchers in Third World communities have tended to overdepend on Western theoretical and methodological models that are often inappropriate for their cultures. The duality of Third World societies calls for more cautious, sophisticated theorizing and innovative methodology. The ecocultural paradigm is considered an appropriate model for research in the Third World because it permits consideration of the terrestrial environment and sociocultural imperatives in Third World contexts. A comprehensive description of the environment is a necessary precondition for sound contextual research. The timetable for such analysis in any society depends on what data already exist and the extent to which the data reflect or explain the embeddedness of the target phenomenon in its context.

11

CONCLUDING STATEMENT

What children become depends entirely on the adult members of our common world. A universal, albeit innocent but unvoiced and usually unconsidered wish of every human offspring is to be reared to become a blessing to the world. Just as children are not party to the decision to be born, so too are most adult humans helpless pawns regarding policies that determine the conditions of their lives. For instance, not quite 20% of the population controls the economic resources and political power in their communities. Worldwide, less than that percentage controls international affairs and the global economic order. The Third World sells cheap but buys expensive and has no voice in the prices of the raw materials they supply for Euramerican industries. Thus the destiny of Third World people lies in the heads and hands of industrialized nations, thence the conditions under which they live. Ojiaku (1974, p. 207) did not hesitate to blame Euramerica "for the low human condition in Africa," particularly in the 19th century, asserting that the condition was more "the result of the rapacious slave-trade perpetuated in Africa by Europe and America for over three centuries." Compared to Africa and Asia, singularly and collectively, "Euro-America has knowledge and power out of proportion to its size and population" (Ojiaku, 1974, p. 204).

As children foreshadow adults, their numbers, status, and nurture are sensitive indicators of the quality of life in diverse societies and reflect our individual and collective values, hopes, and aspirations (McHale & McHale, 1979, p. 4). But the human mind is as sharp an instrument as it can be blunt, a stimulating as well as an inhibiting device; it is as sensitive as it can be insensitive. The genetic code underlies color blindness in an analogous manner that worldview undergirds human injustice and insensitivity to the depravity of the human condition. If these statements are incorrect, how can we explain the following scenarios: pets feed better than millions of children on our planet; a journey of a thousand miles seems shorter for some people than a visit to the next-door neighbor; some of us grieve over the loss of pets but literally stumble unconcerned over homeless people on the street. Technology has rendered our world smaller, but it is increasing interpersonal contacts and distances. How is the world to become interdependent, how is humankind "to control the vast social processes that lead to technological suicide, unless humans learn a great deal about themselves, their relationships with one another, and their relationships with nature in the context of social systems?" (Triandis, 1979, p. 391). With growing awareness of resource interdependence among members of our global village, self-examination and resource allocation should preoccupy individual and collective consciousness. We cannot learn these things without understanding cross-cultural psychological phenomena—how diverse peoples organize life on their own terms. Our hope is that if psychology sheds its petty, over-used monocultural coat and develops into a universal science "it will guide human activities more and more" (Triandis, 1979, p. 392).

SCIENCE AND *HOMO SAPIENS*

Throughout the history of social science the debate about what is science and what is scientific knowledge rages. "It is a question as much for North America or Western Europe as for Africa" (Wallerstein, 1988, pp. 332-333). Doubts about the "science-ness" of psychology thus linger. Perhaps this explains why "the psychologist is never sure that what he does is 'science.' And if what he does is 'science' he is never sure that it is psychology" (Greco, 1967, p. 937). Nevertheless, psychology shares common grounds—systematic approach, openness of mind, objectivity —with other sciences. Science is one way of viewing and exploring phenomena; a critical, systematic way of thinking in the fact-finding process. Obviously, science is not the only means by which we gain knowledge. Other major sources of knowledge are "sensuous penetration, loving participation, ecstacy, and transcendent meditation" (Nchabeleng, 1982, p. 162). We also use logic, casual observation, common sense, and intuition. More importantly, "there are in culture and human experience truths inaccessible to science" (MacGaffey, 1981, p. 229). All the same, scientific psychology may be regarded as "an exercise in creative problem solving"—an empirical endeavor aimed at uncovering the "facts of life" or the principles that govern biobehavioral development (Weiten, 1989, p. 34). But as a scientific discipline, psychology is thus far less than a total success. This is perhaps the case because "scientism imposes a complementary distortion on science itself and particularly on social science" (MacGaffey, 1981, p. 230).

Scientists are not neutral or "unconcerned" fact-finders. They make a priori decisions about research site, "what facet of behavior to study, what measures to use, how to divide up the 'stream of behavior,' how to collect the data, and how to score the data" (Miller, 1989, p. 19). They also decide how to analyze, interpret, and report the findings. Each decision constrains which psychological facts are selected, translated, and published. Scientists usually rely on theoretical or methodological notions, the selective sieves that help them to record some, but not other, "facts." They usually encode "the behavior into words that add connotations" (Miller, 1989, p. 6). But this does not obviate the advantages of scientific psychology; rather, it alerts us to be more critical and somewhat skeptical consumers of research. For example, how can we defend psychology's aspiration to be a universal enterprise when its "data base excludes the majority of . . . [humankind] who live in Asia and the Southern Hemisphere" (Triandis, 1980, p. ix)?

Thus, as it stands today, psychology may be considered as a science of exclusion. Psychology also appears to be an elite science not only because in both Western and non-Western cultures psychologists are usually members of the middle classes, but more so because psychology tends to promote middle-class values to the neglect of lower class psychosocial processes. In the dynamics of race and class relations, there is a claimed superiority and a perceived inferiority. The claimed superiority is an insidious, highly potent ideology, while the felt inferiority is a self-defeating, existential condition. This perhaps explains, at least partially, the stubborn unwillingness to incorporate the behaviors of "inferior humans" into the science of "superior humans"! There is also a lurking, albeit arguable, possibility that available technology and resources cannot yet permit the study of "strange" behavior in exotic parts of our common universe. That current theories, methods, and measures are inadequate tools for a comprehensive study of the African and psychological processes in Africa, there is little doubt. This assertion becomes more compelling in face of the fact that a great deal of African knowledge "is locked in maxims, proverbs and folklore, not easily translatable into Euro-American languages except at the cost of impairment to its essence, or distortion of its full meaning" (Ojiaku, 1974, p. 211). Because "outside observers are often unable to discern" the "keys" of behavior in exotic cultures, they typically "apply more serious interpretative frames to the event taking place than perhaps do the participants in the event themselves" (Ochs, 1988, p. 167). Social science researchers in African cultures usually "ignore the subject-matter: the theories and concepts through which the owners of the culture see their cultural world" (Anyawu, 1975, p. 149). It is thus unfortunate that current social science efforts barely scratch the surface of the African mind and knowledge systems.

The revelation that folk ideas "are not always in agreement with formal psychology" (Goodnow, 1988, p. 287) points to a basic discrepancy between folk epistemology and scientific (Western) epistemology. In other words, what researchers have studied and reported may not be what actually exists "out there" in our homes, farms, factories, offices, streets, or social encounters. For instance, pets have become unprecedented "significant others" in many middle-class Western households, but the extent to which they preoccupy the attention, time, and resources of their owners has yet to be fully reflected in the psychological literature. Many pet owners even seem to spend more time and to relate more intimately with their pets than with members of their own species, for at least some of the time.

The polemics about how members of diverse cultures deal with the environment polarize into two naive positions: They cannot even do anything to their environment; Look at what they have done to their environment. Regardless of the dialectic, the global environmental question today is: What happened to *our* environment? The continuing environmental damages inflicted by modern technology (Triandis, 1979), particularly the greenhouse effect, affects humans everywhere. Increasing environmental awareness is therefore in the best interest of all species, particularly *Homo sapiens*.

Two basic forms of orientation seem to endow human existence with meaning and worth: expressive and instrumental. In expressive cultures the dominant motive for behavior is socio-affective; in instrumental cultures it is techno-economic. Thus expressive cultures tend to encourage human harmony with the environment and to foster socio-affective development, whereas instrumental cultures tend to carpenter the environment and to promote cognitive development. The scientific issue here is not which orientation is right or wrong about the facts, rather it pertains to the extent to which each fosters or stifles understanding, harmony, and solidarity among our planet's diverse peoples.

THIRD WORLD REALITIES: SCIENTIFIC OPTIONS

Every society has at least one theory of knowledge that specifies the limits of knowledge and the path to its acquisition (Ochs, 1988). In the beginning there were diverse human collectives and each had its knowledge system. This is still true, except that the Western epistemologic systems developed an intrusive variant. In the course of history, the African continent, like every part of the Third World, was confronted with "an intrusive ideology which not only rejected the worth" of African epistemology "but also was pervasive in that it took on multiple clothings" (Wallerstein, 1988, p. 331). African resistance to this intrusive, pervasive, newly dominant ideology took ambiguous forms. Whereas "many Africans accepted, seemed to accept, the new universalism, seeking to learn its secrets, seeking to tame this god, seeking to gain its favor," others "(often the same ones) rebelled against it. . . . The situation is such that we can speak of a double bind, in which there was no reaction that could remove the pressure and the oppression" (Wallerstein, 1988, p. 332).

> Admittedly, Africa has knowledge and, logically, power and scholars. But these differ from the Euro-American in one major respect: ever since the early 19th century when the Euro-American presence in Africa began to be noticeably felt in the interior, Africa's knowledge has increasingly ceased to be rooted in the African soil. (Ojiaku, 1974, p. 204)

Like many an import into the continent, African knowledge has increasingly become foreign because conclusions on African scholarship "are significantly influenced by . . . Western societal beliefs, value systems and ideological perspectives" (Ojiaku, 1974, p. 209).

There are "fundamental differences" in the conditions under which psychology is "practiced in developing countries" (Moghaddam & Taylor, 1985, p. 1144) from those in developed nations. W. Russell (1984, p. 1017) stated that "Americans who have not yet had opportunities to see psychologists at work in other countries are often surprised to learn that what psychologists do and how they conceive of their discipline may differ considerably from the American model." All this implies that most Western psychologists know little about social structures, beliefs, value systems, and ways of life in the non-Western World where the bulk of humanity lives.

Judged from where it was three decades ago, one can assert that the current study of Africa and the non-Western World is a laudable *improvement* (Ojiaku, 1974). But "it is only a small minority of Americans who pay careful attention to Africa" (Ungar, 1986, p. 20). Many Westerners see little more than chaos and turmoil in Africa, and the common feeling is that it is a lost cause. The "low regard and little respect the West and its scholars have for Africa" (Ojiaku, 1974, p. 213) is not of course unique to the African continent; the Third World as a whole suffers this second-class status in the academic and intellectual community. This is perhaps why the influence of cross-cultural psychology "on the main body still falls far short of constituting a critical mass" (Jahoda & Lewis, 1988, p. 13). If Third World studies "are unpopular, suspect, or simply insignificant" (Staniland, 1983, p. 77), why should Western scholars care about or need them? Western social scholars claim a universality for their various disciplines. While "many aspects of human development and functioning are no doubt universal, such universality cannot be postulated on the basis of research in a single cultural group; it must be demonstrated empirically across a variety of human populations" (Dasen & Jahoda, 1986, p. 413). If psychology is to become a universal enterprise, it must endeavor to understand cross-cultural psychological phenomena (Triandis, 1979). Adler (1982, p. 88) called for "greater compassion and concerted" action to deal with existing widespread problems, especially the Eurocentric slant in scientific psychology.

International efforts to strengthen Third World psychology (Moghaddam, 1987) have met only partial success. This is because foreign experts and international agencies working in the Third World have a hard time thinking Third World enough to address problems from Third World perspectives directly, or to reach the people in a manner that makes a difference to them. For example, an important factor "sometimes overlooked is the difficulty many people brought to help Africa's economic development have in understanding African ways of thinking and acting" (Creekmore, 1986, p. 39). Thus most intervention programs, including cross-cultural research, in the Third World tend to fail because they are often designed and implemented "with little understanding of the mind of Africa" (Ojiaku, 1974, p. 207). Despite Europe's long-standing contact and presence in Africa, Europeans have starkly failed to "discover" the African. Rather than seek to discover what Africans themselves think they (Africans) are doing, Western scholars more or less "project their mental constructs or 'models' into" Africans "without always realizing that they are doing so" (Beattie, n.d., p. 2).

To play the scientific game in terms of an oppressive system now in crisis, "we must take advantage of the contradictions of the system itself to go beyond it" (Wallerstein, 1988, p. 332). If the psychological world appears to be crumbling onto itself, "how can we know the range of options, and what scientific endeavors will further one or another option?" in the Third World (Wallerstein, 1988, p. 333). First, researchers in Third World contexts might reject Western-based research paradigms, isolate themselves, and try to evolve "their own" science of behavior. To be African psychologists, they must look at, see, understand, and interpret their society with as much completeness as possible on its own terms, rather than through the conceptual systems of others. The emphasis is on the African perspective rather than on African conceptual systems since no coherently systematized African conceptual system exists yet. Second, they might continue to function within Western theoretical periscopes and methodological approaches that permit them to cast Africans entirely in Western molds. Third, by viewing *Homo sapiens* as a global species, they might keenly and critically examine, in light of extant developmental knowledge, how "this organism" develops and behaves in their own niches. They could explore and document this image of humanity from an Afrocentric perspective and ascertain its augmentation of the stock of mainstream psychological knowledge.

Whichever route is chosen, it is essential to note that "indigenous third world psychology could evolve to be far more effective and useful if it were constructively supported by the first and second worlds" (Moghaddam, 1987, p. 917).

DEVELOPMENTAL RESEARCH: THE EXPECTATIONS

The greatest expectation is for cross-cultural developmental research to evolve provincial psychology as well as global psychology to reflect cross-cultural variations (Triandis, 1979) and universals in human development (Kagan, 1981). If the contemporary insular "psychology must be changed to understand the behavior and experience" of *Homo sapiens* as a global species, "then this is a fact of profound importance" (Triandis, 1980, p. ix). "The most important practical action that can be undertaken now is to encourage both American and foreign undergraduate and graduate students to consider child development in a comparative cross-cultural perspective" (Wagner, 1986, p. 301). A second suggestion is to develop the competence of psychologists in the less prosperous half of the world to do creative research (Triandis, 1979). A third expectation is to ascertain relevant, collaborative research and to engage in more genuine cross-exchange of developmental data. But collaborative relationships with colleagues in target cultures should not deteriorate into neocolonial relationships. While the outsider should enjoy some advantage—for example, international status—the insider should also have some other advantage, such as international exposure and publication outlets (Triandis, 1979). The demand for relevant psychology points to the necessity to open up to new theoretical and empirical possibilities for studying the "person-acting-in-setting as the unit of analysis" (Jahoda, 1986, p. 429).

FINAL WORD

Although human beings everywhere endeavor to raise competent offspring, different cultures apply different programs under a variety of ecological conditions, with differing outcomes. For psychologists to be blind to or to undermine such realities is to be expertly ignorant about the content area of their discipline. An urgent challenge facing psychology is to develop tools and strategies to study behavioral development in global perspective. There is thus a dire need to develop new conceptual vocabularies and innovative methods to deal with, explain, and interpret more thoroughly the reality of the human condition among the bulk of humanity in "exotic" cultures. Developmental research is always undertaken in a specific culture. Psychologists should know that compulsive confinement in one cultural niche does not advance "their" science. We ought to intensify and evolve new insights from cross-cultural collaborative research.

REFERENCES

Achebe, C. (1958). *Things fall apart.* Ibadan, Nigeria: Heinemann.

Adler, L. L. (1977). A plea for interdisciplinary cross-cultural research: Some introductory remarks. In L. L. Adler (Ed.), *Issues in cross-cultural research* (Vol. 285, pp. 1-2). New York: Annals of the New York Academy of Sciences.

Adler, L. L. (1982). Cross-cultural research and theory. In B. B. Wolman (Ed.), *Handbook of developmental psychology.* Englewood Cliffs, NJ: Prentice-Hall.

"African economy in brief." (1964, January 20). *The New York Times,* p. 72.

Agar, M. H. (1986). *Speaking of ethnography.* Newbury Park, CA: Sage.

Aiello, J. F., Gordon, B., & Farrell, T. J. (1974). Description of children's outdoor activities in a suburban residential area: Preliminary findings. In R. C. Moore (Ed.), *Childhood city. EDRA 5: Proceedings of the Fifth Environmental Design Research Association Conference* (Pt. 12, pp. 187-196). Washington, DC: Environmental Design Research Association.

Ajayi, O. O. (1980). Taboos and clinical research in West Africa. *Journal of Medical Ethics, 6,* 61-63.

Altman, I. (1975). *The environment and social behavior.* Monterey, CA: Brooks/Cole.

Andah, B. W. (1979). The history of early settlement in Africa before 1000 A.D. In R. K. Udo (Ed.), *Population source book for Sub-Saharan Africa.* Nairobi, Kenya: Heinemann.

Anderson, E. (1969). La notion de Dieu chez quelques tribus Congo-Camerounaises. *Journal of Religion in Africa, II*(2) 96-112.

Andor, L. E. (1983). *Psychological and sociological studies of the black people of Africa, south of the Sahara 1960-1975: An annotated select bibliography.* Braamfontein: National Institute for Personnel Research.

Anyawu, K. C. (1975). African religion as an experienced reality. *Africa: Thought and Practice. Journal of the Philosophical Association of Kenya, 2*(2).

American Psychological Association. (1973). *The consolidated roster for psychology.* Washington, DC: Author.

Ardila, R. (1982). International psychology. *American Psychologist, 37*(3), 323-329.

Asiwaju, A. I. (Ed.). (1984). *Partitioned Africans: Ethnic relations across Africa's international boundaries, 1884-1984.* Lagos, Nigeria: University of Lagos Press.

Atado, Fr. J. C. (1988). *African marriage customs and church law.* Kano, Nigeria: Modern Printers.

Ayisi, E. O. (1979). *An introduction to the study of African culture.* London: Heinemann.

Badri, M. B. (1979). *The dilemma of Muslim psychologists.* London: MWH London Publishers.

Baeta, C. G. (1967). Aspects of religion. In W. Birmingham, I. Neustaadt, & E. N. Omaboe (Eds.), *A study of contemporary Ghana. Vol. 2: Some aspects of social structure in Ghana* (pp. 240-250). London: Allen & Unwin.

Barker, R. G. (1968). *Ecological psychology.* Stanford, CA: Stanford University Press.

Barker, R. G. (1987). Prospecting in environmental psychology: Oskaloosa revisited. In D. Stokols & I. Altman (Eds.), *Handbook of environmental psychology.* New York: John Wiley.

Barrett, L. (1988, April 18). Nigeria: The Sahara closes in. *West Africa, 3688,* 675-718.

Bastide, R. (1967). *Les Amerique Noire: Les civilizations Africaines dans le Nouveu Monde.* Paris: Payot.

Basu, A. (1987). Re-thinking education in the Third World. *Africa Quarterly, 27,* 89-95.

Baum, A., Singer, J., & Baum, C. (1982). Stress and the environment. *Journal of Social Issues, 37*(1), 4-35.

Beattie, J. H. M. (n.d.). Supplements to philosophy. In S. C. Brown (Ed.), *Royal Institute of Philosophy lectures. Series 17: Objectivity and cultural divergence.* London: Cambridge University Press.

Bekombo, M. (1981). The child in Africa: Socialization, education and work. In G. Rodgers & G. Standing (Eds.), *Child work, poverty, and underdevelopment.* Geneva: International Labor Organization.

Bernal, V. (1988). Coercion and influences in African agriculture: Insights from the Sudanese experience. *African Studies Review, 31*(2), 89-108.

Berry, J. W. (1966). Temne and Eskimo perceptual skills. *International Journal of Psychology, 1,* 207-229.

Berry, J. W. (1971). Muller-Lyer susceptibility: Culture, ecology, or race? *International Journal of Psychology, 6,* 193-197.

Berry, J. W. (1975). An ecological approach to cross-cultural psychology. *Nederlands Tijdschrift voor de psychologie, 30,* 51-84.

Berry, J. W. (1976). *Human ecology and cognitive style.* New York: John Wiley.

Berry, J. W. (1979). Culture and cognitive style. In A. J. Marsella, R. G. Tharp, & T. J. Ciborowski (Eds.), *Perspectives on cross-cultural psychology.* New York: Academic Press.

Berry, J. W. (1980). Introduction to methodology. In H. Triandis & W. W. Lambert (Eds.), *Handbook of cross-cultural psychology. Vol. 2: Methodology.* Boston: Allyn & Bacon.

Berry, J. W. (1981). Developmental issues in the comparative study of psychological differentiation. In R. H. Munroe, R. L. Munroe, & B. B. Whiting (Eds.), *Handbook of cross-cultural human development* (pp. 475-500). New York: Garland.

Berry, J. W. (1984). Towards a universal psychology of cognitive competence. *International Journal of Psychology, 19,* 335-361.

Berry, J. W. (1986). The comparative study of cognitive abilities: A summary. In S. E. Newstead, S. H. Irvine, & P. L. Dann (Eds.), *Human assessment: Cognition and motivation* (pp. 5774). Dordrecht, Netherlands: Martinus Nijhoff.

Berry, J. W., et al. (Eds.). (1986). *Cultural adaptations and cognitive development in Central Africa.* Lisse: Swets & Zeitlinger.

Berry, J. W., Irvine, S. H., & Hunt, E. B. (1988). *Indigenous cognition: Functioning in cultural context.* Dordrecht, Netherlands: Martinus Nijhoff.

Berry, J. W., Poortinga, Y. H., Segall, M. H. & Dasen, P. R. (in press). *Cross-cultural psychology: Theory, method and applications.* Cambridge, UK: Cambridge University Press.

Berry, J. W., Trimble, J. E., & Olmedo, E. L. (1986). Assessment of acculturation. In W. J. Lonner & J. W. Berry (Eds.), *Field methods in cross-cultural research.* Newbury Park, CA: Sage.

Boas, F. (1911). *The mind of the primitive man.* New York: Macmillan.

Bornstein, M. H., & Lamb, M. E. (Eds.). (1988). *Developmental psychology: An advanced text.* Hillsdale, NJ: Lawrence Erlbaum.

Boocock, S. (1981). The life space of children. In S. Keller (Ed.), *Building for women.* Lexington, MA: Lexington.

Boserup, E. (1970). *Women's role in economic development.* Geneva: International Labor Organization.

Boulet, J. (1975). *Magoumaz: Etude d'un terroir de Montaigne en pays Mafa.* Yaoundé, Cameroon: OSTROM.

Bowlby, J. (1969). *Attachment.* New York: Basic Books.

Brislin, R. W. (1986). The wording and translation of research instruments. In W. J. Lonner & J. W. Berry (Eds.), *Field methods in cross-cultural research.* Newbury Park, CA: Sage.

Bronfenbrenner, U. (1979). *The ecology of human development.* Cambridge, UK: Cambridge University Press.

Bronfenbrenner, U. (1988). Foreword. In A. R. Pence (Ed.), *Ecological research with children and families: From concepts to methodology.* New York: Teachers College Press.

Bronfenbrenner, U., & Crouter, A. (1983). The evolution of environmental models in developmental research. In W. Kessen (Ed.), *Handbook of child psychology* (Vol. 1, pp. 357-414). New York: John Wiley.

Brown, B. B. (1987). Territoriality. In D. Stokols & I. Altman (Eds.), *Handbook of environmental psychology.* New York: John Wiley.

Brunswick, E. (1956). *Perception and the representative design of psychological experiments* (2nd ed.). Berkeley: University of California Press.

Bryant, B. K. (1985). The neighborhood walk: Sources of support in middle childhood. *Monographs of the Society for Research in Child Development, 210, 50*(3), 1-122.

Busia, K. A. (1954). The Ashanti. In C. D. Forde (Ed.), *African worlds.* London: Oxford University Press.

Busia, K. A. (1967). *Africa in search of democracy.* New York: Praeger.

Campbell, A. (1981). *The sense of well-being in America.* New York: McGraw-Hill.

Campbell, A., & Fiske, D. W. (1959). Convergent and discriminant validation of the multitrait-multimethod matrix. *Psychological Bulletin, 56,* 81-105.

Campbell, D. J., Lev, L., & Holtzman, J. (1980). *Results of a socioeconomic survey in the department of Margui-Wandala and Arrondissement in Meri in North Cameroon, April-May, 1980* (MSU/USAID, Mandara Mountains Research Rep.). East Lansing: Michigan State University, Department of Agricultural Economics.

Caplan, R. D. (1983). Person-environment fit: Past, present, and future. In C. L. Cooper (Ed.), *Stress research: Issues for the eighties* (pp. 35-78). New York: John Wiley.

Carp, F. M., & Carp, A. (1982). Perceived environmental quality assessment scales and their relation to age and gender. *Journal of Environmental Psychology, 2,* 295-312.

Charnov, E. L., & Krebs, J. (1974). On clutch size and fitness. *Ibis, 116,* 217-219.

Che, M. (1985, September). Seminar on languages: Proposes "Fulfulde, Beti, Duala" for Cameroon. *Cameroon Tribune, No. 587,* p. 4.

Cheater, A. (1990). The ideology of "communal" land tenure in Zimbabwe: Mythogenesis enacted? *Africa, 60*(2), 188.

Chilver, E. M. (1962). Nineteenth century trade in the Bamenda grassfields. *Africa und Ubersee, 45*(4), 223-250.

Cleland, J., Verrall, J., & Vaessen, M. (1983). Preferences for the sex of children and their influence on reproductive behavior. *WFS Comparative Studies no 27.*

Cohen, S., Evans, G. W., Krantz, D. S., & Stokols, D. (1980). Physiological, motivational, and cognitive effects of aircraft noise on children: Moving from the laboratory to the field. *American Psychologist, 35,* 231-243.

Cole, M. (1988). Cross-cultural research in the sociohistorical tradition. *Human Development, 31,* 137-157.

Cole, M., Gay, J. A., & Sharp, D. W. (1971).*The cultural context of learning and thinking: An exploration in experimental anthropology.* New York: Basic Books.

Cole, M., & Scribner, S. (1974). *Culture and thought: A psychological introduction.* New York: John Wiley.

Colgate, S. H., Carrière, J. F., Jato, M., & Mounlom, D. (Eds.). (1984). *The nurse and community health in Africa.* Yaoundé, Cameroon: Editions Clé.

Commonwealth Universities yearbook (Vols. 1-4). (1985). London: Association of Commonwealth Universities.

Cooper, C. (1975). *Easter Hill village: Some social implications of design.* New York: Free Press.

Copet-Rougier, E. (1987). Du clan a la chefferie dans l'Est du Cameroun. *Africa, 57*(3), 335-362.

Craik, K. H., & Feimer, N. (1987). Environmental assessment. In D. Stokols & I. Altman (Eds.), *Handbook of environmental psychology.* New York: John Wiley.

Craik, K. H., & Zube, E. H. (1976). The development of perceived environmental quality indices. In K. H. Craik & E. H. Zube (Eds.), *Perceiving environmental quality.* New York: Plenum.

Creekmore, C. (1986). Misunderstanding Africa. *Psychology Today, 12,* 40-45.

Crowder, M. (1985). History of French West Africa until independence. *Africa south of the Sahara* (15th ed.). London: Europa Publications.

Csikszentmihalyi, M., & Rochberg-Halton, E. (1981). *The meaning of things: Domestic symbols and the self.* Cambridge, UK: Cambridge University Press.

Cummings, R. J. (1986). Africa between the ages. *African Studies Review, 29*(2), 1-26.

Cunningham, C. E. (1973). Order in the Atoni house. In R. Needham (Ed.), *Right and left: Essays on the dual symbolic classification* (pp. 204-238). Chicago: University of Chicago Press.

Curran, H. V. (1984). Introduction. In H. V. Curran (Ed.), *Nigerian children: Developmental perspectives.* London: Routledge & Kegan Paul.

D'Alessio, M. (1990). Social representations of childhood: An implicit theory of development. In G. Duveen & B. Lloyd (Eds.), *Social representations and the development of knowledge.* Cambridge, UK: Cambridge University Press.

Dasen, P.R. (1984). The cross-cultural study of intelligence: Piaget and the Baoule. *International Journal of Psychology, 19,* 407-434.

Dasen, P. R., Berry, J. W., & Witkin, H. (1979). The use of developmental theories cross-culturally. In L. Leckensberger, W. Lonner, & Y. Poortinga (Eds.), *Cross-cultural contributions to psychology.* Amsterdam: Swets & Zeitlinger.

Dasen, P. R., Inhelder, B., Lavallee, M., & Retschitzki, J. (1978). *Naissance de l'intelligence chez l'enfant Baoule de Côte d'Ivoire.* Berne: Hans Huber.

Dasen, P. R. & Jahoda, G. (Eds.). Preface. *International Journal of Behavioral Development, 9*(4), 413-416.

Davidson, B. (1985). Africa in historical perspective. *Africa South of the Sahara* (15th ed.). London: Europa Publications.

Davies, A. G. (1974). [Letter to the Editor]. *Bulletin of the Canadian Association of University Teachers, 22*(4), 21.

Davis-Roberts, C. (1986). Indigenous Africa. In A. A. Mazrui (Ed.), *The Africans.* New York: Praeger.

Dawkins, R. (1978). Replicator selection and the extended phenotype. *Zeitschrift Tierpsychologie, 47,* 61-76.

Diaz-Guerrero, R. (1977). Editorial response. *IACCP Cross-cultural Psychology Newsletter, 11,* 3, 4-6.

Dikuk, S. (1989). Women's agricultural production and political action in the Cameroon grassfields. *Africa, 59*(3), 338-355.

Diop, C. A. (1960). *L'Unite culturelle de l'Afrique Noire.* Paris: Presence Africaine.

Diop, C. A. (1987). *Black Africa.* Westport, CT: Lawrence Hill.

Driver, B. L., & Greene, P. (1977). Man's nature: Innate determinants of response to natural environments. In *Children, nature, and the urban environment: Proceedings of a symposium* (General Tech. Rep. NE-30, pp. 63-72). Upper Darby, PA: U.S. Department of Agriculture, Forest Service, Northeastern Forest Experiment Station.

Dubos, R. (1965). *Man adapting.* New Haven, CT: Yale University Press.

Durojaiye, M. O. A. (1983). The role of education, particularly family education, in promoting the physical, emotional and intellectual development of the child. In Federal Republic of Nigeria, *Report of the Nigerian delegation to the Inter-Parliamentary Conference on Policies, Programmes and Legislation for Children in Africa held in Yaoundé, Cameroon, 22nd-26th November, 1982.* Lagos: Federal Government Press.

Durojaiye, M. O. A. (1984). The impact of psychological testing on educational and personnel selection in Africa. *International Journal of Psychology, 19*(1/2), 135-144.

Ekpere, J. A., Oyedipe, F. P. A., & Adegboye, R. O. (1978). Family role differentiation within the Kwara nomadic Fulani. In C. Oppong, G. Adaba, M. Bekombo-Priso, & J. Mogey (Eds.), *Marriage, fertility and parenthood in West Africa.* Canberra: Australian National University Press.

Ellis, J. (1968). *Child-training in Ghana, with particular reference to the Ga tribe.* Unpublished master's thesis, University of Ghana.

Ellis, J. (1978). The child in West African society. In J. Ellis (Ed.), *West African families in Britain.* London: Routledge & Kegan Paul.

Endler, N. S., & Magnusson, D. (Eds.). (1976). *Interactional psychology and personality.* Washington, DC: Hemisphere.

Erikson, E. H. (1950). *Childhood and society.* New York: Norton.

Erny, P. (1968). *L'enfant dans la pensee traditionnelle de l'Afrique Noire.* Paris: Le livre africain.

Erny, P. (1972). *Les premiers pas dans la vie de l'enfant d'Afrique Noire: Naissance et premiere enfance.* Paris: L'Ecole.

Erny, P. (1987). *L'enfant et son milieu en Afrique Noire.* Paris: L'Harmattan.

Esen, A. (1972). A view of guidance from Africa. *Personnel and Guidance Journal, 50*(10), 792-798.

Eveleth, P. B., & Tanner, J. M. (1976). *Worldwide variation in human growth.* Cambridge, UK: Cambridge University Press.

Fafunwa, A. B. (1967). *New perspectives in African education.* London: Macmillan.

Federal Republic of Nigeria. (1983). *Report of the Nigerian delegation to the Inter-Parliamentary Conference on Policies, Programmes and Legislation for Children in Africa held in Yaoundé, Cameroon, 22nd-26th November, 1982.* Lagos: Federal Government Press.

Fisiy, C. F. (1983). The concept and excercise of power in a traditional milieu: A case study of the Bali-Nyonga city state. *Science and Technology Review, 1*(3-4), 117-128.

Food and Agriculture Organization. (1982). *State of food and agriculture, 1982, Production yearbook.* Rome: Author.

Forgas, J. P. (1979). *Social episodes: The study of interaction routines.* New York: Academic Press.

Fortes, M. (1950). Kinship and marriage among the Ashanti. In A. R. Radcliffe-Brown & D. Forde (Eds.), *African systems of kinship and marriage.* Oxford: Oxford University Press.

Fox, L. K. (1967). *East African childhood.* Nairobi: Oxford University Press.

Frank, B. (1990). From village autonomy to modern village administration among the Kulere of Central Nigeria. *Africa, 60*(2), 270-292.

Freud, S. (1956). *A general introduction to psychoanalysis.* New York: Permabooks.

Friedmann, A., Zimring, C., & Zube, E. H. (1978). *Environmental design evaluation.* New York: Plenum.

Frijida, N. H., & Jahoda, G. (1966). On the scope and methods of cross-cultural research. *International Journal of Psychology, 1,* 110-127.

Gardner, H. (1974). The development of competence in culturally defined domains. In R. A. Shweder & R. A. LeVine (Eds.), *Culture theory.* Cambridge, UK: Cambridge University Press.

Gay, J., & Cole, M. (1967). *The new mathematics and an old culture.* New York: Holt, Rinehart & Winston.

Gibson, E. J. (1982). The concept of affordances: The renascence of functionalism. In W. A. Collins (Ed.), *The concept of development: The Minnesota symposia on child development* (Vol. 15, pp. 55-81). Hillsdale, NJ: Lawrence Erlbaum.

Gibson, E. J. (1984). Perceptual development from the ecological approach. In M. E. Lamb, A. L. Brown, & B. Rogoff (Eds.), *Advances in developmental psychology* (Vol. 3). Hillsdale, NJ: Lawrence Erlbaum.

Goodenough, F. (1936). The measurement of mental functions in primitive groups. *American Anthropologist, 38,* 1-11.

Goodnow, J. J. (1984). On being judged intelligent. *International Journal of Psychology, 19,* 391-406.

Goodnow, J. J. (1988). Parents' ideas, actions, and feelings: Models and methods from developmental and social psychology. *Child Development, 59*(2), 286-320.

Goodnow, J. J., Wilkins, P., & Dawes, L. (1986). Acquiring cultural forms: Cognitive aspects of socialization illustrated by children's drawings and judgments of drawings. *International Journal of Behavioral Development, 9,* 485-505.

Goody, J. (1975). Religion, social change and the sociology of conversion. In J. Goody (Ed.), *Changing social structure in Ghana.* London: (International African Institute) Clarke, Doble & Brendon.

Greco, P. (1967). Logique et connaissance. In J. Piaget (Ed.), *Encyclopedie de la Pleiade.* Paris: Gallimard.

Grossen, M., & Perret-Clermont, A. N. (1984). Some elements of social psychology of operational development of the child. *Quarterly Newsletter of the Laboratory of Comparative Human Cognition, 6,* 51-59.

Grusec, J. E., & Lytton, H. (1988). *Social development.* London: Springer-Verlag.

Gump, P. V. (1987). School and classroom environments. In D. Stokols & I. Altman (Eds.), *Handbook of environmental psychology* (pp. 691-732). New York: John Wiley.

Guthrie, G. M. (1979). A cross-cultural odyssey: Some personal reflections. In A. J. Marsella, R. G. Tharp, & T. J. Ciborowski (Eds.), *Perspectives on cross-cultural psychology.* New York: Academic Press.

Guthrie, G. M., & Lonner, W. J. (1986). Assessment of personality and psychopathology. In W. J. Lonner & J. W. Berry (Eds.), *Field methods in cross-cultural research* (pp. 231-264). Newbury Park, CA: Sage.

Guyer, J. I. (1980). Female farming and the evolution of food production patterns amongst the Beti of south-central Cameroon. *Africa, 50*(4), 341-356.

Guyer, J. I. (1984). Women in the rural economy: Contemporary variations. In M. J. Hay & S. Stichter (Eds.), *African women south of the Sahara* (pp. 19-32). New York: Longman.

Gyekye, K. (1984). Akan concept of a person. In R. A. Wright *African philosophy.* Lanham, MD: University Press of America.

Hake, J. M. (1972). *Childrearing practices in Northern Nigeria.* Ibadan, Nigeria: University of Ibadan Press.

Hall, E., Lamb, M. E., & Perlmutter, M. (Eds.). (1986). *Child psychology today.* New York: Random House.

Hefner, R., & DeLamater, J. (1968). National development from a social psychological perspective. *Journal of Social Issues, 24,* 1-5.

Henderson, S., Byrne, D. G., & Duncan-Jones, P. (1981). *Neurosis and the social environment.* Sydney, Australia: Academic Press.

Henn, J. K. (1978). *Peasants, workers, and capital: The political economy of rural Cameroon.* Unpublished doctoral dissertation, Harvard University.

Henn, J. K. (1984). Women in the rural economy: Past, present, and future. In M. J. Hay & S. Stichter (Eds.), *African women south of the Sahara* (pp. 1-18). London: Longman.

Hinde, R. A. (1983). Ethology and child development. In P. H. Mussen (Ed.), *Handbook of child psychology. Vol. 2: Infancy and developmental psychology* (4th ed.). New York: John Wiley.

Hinde, R. A., & Stevenson-Hinde, J. (1990). Attachment: Biological, cultural and individual desiderata. *Human Development, 33*(1), 62-72.

Honig, A. S. (1978). Comparison of child-rearing practices in Japan and the People's Republic of China: A personal view. *International Journal of Group Tensions, 8*(1/2), 6-32.

Hubbard, D. (1985). Economic trends in Africa—1985. *Africa south of the Sahara* (15th ed.). London: Europa Publications.

Hunt, N. R. (1988). "Le bebe en brousse": European women, African birth spacing and colonial intervention in breast feeding in the Belgian Congo. *International Journal of African Historical Studies, 21*(3), 401-432.

Hunter, G. (1962). *The new societies of tropical Africa.* London: Oxford University Press.

Irvine, S. H. (1986). Cross-cultural assessment: From theory to practice. In W. J. Lonner & J. W. Berry (Eds.), *Field methods in cross-cultural research* (pp. 203-230). Newbury Park, CA: Sage.

Irvine, S. H., & Berry, J. W. (Eds.). (1988). *Human abilities in cultural context.* Cambridge, UK: Cambridge University Press.

Ittelson, W. H. (1973). Environmental perception and contemporary perceptual theory. In *Environment and cognition.* New York: Seminar Press.

Ittelson, W. H., Franck, K. A., & O'Hanlon, T. J. (1976). The nature of environmental experience. In S. Wapner, S. B. Cohen, & B. Kaplan (Eds.), *Experiencing the environment.* New York: Plenum.

Jacobi, M., & Stokols, D. (1983). The role of tradition in group-environment relation. In N. R. Feimer & E. S. Geller (Eds.), *Environmental psychology: Directions and perspectives* (pp. 157-190). New York: Praeger.

Jacques, D. C. (1980). Landscape appraisal: The case of a subjective theory. *Journal of Environmental Management, 10,* 107-113.

Jahn, J. (1961). *Muntu.* London: Faber & Faber.

Jahoda, G. (1980). Theoretical and systematic approaches in cross-cultural psychology. In H. C. Triandis & W. W. Lambert (Eds.), *Handbook of cross-cultural psychology. Vol. 1: Perspectives* (pp. 69-141). Boston: Allyn & Bacon.

Jahoda, G. (1982). *Psychology and anthropology.* London: Academic Press.

Jahoda, G. (1986). A cross-cultural perspective on developmental psychology. *International Journal of Behavioral Development, 9,* 417-437.

Jahoda, G., & Lewis, I. M. (1988). Introduction: Child development in psychology and anthropology. In G. Jahoda & I. M. Lewis (Eds.), *Acquiring culture.* London: Croom Helm.

July, R. W. (1974). *A history of the African people.* New York: Allen & Unwin.

Kaberry, P. M. (1952). *Women of the grassfields: A study of the economic position of women in Bamenda.* London: H. M. Royal Stationery Office.

Kagan, J. (1981). Universals in human development. In R. H. Munroe, R. L. Munroe, & B. B. Whiting (Eds.), *Handbook of cross-cultural human development.* New York: Garland.

Kagitcibasi, C. (1984). Socialization in traditional society: A challenge to psychology. *International Journal of Psychology, 19,* 145-157.

Kaplan, S. (1983). A model of person-environment compatibility. *Environment and Behavior, 15,* 311-332.

Kates, R. W. (1976). Experiencing the environment as hazard. In S. Wapner, S. B. Cohen, & B. Kaplan (Eds.), *Experiencing the environment.* New York: Plenum.

Kaye, B. (1962). *Bringing up children in Ghana.* London: Allen & Unwin.

Kennedy, S., Scheirer, J., & Rogers, A. (1984). The price of success: Our cultural science. *American Psychologist, 39,* 996-997.

Kenyatta, J. (1965). *Facing Mount Kenya.* London: Heinemann.

Kimble, G. K. (1984). Psychology's two cultures. *American Psychologist, 39,* 833-839.

Knopf, R. C. (1987). Human behavior, cognition, and affect in the natural environment. In D. Stokols & I. Altman (Eds.), *Handbook of environmental psychology.* New York: John Wiley.

Koenig, D. (1986). Social stratification and labor allocation in peanut farming in the rural Malian household. *African Studies Review, 29*(3), 107-126.

Koenig, D. B. (1977). Sex, work, and social class in Cameroon. Unpublished doctoral thesis, Northwestern University.

Koffka, J. (1935). *Principles of gestalt psychology.* New York: Harcourt, Brace, & World.

Konner, M. J. (1981). Evolution of human behavior development. In R. H. Munroe, R. L. Munroe, & B. B. Whiting (Eds.), *Handbook of cross-cultural human development*. New York: Garland.

Krebs, J. R., & Davies, N. B. (1981). *An introduction to behavioral ecology*. Sunderland, MA: Sinauer Associates.

Kuippers, B. (1982). The "map in the head" metaphor. *Environment and Behavior, 14*(2), 202-220.

Laboratory of Comparative Human Cognition. (1978). Cross-cultural psychology's challenges to our idea of children and development. *American Psychologist, 34*(10), 827-833.

Lamb, M. E., & Bornstein, M. H. (1987). *Development in infancy*. New York: Random House.

Lamb, M. E., Pleck, J. H., Charnov, E. L. & Levine, J. A. (1987). In J. B. Lancaster, J. Atlmann, A. Rossi, & L. Sherrod (Eds.), *Parenting across the lifespan: Biosocial perspectives*. Chicago, Aldine.

Lance, J. (1990). What the stranger brings: The social dynamics of fieldwork. *History in Africa, 17*, 335-339.

Laosebikan, S. (1982, November). *A constituency for clinical psychology in Nigeria: Implications for training*. Paper read at the 2nd Annual Convention of the Nigerian Association of Clinical Psychologists, Benin City, Nigeria.

Laosebikan, S., & Filani, T. (1981, April). *Another view of the African custom of rearing children outside the homes of their biological parents* (Revised version of paper, *Clinical experience with fostered children at Ibadan*), presented at the Nigerian Psychological Society Conference, Jos, Nigeria.

Law, R. (1987). Ideologies of royal power: The dissolution and reconstruction of political authority on the "slave coast", 1680-1750. *Africa, 57*(3), 320-344.

Lawrence, P., & Livingstone, I. (1985). Agriculture in African economic development. In *Africa South of the Sahara* (15th ed.). London: Europa Publications.

Laye, C. (1977). *The African child*. Douglas, Isle of Man: Fontana Books.

Leakey, M. (1979). *Olduvai Gorge: My search for early man*. London: Williams Collins.

Leakey, R., & Lewin, R. (1979). *People of the lake: Man, his origins, nature and future*. London: Williams Collins.

Lee, R. B. (1979). *The !Kung San*. Cambridge, UK: Cambridge University Press.

Leff, H. L. (1978). *Experience, environment, & human potentials*. New York: Oxford University Press.

Leiderman, P. H., Tulkin, S. R., & Rosenfeld, A. (1977). *Culture and infancy: Variations in the human experience*. New York: Academic Press.

Leis, P. E. (1972). *Enculturation and socialization of children in an Ijaw village*. New York: Holt, Rinehart & Winston.

LeVine, R. (1974). Parental goals: A cross-cultural view. *Teachers College Record, 76*(2), 226-239.

LeVine, R. (1977). Child rearing as cultural adaptation. In H. Leiderman, S. Tulkin, & A. Rosenfeld (Eds.), *Culture and infancy* (pp. 15-27). New York: Academic Press.

LeVine, R. A. (1977). In F. M. Okatcha (Ed.), *Modern psychology and cultural adaptation*. Nairobi: Swahili Language Consultants.

Levine, V. T. (1986). Africa in the world. In A. A. Mazrui (Ed.), *The Africans*. New York: Praeger.

Lewin, K. (1936). *Principles of topological psychology*. New York: Harper.

Liebenow, J. G. (1986). *African politics: Crisis & challenges*. Bloomington: Indiana University Press.

Little, B. R. (1972). *Person-thing orientation: A provisional manual for the T-P scale.* Oxford: Oxford University, Department of Experimental Psychology.

Little, B. R. (1976). Specialization and the varieties of environmental experience: Empirical studies within the personality paradigm. In S. Wapner, S. B. Cohen, & B. Kaplan (Eds.), *Experiencing the environment.* New York: Plenum.

Little, B. R. (1987). Personality and environment. In D. Stokols & I. Altman (Eds.), *Handbook of environmental psychology.* New York: John Wiley.

Little, B. R., & Ryan, T. J. (1979). A social ecological model of development. In K. Ishwaran (Ed.), *Childhood and adolescence in Canada* (pp. 273-301). Toronto: McGraw-Hill.

Logli, P. (1985). Industry in Africa. In *Africa South of the Sahara* (15th ed.). London: Europa Publications.

Lonner, W. J. (1980). The search for psychological universals. In H. C. Triandis & W. W. Lambert (Eds.), *Handbook of cross-cultural psychology.* Boston: Allyn & Bacon.

Lonner, W. J., & Berry, J. W. (1986). Preface. In W. J. Lonner & J. W. Berry (Eds.), *Field methods in cross-cultural psychology.* Newbury Park, CA: Sage.

Lubek, I. (1974). Neutralizing the power structure in social psychology. In L. H. Strickland, F. E. Aboud, & K. J. Gergen (Eds.), *Social psychology in transition* (pp. 317-333). New York: Plenum.

Luckham, R. (1985). Political and social problems of development. In *Africa south of the Sahara* (15th ed.). London: Europa Publications.

Lukutati, B. (1983). Social problems and child exploitation: Child labour; juvenile delinquency; prostitution, drugs and alcohol. In Federal Republic of Nigeria, *Report of the Nigerian delegation to the Inter-Parliamentary Conference on Policies, Programmes, and Legislation for Children in Africa held in Yaoundé, Cameroon, 22nd-26th November, 1982.* Lagos: Federal Government Press.

MacDonald, K. B. (1988). The interfaces between sociobiology and developmental psychology. In K. B. MacDonald (Ed.), *Sociobiological perspectives on human development* (pp. vii-xi). New York: Springer-Verlag.

MacGaffey, W. (1981). African ideology and beliefs: A survey. *African Studies Review, 24*(2/3), 227-274.

Maclean, U. (1971). *Magical medicine: A Nigerian case study.* Allen Lane: London: Penguin Press.

Magnusson, D. (1981). Wanted: A psychology of situations. In D. Magnusson (Ed.), *Toward a psychology of situations: An interactional perspective.* New York: Academic Press.

Magnusson, D. (1982). Situational determinants of stress: An interactional perspective. In L. Goldberger & S. Breznitz (Eds.), *Handbook of stress* (pp. 231-253). New York: Free Press.

Manicas, P. T., & Secord, P. E. (1983). Implications for psychology of the new philosophy of science. *American Psychologist, 51,* 164-179.

Maquet, J. (1972). *Africanity.* New York: Oxford University Press.

Marcus, C. C. (1974). Children's play behavior in a low-rise, inner-city housing development. In R. C. Moore (Ed.), *Childhood city. EDRA 5: Proceedings of the Fifth Environmental Design Research Association Conference* (Pt. 12, pp. 197-211). Washington, DC: Environmental Design Research Association.

Marsella, A. J., Tharp, R. G., & Ciborowski, T. J. (Eds.). (1979). *Perspectives on cross-cultural psychology.* New York: Academic Press.

May, J. M. (1968). *The ecology of malnutrition in the French speaking countries of West Africa and Madagascar.* New York: Hafner.

Maynard-Smith, J. (1964). Group selection and kin selection. *Nature, 201,* 1145-1147.

Mayr, E. (1954). Change of genetic environment and evolution. In J. S. Huxley & E. B. Ford (Eds.), *Evolution as a process* (pp. 157-180). London: Allen & Unwin.

Mazrui, A. A. (1986a). Africa is one: A view from the Sahara. In A. A. Mazrui (Ed.), *The Africans.* New York: Praeger.

Mazrui, A. A. (1986b). *The Africans.* New York: Praeger.

Mbiti, J. S. (1970). *African religions and philosophy.* Garden City, NY: Anchor Books.

McCaskie, T. C. (1985). History of British colonialism in Africa. In *Africa south of the Sahara* (15 ed.). London: Europa Publications.

McHale, M. C., & McHale, J., with Streatfeild, G. F. (1979). World of children. *Population Bulletin, 33*(6), 1-49.

Mendonsa, E. L. (1975). The journey to the soul in Sisala cosmology. *Journal of Religion in Africa, 7*(1), 62-70.

Menkiti, I. A. (1984). Person and community in African traditional thought. In R. A. Wright (Ed.), *African philosophy.* Lanham, MD: University Press of America.

Metuh, E. E. (1973). The supreme god in Igbo life and worship. *Journal of Religion in Africa, 5*(1), 1-11.

Milgram, S. (1970). The experience of living in cities. *Science, 167,* 1461-1468.

Miller, P. H. (1989). *Theories of developmental psychology.* New York: Freeman.

Ministry of Plan and Regional Development. (1986). *Six Five Year Economic, Social and Cultural Development Plan 1986-1991.* Yaoundé, Cameroon: Government Printing Press.

Minkus, H. K. (1984). Causal theory in Akwapim Akan philosophy. In R. A. Wright (Ed.), *African philosophy.* Lanham, MD: University Press of America.

Moghaddam, F. M. (1987). Psychology in the three worlds. *American Psychologist, 42*(10), 912-920.

Moghaddam, F. M., & Taylor, D. M. (1985, October). Psychology in the developing world: An evaluation through the concepts of "Dual perception" and "Parallel growth." *American Psychologist,* pp. 1144-1146.

Moore, G. (1987). Environment and behavior research in North America. In D. Stokols & I. Altman (Eds.), *Handbook of environmental psychology.* New York: John Wiley.

Moos, R. (1976). *The human context: Environmental determinants of behavior.* New York: John Wiley.

Morawski, J. G. (1979). The structure of social psychological communities: A framework for examining the sociology of social psychology. In L. H. Strickland (Ed.), *Soviet and western perspectives in social psychology* (pp. 25-56). Elmsford, NY: Pergamon.

More, T. A. (1977). An analysis of wildlife in children's stories. In U.S. Forest Service, *Children, nature, and the urban environment: Proceedings of a symposium* (General Tech. Rep. NE-30, pp. 89-92). Upper Darby, PA: U.S. Department of Agriculture, Forest Service, Northeastern Forest Experiment Station.

Moscovici, S. (1972). Society and theory in social psychology. In J. Israel & H. Tajfel (Eds.), *The context of social psychology* (pp. 17-68). London: Academic Press.

Moshman, D., Glover, J. A., & Bruning, R. H. (1987). *Developmental psychology.* Boston: Little, Brown.

Mostefaoui, A. (1983). Situation of children in Africa. In Federal Republic of Nigeria, *Report of the Nigerian delegation to the Inter-Parliamentary Conference on Policies,*

Programmes and Legislation for Children in Africa held in Yaoundé, Cameroon, 22nd-26th November, 1982. Lagos: Federal Government Press.

Mudimbe, V. Y. (1983). African philosophy as an ideological practice: The case of French-speaking Africa. *African Studies Review, 26*(3/4), 133-154.

Mudimbe, V. Y. (1985). African gnosis: Philosophy and the order of knowledge: An introduction. *African Studies Review, 28*(2/3), 149-233.

Munroe, R. H., Munroe, R. L., & Whiting, B. B. (1981). *Handbook of cross-cultural human development.* New York: Garland.

Munroe, R. L., & Munroe, R. H. (1977). Land, labor and the child's cognitive performance among the Logoli. *American Ethnologist, 4,* 309-320.

Murphy, G., & Kovach, J. K. (1972). *Historical introduction to modern psychology.* New York: Harcourt, Brace, Jovanovich.

Murray, H. A. (1938). *Explorations in personality.* New York: Oxford University Press.

Musoke, L. K. (1975). The African child and his cultural environment. In R. Owor, V. L. Ongom, & B. G. Kirya (Eds.), *The child in the African environment: Growth, development and survival.* Nairobi, Kenya: East African Literature Bureau.

Mytelka, L. K. (1989). The unfulfilled promise of African industrialization. *African Studies Review, 32*(3), 77-137.

Nchabeleng, J. M. (1982). *The concept of play: Its relationship to social science methodology in Africa.* Unpublished doctoral dissertation, Free University of Amsterdam, The Netherlands.

Norris-Barker, C., Stephens, M. A. P., & Willems, E. P. (1982). Behavior varies by environment; Quality of data does not. *Environment and Behavior, 14*(4), 425-442.

Nsamenang, A. B. (1981). *Premarital perception of marriage and family life among young Cameroonians in Bamenda and Kimbo.* Unpublished manuscript.

Nsamenang, A. B. (1983). *Experimental improvement of the quality of fathering among a group of Cameroonians.* Unpublished doctoral thesis, University of Ibadan, Nigeria.

Nsamenang, A. B. (1987). A West African perspective. In M. E. Lamb (Ed.), *The father's role: Cross-cultural perspectives* (pp. 273-293). Hillsdale, NJ: Lawrence Erlbaum.

Nsamenang, A. B. (1988). *Kinship networks and the socialization of children: A Bamenda Grassfields profile.* Unpublished manuscript.

Nsamenang, A. B. (1989a, May). *Another style of socialization: The caregiving child.* Poster presented at the (Iowa) International Conference on Personal Relationships, Iowa City, IA.

Nsamenang, A. B. (1989b, December). The *Journal of African Psychology:* What's in a name? *Journal of African Psychology, 1*(3), 1-5.

Nsamenang, A. B. (1989c, July). *The social ecology of Cameroonian childhood.* Poster presented at the Tenth Biennial Meetings of the International Society for the Study of Behavioral Development, Jyvaskyla, Finland.

Nsamenang, A. B. (1992). Early childhood care and education in Cameroon. In M. E. Lamb et al. (Eds.), *Day Care in context.* Hillsdale, NJ: Lawrence Erlbaum.

Nsamenang, A. B., & Lamb, M. E. (1988). *Parent interview guide.* Unpublished interview schedule.

Nsamenang, A. B., & Laosebikan, S. (1981, April). *Father-child relationship and the development of psychopathology: Two clinical examples.* Paper presented to the Nigerian Psychological Society Conference, Jos, Nigeria.

Nwogugu, E. I. (1974). *Family law in Nigeria.* Ibadan, Nigeria: Heinemann.

Nyerere, J. (1977, August). *The plea of the poor* [Presidential address]. Washington, DC: Howard University.

Nyiti, R. M. (1982). The validity of "cultural differences explanations" for cross-cultural variation in Piagetian cognitive development. In D. A. Wagner & H. W. Stevenson (Eds.), *Cultural perspectives on child development.* San Francisco: Freeman.

O'Barr, J. (1984). African women in politics. In M. J. Hay & S. Stichter (Eds.), *African women south of the Sahara* (pp. 140-155). New York: Longman.

Obiechina, E. N. (1975). *Culture, tradition and society in the West African novel.* Cambridge, UK: Cambridge University Press.

Ochs, E. (1986). Introduction. In E. Ochs & B. B. Schieffelin (Eds.), *Language socialization across cultures.* Cambridge: Cambridge University Press.

Ochs, E. (1988). *Culture and language development.* Cambridge: Cambridge University Press.

Ogbu, J. U. (1988). Cultural diversity and human development. In D. T. Slaughter (Ed.), *Black children and poverty: A developmental perspective.* San Francisco: Jossey-Bass.

Ogbu, J. U. (1991). From cultural differences to cultural frame of reference. In P. Greenfield & R. Cocking (Eds.), *Continuities and discontinuities in the cognitive socialization of minority children.* Hillsdale, NJ: Lawrence Erlbaum.

Oguah, B. E. (1984). African and Western philosophy: A comparative study. In R. A. Wright (Ed.), *African philosophy.* Lanham, MD: University Press of America.

Ohuche, R. O., & Otaala, B. (1981). *The African child in his environment.* Oxford: Pergamon.

Ojiaku, M. O. (1974). Traditional African social thought and Western scholarship. *Presence Africaine, No. 90,* 2nd Quarterly.

Okeke, Fr. H. O. (1988). Preface. In Fr. J. C. Atado, *African marriage customs and church law.* Kano, Nigeria: Modern Printers.

Okonji, O. M. (1971). The effects of familiarity on classification. *Journal of Cross-Cultural Psychology, 2,* 339-349.

Olurunsola, V., with Muhwezi, D. (1986). A Garden of Eden in decay. In A. A. Mazrui (Ed.), *The Africans.* New York: Praeger.

Onwuanibe, R. C. (1984). The human person and immortality in Ibo metaphysics. In R. A. Wright (Ed.), *African philosophy.* Lanham, MD: University Press of America.

Oppong, C. (Ed.) (1983). *Male and female in West Africa.* London: Allen & Unwin.

Organization of African Unity. (1981). *Lagos plan of action for economic development of Africa, 1980-2000.* Geneva: International Institute of Labor Studies.

Osmond, H. (1957). Function as the basis of psychiatric ward design. *Mental Hospitals (Architectural Suppl.), 8,* 23-29.

Ouden, J. H. B. den (1987). In search of personal mobility: Changing interpersonal relations in two Bamileke chiefdoms, Cameroon. *Africa, 57*(1), 3-27.

Oyebola, A. (1976). *Blackman's dilemma.* Ibadan, Nigeria: Academic Press.

Paxton, J. (1987). *The statesman's year-book.* New York: St. Martin's.

Peil, M. (1977). *Consensus and conflict in African societies.* London: Longman.

Pellegrini, A. D. (1987). *Applied child study: A developmental approach.* Hillsdale, NJ: Lawrence Erlbaum.

Pence, A. R. (1988). *Ecological research with children and families: From concepts to methodology.* New York: Teachers College Press.

Pervin, L. A. (1978). Definitions, measurements, and classifications of stimuli, situations, and environments. *Human Ecology, 6,* 71-105.

Petzold, M. (1984). Psychology and the developing world. *International Society for the Study of Behavioral Development Newsletter, 1*(5) 5-6.

Piaget, J. (1970). Piaget's theory. In P. Mussen (Ed.). *Carmichael's manual of child psychology* (Vol. 1, pp. 703-732). New York: John Wiley.

Plomin, R. (1986). *Development, genetics, and psychology*. Hillsdale, NJ: Lawrence Erlbaum.

Plomin, R., & DeFries, J. C. (1985). *Origins of individual differences in infancy*. Orlando, FL: Academic Press.

Plomin, R., & Rende, R. (1991). Human genetics. *Annual Review of Psychology, 42*, 161-190.

Poincaré, J. H. (1908). *Science and hypothesis*. New York: Dover.

Poortinga, Y. S., & Malpass, R. S. (1986). Making inferences from cross-cultural data. In W. J. Lonner & J. W. Berry (Eds.), *Field methods in cross-cultural research*. Newbury Park, CA: Sage.

Posnansky, M. (1986). Anatomy of a continent. In A. A. Mazrui (Ed.), *The Africans*. New York: Praeger.

Preston, V., Taylor, S. M., & Hodge, D. C. (1983). Adjustment to natural and technological hazards: A study of an urban residential community. *Environment and Behavior, 15*(2), 143-164.

Radcliffe-Brown, A. R. (1952). *Structure and function in primitive society*. London: Cohen & West.

Raum, O. F. (1967). *Chaga childhood*. London: Oxford University Press.

Redfield, R. (1959). The anthropological study of man. *Anthropological Quarterly, 32*(1), 4.

Riddell, J. C., & Campbell, D. J. (1986). Agricultural intensification and rural development: The Mandara mountain of North Cameroon. *African Studies Review, 29*(3), 89-106.

Riesman, P. (1986). The person and the life cycle in African social life and thought. *African Studies Review, 29*(2), 71-138.

Ritzenthaler, R. (1962). Cameroons village: An ethnography of the Bafut. *Anthropology, No. 8*. Milwaukee: Milwaukee Public Museum.

Robertson, C. C. (1984). Women in the urban economy. In M. J. Hay & S. Stichter (Eds.), *African women south of the Sahara* (pp. 33-49). New York: Longman.

Rotberg, R. I. (1986). Exploitation. In A. A. Mazrui (Ed.), *The Africans*. New York: Praeger.

Rowles, G. D. (1980). Growing old "inside": Aging and attachment to place in an Appalachian community. In N. Datan & A. Lahmann (Eds.), *Transitions of aging* (pp. 153-170). New York: Academic Press.

Russell, J. A., & Snodgrass, J. (1987). Emotion and environment. In D. Stokols & I. Altman (Eds.), *Handbook of environmental psychology*. New York: John Wiley.

Russell, J. A., & Ward, L. M. (1982). Environmental psychology. *Annual Review of Psychology, 33*, 651-688.

Russell, W. R. (1984). Psychology in its world context. *American Psychologist, 39*(9), 1017-1025.

Sameroff, A. J., & Feil, L. A. (1985). Parental concepts of development. In I.E. Sigel (Ed.), *Parental belief systems*. Hillsdale, NJ: Lawrence Erlbaum.

Sampson, E. E. (1981). Cognitive psychology as ideology. *American Psychologist, 36*, 730-743.

Sanchez, E., Wiesenfeld, E., & Cronick, K. (1987). Environmental psychology from a Latin American perspective. In D. Stokols & I. Altman (Eds.), *Handbook of environmental psychology*. New York: John Wiley.

Sanneh, L. (1986). New gods. In A. A. Mazrui (Ed.), *The Africans*. New York: Praeger.

Sattler, J. M. (1988). *Assessment of children*. San Diego, CA: Jerome M. Sattler.

Scarr, S. (1985). Cultural lenses on mothers and children. In L. Friedrich-Cofer (Ed.), *Human nature and public policy*. New York: Praeger.

Scarr, S., & Kidd, K. K. (1983). Developmental behavioral genetics. In P. H. Mussen (Ed.), *Handbook of child psychology. Vol. 2: Infancy and developmental psychology* (4th ed.) (pp. 345-433). New York: John Wiley.

Scarr, S., & McCarthney, K. (1983). How people make their own environments: A theory of genotype-environment effects. *Child Development, 54*(2), 424-435.

Scarr, S., & Weinberg, R. A. (1983). The Minnesota adoption studies: Genetic differences and malleability. *Child Development, 54*(2), 260-267.

Schildkrout, E. (1981). The employment of children in Kano. In G. Rodgers & G. Standing (Eds.), *Child work, poverty and underemployment*. Geneva: International Labor Organization.

Schultheis, M. J. (1989a). A symposium: Refugees in Africa—The dynamics of displacement and repatriation. *African Studies Review, 32*(1), 1-2.

Schultheis, M. J. (1989b). Refugees in Africa: The geopolitics of forced displacement. *African Studies Review, 32*(1), 3-29.

Scribner, S., & Cole, M. (1973). The cognitive consequences of formal and informal education. *Science, 182*, 553-559.

Sears, R., Maccoby, E., & Levin, H. (1957). *Patterns of childrearing*. Evanston, IL: Row & Peterson.

Segall, M. H. (1979). *Cross-cultural psychology: Human behavior in global perspective*. Monterey, CA: Brooks/Cole.

Segall, M. H. (1986). Assessment of social behavior. In W. J. Lonner & J. W. Berry (Eds.), *Field methods in cross-cultural research* (pp. 265-290). Newbury Park, CA: Sage.

Segall, M. H., Dasen, P. R., Berry, J. W., & Poortinga, Y. H. (1990). *Human behavior in global perspective*. Elmsford, NY: Pergamon.

Serpell, R. (1976). *Culture's influence on behavior*. London: Methuen.

Serpell, R. (1984) Commentary on the impact of psychology on Third World development. *International Journal of Psychology, 19*, 179-192.

Serpell, R. (1990). Audience, culture and psychological explanation. *Quarterly Newsletter of the Laboratory of Comparative Human Cognition, 12*(3), 99-132.

Sexton, V. S., & Misiak, H. (1984). American psychologists and psychology abroad. *American Psychologist, 39*(9), 1026-1031.

Sharan, P. (1988). One view of the cultural context for the study of childrearing in India. *International Society for the Study of Behavioral Sciences Newsletter, 1*(13), 1-3.

Sharp, E. (1970). *The African child*. Westport, CT: Negro University Press.

Sheet, H., & Morris, R. (1974). *Disaster in the desert*. Washington, DC.: Carnegie Endowment for International Peace.

Sicault, G. (Ed.). (1963). *The needs of children* (UNESCO). New York: Free Press.

Sinha, D. (1983). Cross-cultural psychology: A view from the Third World. In J. B. Deregowski, S. Dziurawiec, & R. C. Annis (Eds.), *Expiscations in cross-cultural psychology*. Lisse: Swets & Zeitlinger.

Skinner, E. P. (1986). The triple heritage of lifestyles. In A. A. Mazrui (Ed.), *The Africans* (pp. 60-81). New York: Praeger.

Skinner, E. P., & Mikell, G. (1986). A conflict of cultures. In A. A. Mazrui (Ed.), *The Africans* (pp. 212-231). New York: Praeger.

Sommer, R. (1969). *Personal space*. Englewood Cliffs, NJ: Prentice-Hall.

Sorensen, J. H. (1983). Knowing how to behave under the threat of disaster: Can it be explained. *Environment and Behavior, 15*(4), 438-457.

Southall, A. (1988). Small urban centers in rural development: What else is development other than helping your own home town? *African Studies Review, 31*(3), 1-15.

Staniland, M. (1983, September/December). Who needs African studies? *African Studies Review, 26*(3/4), 77-98.

Stapleton, P. (1978). The West African background. In J. Ellis (Ed.), *West African families in Britain.* London: Routledge & Kegan Paul.

Stapp, J., Tucker, A. M., & VandenBos, G. R. (1985). Census of psychological personnel: 1983. *American Psychologist, 40,* 1317-1351.

Staudt, K. (1986). Stratification, implications for women's politics. In C. Robertson & I. Berger (Eds.), *Women and class in Africa* (pp. 197-215). New York: Holmes & Meier.

Sternberg, R. J. (1984). A contextualist view of the nature of intelligence. *International Journal of Psychology, 19,* 307-334.

Stokols, D. (1987). Conceptual strategies of environmental psychology. In D. Stokols & I. Altman (Eds.), *Handbook of environmental psychology.* New York: John Wiley.

Stokols, D., & Altman, I. (1987). *Handbook of environmental psychology.* New York: John Wiley.

Stokols, D., & Novaco, R. W. (1981). Transportation and well-being: An ecological perspective. In I. Altman, J. F. Wohlwill, & P. B. Everett (Eds.), *Transportation environment: Advances in therapy and research* (pp. 85-130). New York: Plenum.

Stokols, D., & Shumaker, S. A. (1981). People in places: A transactional view of settings. In J. Harvey (Ed.), *Cognition, social behavior and the environment* (pp. 441-488). Hillsdale, NJ: Lawrence Erlbaum.

Students go on rampage. (1988, April 25). *West Africa, 3689,* pp. 723-762.

Suedfeld, P. (1987). Extreme and unusual environments. In D. Stokols & I. Altman (Eds.), *Handbook of environmental psychology* (pp. 863-887). New York: John Wiley.

Super, C., & Harkness, S. (Eds.). (1980). *Anthropological perspectives on child development.* London: Jossey-Bass.

Super, C. M., & Harkness, S. (1986). The developmental niche: A conceptualization at the interface of child and culture. *International Journal of Behavioral Development, 9,* 545-569.

Susman, L. (1989). Biology-behavior interactions in behavioral development: Current status and future perspectives. *International Society for the Study of Behavioral Development Newsletter, 1*(15), 1-3.

Tangwa, G. B. (1988). *Ethical problems in genetic technology.* Revised version of a paper read before the Nigerian Philosophical Association (NPA), Benin City, Nigeria.

Tapé, G. (1977). Les activites de classification et les operations logiques chez les enfants ivoiriens. *Annales de l'Université d'Abidjan serie D 10,* 155-163.

Taylor, J. V. (1963). *The primal vision.* London: SCM Press.

Tchanou, Z. (1976). *Ecologie du Sahel: Une analyse des freins au developpement en vue d'une intervention forestiere.* Faculte de Forestiere et de Geodesie de l' Université Laval: Essai presente pour obtention du grade de maitre es sciences.

Tetteh, P. A. (1967). Marriage, family and household. In W. Birmingham, I. Neustadt, & E. N. Omaboe (Eds.), *A study of contemporary Ghana. Vol 2: Some aspects of social structure in Ghana* (pp. 201-216). London: Allen & Unwin.

Thomas, B. P. (1988). Household strategies for adaptation and change: Participation in Kenyan rural women's association. *Africa, 58*(4), 401-422.

Tinbergen, N. (1963). On aims and methods of ethology. *Zeitschrift Tierpsychologie, 20,* 410-433.

Tolman, E., & Brunswick, E. (1935). The organism and the causal texture of the environment. *Psychological Review, 42,* 43-77.

Tolsdorf, C. C. (1976). Social networks, support and coping: An exploratory study. *Family process, 15,* 407-417.

Touré, M. (1983). Urbanization and social problems in Africa. *Africa Development, 14*(3), 1-11.

Trevor, J. E. (1955). Race. *Encyclopaedia Hebraica.*

Triandis, H. C. (1979). The future of cross-cultural psychology. In A. J. Marsella, R. G. Tharp, & T. J. Ciborowski (Eds.), *Perspectives on cross-cultural psychology.* New York: Academic Press.

Triandis, H. C. (1980). Introduction to Handbook of cross-cultural psychology. In H. C. Triandis & W. W. Lambert (Eds.), *Handbook of cross-cultural psychology.* Boston: Allyn & Bacon.

Triandis, H. C., & Brislin, R. W. (1984). Cross-cultural psychology. *American Psychologist, 39*(9), 1006-1016.

Triandis, H. C., & Heron, A. (Eds.). (1981). *Handbook of cross-cultural psychology. Vol. 4: Developmental psychology.* Boston: Allyn & Bacon.

Trivers, R. L. (1974). Parent-offspring conflict. *American Zoologist, 14,* 249-264.

Tuan, Y. F. (1971). *Man and nature* (Commission on College Geography resource paper No. 10). Washington, DC: Association of American Geographers.

Turrittin, J. (1988). Men, women and market trade in rural Mali, West Africa. *Canadian Journal of African Studies, 22*(3), 583-604.

Uchendu, U. C. (1965). *The Ibo of southeast Nigeria.* New York: Holt, Rinehart & Winston.

Udo, R. K. (1978). *A comprehensive geography of West Africa.* New York: Africana.

Udo, R. K. (1982). *The human geography of tropical Africa.* Ibadan, Nigeria: Heinemann.

Uka, N. (1966). *Growing up in Nigerian culture.* Ibadan, Nigeria: Ibadan University Press.

Ulrich, R. S. (1981). Natural versus urban scenes: Some psychophysiological effects. *Environment and Behavior, 13*(5), 523-556.

Ungar, S. J. (1986). *Africa.* New York: Simon & Schuster.

United Nations. (1975). *Demographic handbook for Africa.* Addis Ababa: Economic Commission for Africa.

United Nations. (1986). *Demographic yearbook.* New York: United Nations.

Valsiner, J. (1988). Organization of children's social development in polygamic families. In J. Valsiner (Ed.), *Cultural context and child development: Toward a culture-inclusive developmental psychology.* Toronto: C. J. Hogrefe.

Vatican City. (1987). *Liberia Editrice Vaticana.* Vatican City: Author.

Wagner, D. A. (1986). Child development research and the Third World. *American Psychologist, 41*(3), 298-301.

Wagner, D. A., & Stevenson, H. W. (Eds.). (1982). *Cultural perspectives on child development.* San Francisco: Freeman.

Wallerstein, I. (1988). A comment on epistemology: What is Africa? *Canadian Journal of African Studies, 22*(20), 331-334.

Ware, H. (1975). *The changing African family in West Africa.* Paper presented to the Commonwealth Students' Children Society, Report of Ibadan Seminar on the African child in Great Britain, Ibadan, Nigeria.

Ware, H. (1983). Male and female life cycles. In C. Oppong (Ed.), *Male and female in West Africa.* London: Allen & Unwin.

Warren, N. (Ed.). (1980). *Studies in cross-cultural psychology* (Vol. 2). London: Academic Press.

Warwick, D. P. (1980). The politics and ethics of cross-cultural research. In H. C. Triandis & W. W. Lambert (Eds.), *Handbook of cross-cultural psychology. Vol. 1: Perspectives.* Boston: Allyn & Bacon.

Weisner, T. S., & Gallimore, R. (1977). My brother's keeper: Child and sibling caretaking. *Current Anthropology, 18*(2), 169-190.

Weisner, T. S., & Weibel, J. C. (1981). Home environments and family lifestyles in California. *Environment and Behavior, 13*(4), 417-460.

Weisz, J. R. (1978). Transcontextual validity in developmental research. *Child Development, 49,* 1-12.

Weiten, W. (1989). *Psychology: Themes and variations.* Pacific Grove, CA: Brooks/Cole.

Werner, E. E. (1979). *Cross-cultural child development.* Monterey, CA: Brooks/Cole.

Werner, E. E. (1988). A cross-cultural perspective on infancy: Research and social issues. *Journal of Cross-cultural Psychology, 19*(1), 96-113.

Werner, H. (1978). *Developmental processes: Heinz Werner's selected writings.* S. S. Barten & M. B. Franklin (Eds.). New York: International Universities Press.

Westermann, D. (1935). *Africa and Christianity, 74.*

White, L. (1984). Women in the changing African family. In M. J. Hay & S. Stichter (Eds.), *African women south of the Sahara* (pp. 53-67). New York: Longman.

Whiting, B. B., & Whiting, J. W. M. (1975). *Children of six cultures.* Cambridge, MA: Harvard University Press.

Wipper, A. (1982). Riot and rebellion among African women: Three examples of women's political clout. In J. O'Barr (Ed.), *Perspectives on power: Women in Africa, Asia, and Latin America* (pp. 50-72). Durham, NC: Duke University Center for International Studies.

World Health Organization. (1976). The African region of WHO. *WHO Chronicle, 30*(1), 2-48.

World Health Organization. (1982). The contribution of human genetics to health for all. *WHO Chronicle, 36*(5), 186-190.

Wicker, A. W. (1987). Behavior settings reconsidered: Temporal stages, resources, internal dynamics, context. In D. Stokols & I. Altman (Eds.), *Handbook of environmental psychology.* New York: John Wiley.

Williams, G. C. (1966). *Adaptation and natural selection.* Princeton, NJ: Princeton University Press.

Winkel, G. H. (1987). Implications of environmental context for validity assessments. In D. Stokols & I. Altman (Eds.), *Handbook of environmental psychology* (pp. 71-97). New York: John Wiley.

Wiredu, J. E. (1984). How not to compare African thought with Western thought. In R. A. Wright (Ed.), *African philosophy.* Lanham, MD: University Press of America.

Witkin, H. A., & Berry, J. W. (1975). Psychological differentiation in cross-cultural perspective. *Journal of Cross-Cultural Psychology, 6,* 4-87.

Wober, M. (1975). *Psychology in Africa.* London: International African Institute.

Wohlwill, J. F. (1978, November). *Ecological representativeness in developmental research: A critical view.* Paper presented at the Institute of Psychology of the Technological University of Berlin, Berlin.

Wohlwill, J. F., & Heft, H. (1987). The physical environment and the development of the child. In D. Stokols & I. Altman (Eds.), *Handbook of environmental psychology* (pp. 281-328). New York: John Wiley.

World Bank. (1981). Accelerated development in sub-Saharan Africa. Washington, DC: Author.

World Bank. (1980). *Poverty and human development.* New York: Oxford University Press.

Wright, R. A. (1984). Preface to the first edition. In R. A. Wright (Ed.), *African philosophy.* Lanham, MD: University Press of America.

Zelizer, V. A. (1981). *Pricing the priceless child.* New York: Basic Books.

Zempleni-Rabain, J. (1973). Food and the strategy involved in learning fraternal external exchange among Wolof children. In P. Alexandre (Ed.), *French perspectives in African studies.* London: Oxford University Press.

Zukow, G. P. (1989). Communicating across disciplines: On integrating psychological and ethnographic approaches to sibling research. In P. G. Zukow (Ed.), *Sibling interaction across cultures.* New York: Springer.

Zuniga, R. B. (1975, February). The experimenting society and radical social reform: The role of the social scientist in Chile's Unidad Popular experience. *American Psychologist,* 99-115.

INDEX

ABOUT THE AUTHOR

A. Bame Nsamenang is a researcher at Cameroon's Institute of Human Sciences, Bamenda. He was educated in Kitiwum and Bamenda (Cameroon), and in Ibadan (Nigeria) where he earned a Ph.D. in child psychology in 1984. From October 1987 to May 1990 he was a Fogarty (postdoctoral) Fellow at NICHD, Bethesda, MD, where he worked under the mentorship of Dr. Michael E. Lamb.

Nsamenang's research interests are in the ecology of infancy, socialization, parental knowledge, and collaborative cross-cultural work. His research strategy is to build up, systematically and in collaboration with related disciplines and other researchers, a database on Cameroonian childhood. He tries to point out the policy implications of his research, with particular reference to health and welfare issues. In this regard, Nsamenang hopes to convert his Father Involvement Training (FIT) program into a Parent Education Program (PEP) for parent education in the face of conflicting traditional and "modern" directives regarding child survival and parenting. Furthermore, he endeavors to show how developmental knowledge from a non-Western culture fits into mainstream developmental literature.

His major publications include: "A West African Perspective", in M. E. Lamb, *The Father's Role: Cross-Cultural Perspectives*; "Differences in Nso (Cameroon) Perceptions of Parenthood," in B. Hewlett, *Father-Child Relationships: Cross-Cultural Perspectives*; "Early Childhood Care and Education in Cameroon," in M. E. Lamb et al., *Daycare in Context*; and "Socialization Values in Two Generations of Bamenda (Cameroon) Grassfields Families" (co-authored with M. E. Lamb), in P. Greenfield and R. Cocking, *Continuities and Discontinuities in the Cognitive Socialization of Minority Children*.